"Geter's expansive vision becomes much more than a self-portrait as it confronts how the human body keeps score—and survives. This poetic memoir delivers." —*Publishers Weekly*

"Among the most evocative and intellectually dazzling memoirs of recent times." —SUKETU MEHTA, author of *This Land Is Our Land*

"A book of extraordinary ambition, at once bracing, beautiful, and necessary—I couldn't put it down."
—MEGHAN O'ROURKE, author of *The Invisible Kingdom*

"An absolutely stunning literary experience . . . Hafizah Augustus Geter has written a classic." —KIESE LAYMON, author of *Heavy*

"A stellar example of the brilliance it requires to walk the tightrope of offering a full portrait of a life . . . a triumph of the form."
—HANIF ABDURRAQIB, author of *A Little Devil in America*

"Hafizah Augustus Geter announces herself as a storyteller, truth seeker, and pathfinder. This is a work that interrogates as it both mourns and celebrates."
—TAYARI JONES, author of *An American Marriage*

"A brilliant evocation of artistic and political restlessness . . . a record of sustaining joy." —ALEXANDER CHEE, author of
How to Write an Autobiographical Novel

"An affirmation of the strongest sort . . . a simple and beautiful statement of our inevitability."
—UZODINMA IWEALA, author of *Speak No Evil*

"An essential read for all of us concerned with navigating the century ahead . . . *The Black Period* is a triumph."

—CHANDA PRESCOD-WEINSTEIN, author of *The Disordered Cosmos*

"An indictment, an elegy, and above all a work of brilliance."

—ALEX MARZANO-LESNEVICH, author of *The Fact of a Body*

"Overflows with stories, family histories, disarming images, and arresting truths." —JESS ROW, author of *White Flights*

"A journey of greater breadth and depth than nearly anything else being written today."

—JOHN MURILLO, author of *Kontemporary Amerikan Poetry*

"A beautiful combination of personal memoir, cultural criticism, and visual art created by her father . . . [Geter] delves into art and music, migration and activism, queer community and grief."

—*Book Riot*

BY HAFIZAH AUGUSTUS GETER

The Black Period
Un-American

THE BLACK PERIOD

HAFIZAH
AUGUSTUS GETER

THE
BLACK
PERIOD

ON PERSONHOOD, RACE, AND ORIGIN

A MEMOIR

RANDOM HOUSE
NEW YORK

Published in the United States by Random House, an imprint and division of Penguin Random House LLC, New York.

RANDOM HOUSE and the HOUSE colophon are registered trademarks of Penguin Random House LLC.

Originally published in hardcover in the United States by Random House, an imprint and division of Penguin Random House LLC, in 2022.

Library of Congress Cataloging-in-Publication Data
Names: Geter, Hafizah, 1984– author.
Title: The Black period: on personhood, race, and origin / Hafizah Augustus Geter.
Other titles: On personhood, race, and origin
Description: First edition. | New York: Random House, 2022 | Includes bibliographical references.
Identifiers: LCCN 2022001107 (print) | LCCN 2022001108 (ebook) | ISBN 9780593448663 (trade paperback) | ISBN 9780593448656 (ebook)
Subjects: LCSH: Geter, Hafizah, 1984– | Geter, Hafizah, 1984– Family. | Nigerian Americans—Biography. | Lesbians, Black—United States—Biography. | Immigrants—United States—Biography. | Nigeria—Biography. | United States—Race relations.
Classification: LCC E184.N55 G48 2022 (print) | LCC E184.N55 (ebook) | DDC 305.896/69073—dc23/eng/20220124
LC record available at https://lccn.loc.gov/2022001107

Printed in the United States of America on acid-free paper

randomhousebooks.com

Illustrations by Tyrone Geter. Used by permission of the artist.

9 8 7 6 5 4 3 2 1

Book design by Jo Anne Metsch

FOR

Brandon and Connor Moore

I mean to tell you that everywhere I go
I hear us singing to each other.

—ARACELIS GIRMAY

This can still happen anywhere. Not everything is lost.

—NAOMI SHIHAB NYE

CONTENTS

List of Illustrations xv

In the Beginning. xix

∞

I.

Age I—Reverberation, Reverberation: The Body 3

Age II—Simulacra: Identity Wars 29

Age III—Kujichagulia: Self-Determination 59

Age IV—God's Country: Narrative 75

Age V—Theatre of Forgiveness: Black Rage 101

Age VI—A Political Condition: Luck 133

II.

Age VII—The Way Light Holds the Blues: Queer 165

Age VIII—On Haints: Transformation. 187

Age IX—This Can Still Happen Anywhere: Testimony 227

Age X—Where the People Could Fly: Inheritance 247

III.

Age XI—Earth, Wind & Fire: Revelations 269

Age XII—Weighing of the Hearts: Joy 289

Age XIII—Me, We! Muhammad Ali!: Love 337

IV.

The Black Period: Rememory 359

∞

Epilogue: Black Light 383

∞

Acknowledgments 393

Selected Bibliography 397

LIST OF ILLUSTRATIONS

ALL ART BY TYRONE GETER

xxviii *Keeper of the Watchman*, charcoal on paper, 1980, 30" x 28"

4 *Griot*, from the series *Living in the Light of Hell's Shadow*, charcoal and torn paper, circa 2014–2015, 96" x 48"

14 *Target*, charcoal and torn paper, circa 2018, 40" x 60"

19 *Where Are the Girls?*, charcoal and torn paper, 2020, 60" x 40"

30 *Street Creds*, from the series *The Art of the Misdirect*, charcoal on paper, 2014, 40" x 60"

38 *Call to Council*, charcoal on paper, 1983, 86" x 48"

45 *Mississippi*, pencil, circa 1978, 60" x 38"

52 *Paper Doll*, charcoal and torn paper, 1997, 40" x 60"

60 *The Confrontation of X*, charcoal, 1994, 30" x 28"

69 *Urban Warrior—The Camouflage of Deceit*, charcoal and torn paper, circa 2016–2017, 48" x 96"

76 *Black Face, White Face*, charcoal and torn paper, 2015, 96" x 48"

81 *Just Brother Stylifying*, from the series *A Hoodie Ain't Nothing Like You Heard*, charcoal and torn paper, 2016, 44" x 40"

87 *Hands Up*, charcoal and torn paper, circa 2014–2015, 96" x 48"

94 *Obama and the Struggle Against the Void*, charcoal, torn paper, white chalk, 2010, 48" x 42"

102 *Flight,* charcoal and torn paper, circa 2002, 42" x 86"

110 *Tomorrow's Children,* charcoal, 1982, 36" x 36"

116 *Pirate Like,* charcoal and torn paper, circa 2008, 32" x 38"

123 *Juma,* charcoal, 1980, 40" x 32"

134 *Just Ain't What You're Thinking,* from the series *A Hoodie Ain't Nothing Like You Heard,* charcoal and torn paper, 2016, 40" x 46"

142 *Mother, Africa and Child,* charcoal, 1983, 32" x 32"

148 *Hooding with Some Style,* from the series *A Hoodie Ain't Nothin' Like You Heard,* charcoal, 2016, 60" x 40"

152 *Fear,* charcoal and torn paper, 2015, 28" x 32"

158 *Water, Water,* charcoal, 1986, 46" x 58"

166 *Enough,* charcoal, lace, torn paper, 1996, 42" x 54"

172 *Rooted in the Past of Our Future,* charcoal, 2010, 60" x 40"

179 *Twins,* charcoal and torn paper, circa 2003, 28" x 24"

188 *A Kettle of Friends,* charcoal and torn paper, 2022, 28" x 58"

202 *The Contemplation of X,* charcoal, 1994, 34" x 36"

207 *Just Shut Up Moscow and Drink the Kool Aid,* charcoal, circa 2018–2020, 38" x 50"

215 *Herdsman,* charcoal on paper, 1983, 45" x 45"

228 *Backache,* charcoal and torn paper, circa 2014–2015, 50" x 40"

240 *Fakin' the Fear,* from the series *A Hoodie Ain't Nothing Like You Heard,* charcoal, pencil, torn paper, hoodie, 2016, 60" x 40"

248 *Spirits No. 2 Ancestors,* charcoal, circa 1984, 54" x 48"

258 *I Don' Old, I Don' Tire, but I Ain't No Ways Don',* charcoal, 2013, 40" x 65"

270 *Homeless in the Promised Land,* charcoal, cloth, torn paper, objects, 2016, 15' x 18'

278 *Living the Li(f)e,* from the series *Hats and Mats,* charcoal and torn paper, 2016, 72" x 71"

285 *Fulani,* charcoal, 1986, 100″ x 50″

290 *Spirits #3 Metamorphosis,* charcoal, 1989, 50″ x 30″

298 *Drought,* charcoal, 1986, 38″ x 50″

307 *Untitled,* charcoal, 2006, 22″ x 28″

314 *Yusef Lateef Later in Africa,* charcoal, 1985, 24″ x 36″

326 *The Lesson,* from the series *Brave New World,* charcoal and
found objects, 2021, 48″ x 96″ x 36″

332 *Shy,* charcoal on paper, 1980, 36″ x 40″

338 *My Soul Looks Back in Wonder,* charcoal and torn paper, 2006,
38″ x 36″

345 *Garvey,* charcoal on paper, 1987, 28″ x 32″

350 *The Jester,* charcoal and torn paper, 1998, 34″ x 40″

362 *Umbilical Connection,* charcoal, torn paper, wood, found
objects, 2001, 32″ x 96″ x 10″

371 *Man with Big Hat,* charcoal, 2014, 28″ x 32″

382 *Dancers,* charcoal and torn paper, 2010, 60″ x 40″

388 *Daylight Savings: The Dimming of the Light,* charcoal, 2022,
60″ x 40″

INSERT ONE

1 *Saffron,* pastels collage, 2016–2017, 60″ x 40″

2 *Jubilation at the Gate,* oil on board, circa 2014, 48″ x 36″

3 *My Beauty Is Not My Beast,* mixed media: torn paper and
pastels, 2016–2017, 48″ x 96″

4 *Rebirth of Rhythm,* oil on canvas, circa 1997, 54″ x 57″

5 *Sissy,* oil on canvas, circa 1987, 36″ x 50″

6 *Totem,* oil on canvas, 1997, 52″ x 56″

7 *God's Country,* pastels, torn paper, African textile, circa 1995,
48″ x 86″

8 *I See You,* charcoal, torn paper, pastels, circa 2005, 36″ x 32″

INSERT TWO

1 *White Socks Only,* oil on paper, 1996, 16″ x 20″

2 *Lucy,* oil on board, 2021, 60″ x 40″

3 *9 Months,* oil on canvas, 1984, 36″ x 65″

4 *Young Fulani Maidens,* pastels on paper, 2008, 72″ x 42″

5 *The Breakfast Table,* oil on paper, circa 1990, 28″ x 32″

6 *Sometimes I Felt Like I Didn't Have No Life,* oil on canvas, 1981, 26″ x 30″

7 *The Good Lord Don' Give Me Wings but My People Taught Me to Fly,* water soluble oil on paper, torn paper, circa 2011, 48″ x 56″

8 *When the Spirit Moves You,* water soluble oil on paper, torn paper, 2012, 20″ x 16″

IN THE BEGINNING

"WHAT DOES MY NAME MEAN?" I LOVED asking my mother. With a seriousness that opened her face, she'd reply: *protector, watcher, guardian, memory.* It is an ancient name, derived from the seventh-century Arabic word "hafiz"—one who memorized all eighty thousand words of the Quran. Later, Hafiz was a fourteenth-century Persian poet, a guardian of memory who wrote about hypocrisies, fear, and the moon. I took my mother seriously from the start. For her, for me, for all of us, I wanted to be memory, protector, *and* the protector of memories.

I spent my childhood watching my father remake us into charcoal, oil, and pencil. I wanted to preserve something I loved like that. He taught me the mirror trick for drawing faces. I held the world I'd drawn up to a mirror and by that small shift in looking, what I'd drawn was new, full of miscalculations: an eye too low, the mouth too crooked. It quaked something in the soft part of me to know what was there to see was seldom what the bare eye saw. *It's okay,* my father told me. There was always time for starting over or revision. Like him, I wanted to be an accurate witness. There was as much to guard as there was to see.

For a time, whatever image America tried to draw of me and the world, my mother's stories and presence and my father's art were there to correct. My father is still like this: a man trying to hold up a promise made to his dead wife, to set their children's world right. When did I put my parents' lessons down?

My therapist, who is a Black woman, had me look up "dissociation." Dr. Lamb has heard me say more than once how, after my mother died—I was nineteen, and my father so stunned that six weeks later he needed a triple bypass—my world picked up a tornado's wind.

Having seen how the world's vision of me was marred with anti-Blackness and homophobia, instead I took up the work of self-surveillance. How American, to mistake policing for protection, to confuse the hunter for a guardian. With my mother gone and my father, quite literally, heartsick, there was no one to correct the story. My mirrors shattered, I stood with my hands up in the eye of the storm.

There are years I barely remember, so deeply entrenched was I in grief and shame's blackout. There are years I can tell you exactly where the tornado blew *every single* thing. Years I forgot the meaning of my name. There were years it felt like I had no body. Years so angry, it felt like I had no heart. Lost in grief, I'd lost track of what my parents had taught me about myself. Instead, I swallowed America's messages. In Dr. Lamb's naming, I began to draw a map out.

I saw the Patriot Act and 9/11 as being knotted up with my difficulty grieving my Nigerian and Muslim mother. I saw anti-Blackness and Islamophobia laying the building blocks for my young terror over everything, including my own queerness. I understood the shame I carried over my chronic pain and my families' ailing bodies as state designed. After all that, there was still more to know.

How had climate change become another one of America's tools, catalyzing Black and brown death? Was it my colonizer's tongue that was poisoning me? Was it the darkness that surrounds a queer woman before she's opened her closet? I'd lost the thread to my own story.

By the time the immigration detention centers were flooding the news in early 2016, I could see clearly that what history had unleashed on Black people was being used as a road map to harm others, and what was I supposed to do about that? What did I owe non-Black oppressed people? And what did it mean to want love from a nation built on someone else's erasure, on genocide, on stolen land?

I felt complicity for what I'd been forced to inhabit, and for what I'd gotten too comfortable with to disavow. Why do I have this mouthful of grief for people I'll never know, never meet?

I roamed like a zombie from physical therapy to my chiropractor's office to pain management centers. My body was constantly seeping with pain. I didn't know what to do with all my compounding hurts, but understood the stress of America had latched itself to the wound. More than anything, I wanted to know: How long is history? And how long would I have to be responsible for it? I needed healing and, in every beginning, found the violences of history. I looked and looked and looked at Black people until what I'd forgotten about us began to come back. I expected each violence unearthed to be a new wound. But no. History uncovered was my mind's salve.

I was trying to emerge from erasure.

Suddenly, I was standing at the cliff of my own life, remembering. White America had palimpsested itself over us. But scrape the picture back with one of my father's palette knives, and the world became splashed in colors once again. When I got to what I thought was *my* beginning, I had to go even further back. We, too, were a palimpsest written over someone else's origin story, someone else's land. There was a two-stranded twist where Black and Indigenous life wrapped around each other. There was a liminal space where our ancestors were obligated to each other, and where we were kin. My work was to find it. I'd know I'd arrived because there, our responsibilities to each other would be recognized as our good fortune.

I had to go back and then I had to go even further back again, until I'd gone so far, I ended up at *time's* beginning. There, I saw: I'd been living inside the story begotten by white America, but I'd been born into something else—*what was it?*

To find it, first I'd have to name it.

I was doubling back for what I'd lost—forgotten. I found that what haunted me was the *rest* of the story. The stories America intentionally forgot, obscured, mistold, hid. I took one step backwards, then another, preparing for each step to feel like quicksand. I knew a beginning was more than a starting point, it was a course of action. From earth's 4.5-billion-year history, I knew a beginning could be the longest road ever toed.

Theologians of the earth, geologists understand time and history in millions and billions of years, and through the formation and changing of the earth's rocks. They give time its own unique monikers: eons, eras, periods, epochs, ages. But my favorite thing about geology has always been how it makes time physical. Geology insists that time and history are matters of space, place. We know the Grand Canyon is six million years old because its Precambrian rocks tell us so. Hadn't *I* always been obsessed with time?

In elementary school, one of my favorite stories was *The Land before Time*. A group of trembling young dinosaurs flee famine, survive drought, earthquakes, a mother's death—though the dead mother's voice remains as a ghost in the ether. Her vestige guides them to safety and an oasis known as the Great Valley, which gapes back at them with still fifty-nine million years to go before the Grand Canyon is born. Their worlds have ended—their mother, their origin story, is gone. Their hand forced, they must begin something else.

How long it takes to start over was another way to measure time.

I peered into the earth's crust, and I saw time. In illustrated textbooks, time stretched longer the closer I got to the earth's fiery heart. I memorized landmasses. A valley was a low place that could take one hundred thousand years to form. Hills were born from the time-consuming buildup of deposits. Faults were exactly what I feared: with enough time, even the earth could fracture. My favorite lesson was always the supercontinent Pangea. Two hundred eighty million years ago was a geology where all was connected and the continents kissed. I was searching for a beginning like this.

"The mysteries of time are bound up in the great unknowns of the body and universe, from consciousness to black holes," writes book critic Parul Sehgal in "In Search of Time Lost and Newly Found." "But we've always reached for it." Since the very beginning of time, humans have attempted to fix it, "in language or theory, to possess it, reclaim it—"

When it came to time, my mother couldn't keep track of it, disappeared into it—severed her daughters from it by rarely speaking of her past. From me, grief and shame plundered years. As a child, the Black adults around me talked time incessantly. We didn't have any/we were running out/we'd been robbed—still could be. We measured time not in rock or fossils but with stories and through ancestors.

They made us that same kind of sturdy. Our ancestors were our Genesis, and I was trying to retrace/outrun/name *the Fall*. Had there ever been *any* kind of Eden?

In search of a new creation story, I looked to my father's early drawing lessons. I wanted to know, in the darkness, what else could be made.

My father has always loved the Spanish painter Francisco Goya's Black Paintings, which depict Greek myth, witches, goblins, and the violent heart of humankind in landscapes lit with ghostly blacks. Where, on Goya's canvases, I saw darkness, my father saw an expert in light—he saw skill. In that turn of my father's looking, I learned there was always more to see. As a child, when we drew together, my father pushed his pencil from the white point to the darkest dark. He told me, *In nature, black absorbs the light*—the pressure of his hand turning the shadows beneath his pencil blacker and blacker until what he was drawing became illuminated—3-D—somehow alive on the page—blackness converting light into energy.

Taking my cue from art, I named what I had lost—what I was attempting to remake: the Black Period.

Could I let the light back in?

Here lies the Fall: My body, my spirit, my mind—it had tumbled. As though down a beanstalk. I'd woken up in white America. And that world wanted the door of me kicked in. Every day, America painted over the Black Period, which nurtured and loved me. In my naming of the Black Period—like reading a sundial—life began to make sense.

More than the Age of Innocence, the Age of Aquarius, or the Age of Exploration, I saw "identity wars," the suppression of my rightfully earned rage, state-generated terrorism, erasure, exile, the disposability of life, and a rapid slide into climate disaster. White America was marking time with oppressions. But slowly, like a body revealing itself from a sculptor's marble, I saw: there was more to the story. I was remembering where I had come from.

It took me decades after forgetting to remember that what I've named the Black Period was more than the shelter I'd constructed in my imagination—it had a history deeper than the life that I build for myself every day, now.

The Black Period was the canvas where anything was possible—where old truths could be rescued. New ones made.

The Black Period is what, as a child, the Black and African adults that surrounded me were constantly drawing/writing/storytelling for us. Carrying their lessons, their histories and stories, forward, the Black Period is what I've learned—am still learning—to never stop rendering for myself as a Black queer woman in a world antagonistic to all these identities.

The Black Period was a state of mind, a position, a duration, something physical to hold in my hands. It was the soil that we planted our houses in. The Black Period was the entire expanse of what the Black adults around me called time and history. It was the stories they wrote and painted inside of us in order that our souls might survive the constant assaults awaiting our minds and bodies. The Black Period was something I could render once again.

Black people perpetually codeswitched between different worlds, but in the Black Period, *we* were the default. In the Black Period we were scientists, inventors, singers, poets, runaways, mathematicians, martyrs, abolitionists, and artists.

In the Black Period of my childhood, the houses were smaller than my white classmates' but larger than the shotgun houses my father, his siblings, and their aunties and uncles all seemed to be born in and larger than the dirt-floor house in Nigeria where my mother took her first breath. In the Black Period, the stoves never turned off. There was always something cooking in the kitchens. In this world, though hips and knees still hurt, the adults around me relaxed their shoulders a bit more.

The Black Period was a truth that, in the places I called home, was clear as day. It was as clear as the way Jesus and a church choir could lift my aunt Sarah's burdens. In the Black Period, almost any uncle could fix your car. My older cousin Andy could disassemble a military plane and put it back together. In the Black Period, we were magicians of accounting. We knew how to put even the laziest penny in our pockets to good work. Here, Aunt Liz read more books than even I did. I knew we were a family of records.

A child of the eighties and nineties home-video boom, I pressed play on one old 8mm home videocassette, then another. The past unfolded rapidly in hundreds of hours. There was Ms. India, dressed like a modern Nefertiti, in our Akron living room, her hands gripping the kinara that held the red, black, and green candles we lit every Kwanzaa. Like we were remaking the world, we lit a candle for each of the seven days of celebration. "And he rested on the seventh day from all his work which he had made," said bibles, nuns, and my Catholic school. But on Kwanzaa's seventh day we shouted, "Imani." The white world could be hopeless, but in one another we kept the "faith." Remixing my father's making methods, I found words.

I say "the Black Period," and mean "home" in all its shape-shifting ways. I walked around trying to imagine the feeling of emancipation. The Black Period was calling me back. It was possible to emerge from erasure. But first, there were things I had to know.

A writer, I read and read and read. Like bell hooks, "I came to theory because I was hurting . . . I came to theory desperate, wanting to comprehend." Having strayed so far from the Black Period, I needed a language. As hooks writes, I needed a naming in order to "grasp what was happening around and within me."

I began to name my shame what it really was: America testing how long its history could last.

To tell you everything I have to tell you, we'll have to arrive at the brink of exhaustion. You'll have to believe me when I say history is a magic trick. To arrive at the particular predicament of our present, I could begin anywhere: 1492, 1776, 1865, 1954, 2016, 2020. Pick a number, any number.

In the beginning—

REVERBERATION,
~~REVERBERATION~~

AGE I

THE BODY

STARE OUT AT THE GRAND CANYON'S PRECAMBRIAN ROCK, searching for the oldest way to know a country. Red cliffs thrust into vanishing violets. Some borrow the blue of the sky. This canyon aches inside me. My wife, Stephanie, my best friend Camille—her belly at the end of its first trimester—Andrey, her Belarusian husband, and I have come to see the rarest thing of all: a beginning. Have come in search of a reminder that beyond these bodies, we are rock, river, gully. Though, too, we are a fee we've paid the U.S. government to access once-sovereign sites of emergence for the Hualapai, Havsuw 'Baaja, Hopi, Yavapai Apache, Diné, Zuni, and Paiute Nations—as a small plaque, designed to be barely visible in our minds, tells us.

Across their kidnapped landscape, white cliffrose and pink Apache plume bloom. Moss, green and purplish shrubs patch the expanse. Shale, sand, and limestone glimmer in the March sun. The Grand Canyon is something both brand-new and familiar, like the hues my father used in the children's books he illustrated me and my sister, Jamila, into—it's like holding each of my nephews for the very first time. Above, the clouds ink up every color. I consider the status of my back. It's been a decade of chiropractors, cortisol shots, these invisible bricks the size of my country that live at my back, neck, and shoulders. Pain has lived in me, with me so long, I no longer name it.

Unlike our white partners, Camille and I have never been to this part of America before. This 1,902-square-mile canyon stretching out in front of us is so beautiful it veers on incomprehensible. Called Ongtupqa by the Hopi, Bidáá' Ha'azt'i' Tsékooh by the Diné, and Wi:ka'i:la by the Yavapai, the white colonizers first referred to it as "The Great Unknown." They drew it as a literal blank spot on their maps, but my father would paint this scene blue-violet, paint it into the in-betweens of color to remind me that value, a gradient between light and dark, is an interpretation by the hand of the creator.

My father would say: *They can't even look over their shoulders and find a hero.* A man aging more and more into non sequiturs, I know he means truth, legacy, and white people. He means beginnings and us. When my father speaks of beginnings, he means this nation is a dangerous place to be stuck. A bad beginning, he's warned me, can make you mistake treading water for swimming. It can be the wrong end of a stick, while the right beginning can be a rescue.

GAZING OUT AT ONE ORIGIN, I FIND IT IMPOSSIBLE NOT TO CONsider the end of mine. My father came home on his lunch break to catch my mother in his arms as she died from a single massive stroke. Her brain burst like a colossal star. I was a sophomore in college. Now, she's been gone so long, is all that's left of her, her propagation? Me, my sister, the grandchildren she loves but will never meet or know.

I don't see the capital of the Havasupai Indian Reservation, the village of Supai, at the base of the canyon. I'm too far away to see the fresh footprints on their ancestral footpaths. Still, I know, like all Indigenous peoples, the Havsuw 'Baaja have to fight for their ancestral lands inside the young laws of illegitimate governments. They have had to take "beginnings" to court, despite having called the base of the canyon home since AD 1300. For both Native and Black folks, white America tries to legislate the start of our narratives, overwriting our beginnings with "manifest destiny," smiling slaves, mascots, in classrooms—on TV, in history and children's books—and through marginalizing tactics like redlining, censorship, and incarceration and policing. This need to guard our origin stories I recognize as one of the many things our people have in common.

"We didn't ask to be put on a reservation . . . [this] was imposed on us," Coleen Kaska, a former Havasupai tribal council member, tells a reporter in 2017, reminding me of the 1964 Malcolm that so many of the Black adults of my childhood loved to shout: "We didn't land on Plymouth Rock! The rock was landed on us!"

Kaska, whose parents taught her that her duty was "to grow up and pursue the lands that we have lost."

But I won't read Kaska's words until months later when I finally google this place I've come to so easily, not knowing much of anything about it. For now, from our vantage point, it is easy to assume that there is no one here but us.

THE HAVSUW 'BAAJA ARE "THE BLUE CREEK PEOPLE," NAMED THE Havasupai tribe by the federal government. They are the first people documented in North America, more than twenty thousand years ago, and their language is suspected to be the first spoken in the Americas. This land—Red Butte, "mountain of the clenched fist"— which they have occupied for centuries, is one of their most sacred spaces. In the Havsuw 'Baaja people's creation story of themselves and humankind, they were birthed from a tributary of the Grand Canyon. The first people, they are its protectors and stewards.

As history goes, the U.S. government stole most of the Havsuw 'Baaja's land, restricting them, in 1882, to a 518-acre reservation, and devastating an existence which heavily relied on its ecosystems. Today, the tribe lives at the canyon's base year-round, though before the land theft it was their summer home, and they migrated to the higher plateaus in the winter.

"My tribe has lost over 500 million acres, which includes all the plateau lands up here and Grand Canyon National Park. We were told that we could not live there anymore," Kaska told the conservation nonprofit Grand Canyon Trust in 2019 for their oral history project. Not until 1975 did the Havsuw 'Baaja succeed in suing the federal government for the return of 185,000 acres.

In me and Jamila, my mother's language didn't survive the journey over the Atlantic, but an astonishing 95 percent of the tribe speak dialects of their Yuman tongue, making it the only Native language spoken by almost its entire population. I'm learning how cunningly, how quickly—and how frequently—stolen beginnings can be discarded or renamed "lost" inside something as vast as empire. Whether we want to know it or not, when we say "the Grand Canyon," we are always speaking of the Havsuw 'Baaja. These days, the Havsuw 'Baaja refer to the Grand Canyon as Wambodajwogo—"where the train stops."

THE VILLAGE OF SUPAI IS A TOURIST HOT SPOT. IT HOLDS A HELI-copter landing pad, a tourist office, a small museum, rodeo grounds, and a café. With a population of around 450, Supai has a small elementary school of approximately seventy K-through-sixth-graders. Supai's only school, it opened in 1895 before being shuttered by the U.S. government in 1976.

In 1982, the tribe reopened what is still known today as Havasupai Elementary. After twenty years—and due to a lack of financial and administrative support from the Bureau of Indian Affairs (BIA)—the tribe, denied resources, couldn't meet the standards of the 2001 No Child Left Behind Act—legislation that would do just that: leave behind poor students, students with disabilities, and due to systemic racism in schools, students of color. The tribe's hand forced, control of the school was transferred to the Bureau of Indian Education (BIE).

Because the federal government does not provide Supai the funding or resources for a high school, parents must choose between moving their families away from their homes or boarding their children out to neighboring areas for semesters at a time, or even years. As of 2017, none of the teachers are from the reservation. Instead, like tourists, they fly in and out of Supai by helicopter during the school week.

As a child attending an almost-all-white, all-girls Catholic school, I'd spent most of fourth grade in libraries obsessively reading books about Native-assimilation schools. Page after page, I read about Native children who'd been kidnapped from their communities, held hostage in classrooms where they were punished for their language, their culture, their sovereignty, their clothing, their hair, their home—all that gave color to *their* Black Periods.

In those books about Native-assimilation schools, it was the white people—the teachers, the nuns—and their structures that all felt so familiar. How their tenderness could vanish in response to my skin. How their faces could betray a distaste that left a cold stone in my belly. In those library books, I recognized that America also responded to me as less of a someone. I was a some*thing* that needed to be watched, needed correction.

FORTY-THREE HUNDRED FEET BELOW US, THE COLORADO RIVER rushes like frothy tap water, or like time, this measure well understood by Indigenous peoples, Black folks, and geologists. If my mother were still alive, she'd only be sixty-eight years old, a reminder that, after being gone seventeen years, she could still be so young. But she is an apparition that, in the past, my grief rarely allowed me to call to the present.

I try my hand at remembering. An origin story is what you make of it. It can be a culture, a treasured heirloom, or a history, reduced. Like the shore village my family and I visited the year before, near Kunta Kinteh Island in The Gambia—one of the transatlantic slave trade's earliest ports, in my brother-in-law's home country—tourism is Supai's largest income driver. This knowledge feels cruel. But what is the difference between looking, knowing, and memory?

If my mother's goneness is a river, I'd say it took me fifteen years to cross. But standing at the top of the Grand Canyon, I see her clearly now, smiling wide in front of Chautauqua Lake. It's 1994, my mother forty-two. I'm ten and we're about to leave *Highlights* magazine's artist retreat for children's authors, where my father, also an illustrator, has been invited. She has yet to cut her hair into an afro, and her green scrunchy holds back a long pony.

In the home video taken that last day, sailboats line the dock. The occasional seagull dashes in and out of view, fussing up the camera's autofocus. Jamila, thirteen, wears iconic nineties Black girl bangs and her usual ballet flats.

"Let's see if my ship is out there, waiting to sail," our mother says as she moves her body to the edge of the water. The pitch of her voice, high and soft enough that it competes with the birds. Like the way she says the word "lettuce," British colonization injects something a hint British into her Nigerian accent. Smiling, our mother asks the wind and her daughters if where she really wants to sail is off to Nigeria. "Or do I want to go sightseeing to places I've never been before?" Now—is it me or Jamila who holds the camera?

Our mother's dimples indent her face like two stars punching the night with light. Laughing, she calls the day "Saturday, the twenty-third of September," until my know-it-all sister interjects.

It's 7:30 and an ever-shifting blue dusk falls over the lake. "I'm sorry, it's July—I'm ahead of my time," our mother says to remind the me now she could be this funny.

"You see what happens when you're amongst all this literature, and its poets, and artists," she says, shoving an arm out toward a horizon that's seeing its way to purple.

Wind, and me and Jamila's bickering, knocks the sound of our mother to unintelligibility, but after ten minutes in iMovie, I can make out a few of her words. Something about a concert by Simon and Garfunkel, who she taught me to love. She calls them writers, inspirations. Says her "creative juices are flowing."

Standing in front of a lake whose name is derived from the now-dormant Erie language of the "no-longer-extant" Erie people, as described by the Oklahoma Historical Society, my dead mother gestures back to the conference we've left—I'm staring into a moment where everything is gone.

She quotes one of the speakers: "A writer always carries a pen." Her neck is so long, she looks like a crane that might fly away. "I don't have a pen on me, but the writer in me, in my veins, is telling me exactly what to say," my mother says, and the me now doesn't know what to think. Even as a child, I recognized that she had a whole sky inside her, but did my mother fashion herself a writer?

I see her blue ink ball pen writing *thank you* across the only journal page she ever wrote. Her handwriting still more like Jamila's than it will ever be mine.

She's forty-seven. There's four more years of life left in her.

May 6, 1999

In the name of God the merciful, the benefactor after so many years of wanting to start a journal, I have finally started one myself. Thanks to Oprah Winfrey & her reruns & inspiration from speakers like Iyanla Vanzant, John Gray, Suze Orman & so many others.

I started off the day with PBS at 5:30am with inspiration from Desmond Tutu of the South African Reconciliation Tribunal. With people like him & Nelson Mandela—they give hope to the world and I thank God for sending them & giving them the courage to do what they did.

I also thank God for my family, my husband & my children. I also thank God for the good people who have touched our lives.

Every time I read it, I can't help myself—I laugh. Both of us finally having risen to our own "other side." She's cooking jollof rice at the stove. She's kiki-ing on the phone with a cousin in Nigeria. She's spreading her prayer mat East. She's in her garden, bent over a crown of marigolds. I recognize the miracle of a clearing.

∞

If history is an indicator, my mother would be staring at the Grand Canyon's views from a wheelchair. Toward the final years of her life, her legs constantly ached, she took naps during the day, but the only explanation her doctor could give her was hypertension. Dr. Washington was a Black man with the kind of beard that grew so thick, even with a close trim, it looked painted on. He had the habit of speaking to my mother as if he were trying to piss me off. He spoke *reeeeaaalll* slow—amused, as if he couldn't comprehend a world where English was the national language of an African woman.

One afternoon, my parents and I drove to the airport to pick my sister up. Maybe I was sixteen. Jamila—whose name, in Arabic, means "beauty"—was nineteen or twenty, and returning from one of her many stints abroad. My mother had already begun to look like a faded picture. At the airport, with my mother's body mysteriously exhausted, an airport attendant pushed her in a wheelchair as my parents smiled widely in anticipation of seeing my sister.

I didn't understand why, but shame flooded my body to see my mother in a wheelchair. Neither of my parents had explained to me what was going on. Why was my mother tired all the time? Why had dark flecks suddenly begun appearing in her eyes? Between us, there was only the silence that flooded the ailing, failing body that was my origin story.

The poet and writer Leah Lakshmi Piepzna-Samarasinha argues that for Indigenous and Black folks and POC communities, "being sick or disabled can just be 'life.'" It's an origin story that reveals to me my family's entire world. By my freshman year of college, my father, like my grandmother, had become a diabetic. After a decade of limping, he survived two painful hip replacements. He's endured triple bypass heart surgery, stents. Most recently lung cancer robbed him of a lobe. My grandfathers are young, dead—different kinds of missing. I see my American grandmother and remember, toward the end, she could barely walk. Gone by the time I was sixteen, she lived the last years of her life in a nursing home, a stroke leaving her unable to move anything other than her eyes. Yaya, my mother's mother, like my father's, also survived her share of strokes. Each one ate away at their bodies. In the end Yaya, having outlived my mother, was paralyzed down one side. And then there was the world beyond my relations. Those who, to me, still felt like kin.

There was Erica Garner—daughter of Esaw Garner Snipes and Eric Garner. Dead from an asthmatic attack that triggered cardiac arrest at twenty-seven, Erica was the mother of two young children, and grieving in a world where images and videos of her father's murder by the hands of the police circulated like wind. There was Shalon Irving, CDC epidemiologist, brand-new mother, and dead at thirty-six from complications due to hypertension and the refusal of a system to believe Black mothers or offer them adequate postpartum healthcare. And there was Shalon's mother, Wanda, raising the baby left behind.

Whether physical, psychological, or cognitive, it's estimated that, globally, one in seven people live with a disability—a number that is rising due to large aging populations such as baby boomers, as well as an increase in illnesses ranging from cancers to strokes to long Covid. Eighty percent of people living with disabilities—including children—have disabilities that are invisible to others, such as ADHD, autism, complex trauma, depression, hypertension, autoimmune disorders, my chronic pain and anxiety, my father's diabetes and arthritis. Our pain, in/visible as the chronic fatigue that stalked my mother at the end of her life.

LIKE BLACK PEOPLE, THE HAVSUW 'BAAJA MUST FIGHT THE UNITED States for their right to everything: their land, natural resources, their own narratives, ownership of their DNA, their living and ancestral bodies, their children's education. But unlike any other group in the United States, the Havsuw 'Baaja, like all Native people in the U.S., are indigenous to the U.S. and have an inherent right to their home-lands given to them by their creator/s, though they suffer from centu-ries of land theft at the hands of the U.S. government. Standing atop someone else's home, I don't yet know that at Havasupai Elementary, approximately half the students have disabilities ranging from physi-cal to developmental to behavioral.

I don't yet know that since 2017, the Native American Disability Law Center (NADLC) has been in federal court suing the BIE on behalf of nine Havasupai Elementary students with disabilities—ages six through fifteen—and their families. Their diagnoses vary: ADHD, emotional disturbances, and specific learning disabilities (SLD).

The Americans with Disabilities Act defines disability as "a condi-tion of the body or mind (impairment) that makes it more difficult for the person with the condition to do certain activities (activity limita-tion) and interact with the world around them (participation restric-tions)." The very name of the act implying protection be reserved for Americans, a designation that defaults to white. But because the cu-mulative effects of systemic racism—from environmental concerns to education to immigration to gun and police violence—are disabling, Indigenous communities, followed by Black people, have the highest disability rates across both children and working-age adults.

At Havasupai Elementary, there are no systems and nowhere near enough trained staff to accommodate students. Instead, children with disabilities are sent home. They are limited to reduced hours, in some cases as few as three a week. At times, teachers and administrators rely on law enforcement to respond to behavioral issues that are man-ifestations of students' complex traumas and disabilities. I'll be too overwhelmed by the cruelty to understand the words on the page when I first read that, in 2017, an eleven-year-old Havasupai Elemen-tary child was arrested and indicted in federal court for yanking a cord out of the back of a computer monitor—the case only thrown out because the cops got the time and the boy's name wrong. But it's the same school-to-prison pipeline that targets my people.

All the students in the NADLC's case experience complex trauma—an invisible disability—which researchers have shown can lead to palpable physiological harm in developing brains. In her seminal 1992 text, *Trauma and Recovery: The Aftermath of Violence—From Domestic Abuse to Political Terror*, Judith Herman introduced the concept of complex trauma to describe how people respond to prolonged exposure to interpersonal stress, and how these traumas and stressors accumulate in us over time. In Black people, this accumulation is called "weathering"—a concept first developed by public health researcher Arline T. Geronimus to explain the cumulative impact of the racism, both subtle and overt, that Black people experience daily, from institutional bias to overpolicing to political disenfranchisement to the social alienation in communities and across our intimate relationships. State-induced trauma causes our biological clocks to run fast, aging us, on average, 6.1 years faster than our white counterparts. Psychological anthropologists Janis H. Jenkins and Bridget M. Haas historicize trauma as "empire," a description that feels so apt I can almost touch its walls. "Black don't crack," but the systemic and interpersonal racism we experience daily erodes us away.

ALL AROUND ME, BRIGHT-ORANGE GLOBEMALLOWS, PURPLE LU-pines, and neon Yellow Queens groom the cliffs. The Grand Canyon is a place where music needs no sound. Each layer of rock like waveforms on an audio graph, color-splashed by ancient history.

As natural resources, canyons are unusual. To shape them, nouns turn into verbs. Over millions and billions of years, wind, sand, and water become actions that author the landscape. Nature never ceases. Canyons are not only repositories of history: like us, canyons are history recording itself in real time.

Canyons are one of the rare places in the world where we can see the earth's past, layer by spectacular layer—its origin stories. The Grand Canyon makes visible millions of years, and in stark color contrast. Each layer reveals not just length of time but chronology. Whereas "for Europeans, ownership of land is a dominant value," writes Maria Yellow Horse Brave Heart and Lemyra M. DeBruyn in "The American Indian Holocaust: Healing Historical Unresolved Grief," "for American Indians, land, plants, and animals are considered sacred relatives, far beyond a concept of property. Their loss became a source of grief."

The conditions of Havasupai Elementary students' complex traumas are historical, stemming from centuries of displacement, overpolicing, overincarceration, racism, and the poverty of their communities due to centuries of theft. These forces combine to exacerbate and increase incidents of addiction and violence. I say this no longer knowing who I'm talking about, us or them.

Journalist Adam Serwer argues, "The cruelty is the point." But, I think, it's also the theft. It's through Black and brown people's exploitation that whiteness plunders its riches. We are priceless—though our oppressors settle, time and time again, for a king's ransom.

Black and Indigenous communities are sequestered into the bull's-eye of this country. Though separate, we are also a we. Though the United States positions us to forget by pitting our communities against each other, as with the Creek Freedmen and Choctaw Freedmen—the Afro-Indigenous descendants of enslaved people owned by Indigenous tribes, who to this day, due in part to anti-Blackness in Native communities, are still denied their tribal citizenship.

A few months away from this canyon, I will know everything Google and the NADLC can tell me about Havasupai Elementary's cruel conditions. I'll recognize it all in disbelief. Every telling revealing that there's more to the story—*where can I find it?*

I'll think of *In the Wake,* a book about the afterlife of enslavement—Christina Sharpe looking at a Haitian girl after Haiti's 2010 earthquake. The girl wears a piece of transparent tape across her forehead that reads, *Ship.* Sharpe asks, "What is the look in her eyes? What do I do with it?"

I'll read the NADLC's suit almost obsessively, page after page of neglect unfolding—*make it make sense*—what do I do with it?

I don't know, but recognize the answer lies somewhere inside the very achievable dream of abolition. This desire to build, which activist and organizer Mariame Kaba describes in *We Do This 'Til We Free Us* as a "a vision of a restructured society in a world where we have everything we need: food, shelter, education, health, art, beauty, clean water, and more things that are foundational to our personal and community safety"—this ultimate Black Period. Abolition, rooted in our refusal to surrender our right to dream.

NEXT TO ME, CAMILLE ISOLATES HERSELF ATOP A LARGE BOULDER in the middle of the viewpoint, mindful of the crowd, the Black-Belarusian-Jamaican-American baby boy who grows inside her, and a virus whose name we barely know. The clouds cascade sunlight across the canyon's open mouth. She rubs the child in her belly who we'd all, long ago, begun to love. Like this canyon, her mothering is eons in the making—in my mind, mine says: repeat after me. My mother quotes Nikki Giovanni, June Jordan, Langston Hughes. With almost a song in her voice, she sounds off Audre Lorde's "The master's tools will never dismantle the master's house." I see my father walking around my childhood in paint-splattered jeans. He's humming Nancy Wilson, Sam Cooke. He's been painting all day and it's made something in him—and thus in me and Jamila—so much lighter. Did my parents know then that dreaming was a requirement of freedom?

But while we canyon-gaze, Havasupai Elementary's school day marches on. Three thousand feet below, students receive, at best, an inconsistent education in math, reading, and writing. I've read about the school before, but standing at the lip of their ancestral cliffs, I won't remember until I'm gone. Above them, a rainbow hangs in the gap.

Black, queer, a woman with a Nigerian Muslim mother and a Black American father, in the present, I don't know how to balance the ledgers of this life I make on colonized land. The students at Havasupai Elementary, along with another forty-six thousand Indigenous students across twenty-three states, attend schools run by BIE. Instead of the Department of Education, the BIE is overseen by the Interior, whose function has nothing to do with young people's education but is primarily responsible for overseeing national parks and resources.

"Throughout our history, we have fought to provide a quality education to our children," writes the tribe's chairman, Don E. Watahomigie in a 2017 statement to the press. "The Havasupai Tribal Council has approached the BIE many times about its failures to provide adequate staff, a complete curriculum, accommodations to disabled students, involvement of a local school board, and the list goes on and on. And each time we raise these issues we are given promises that are never delivered upon."

At Havasupai Elementary, as of 2020, there is no science, no history, no social studies, no foreign languages, no art programs, no PE, no field trips, no library, and not enough textbooks to allow students to take them home. It's less 2020, more Jim Crow.

ANOTHER WAY WE CAN UNDERSTAND COMPLEX TRAUMA IS THROUGH what philosopher Jill Stauffer calls *ethical loneliness*—"the experience of having been abandoned by humanity compounded by the experience of not being heard."

Ethical loneliness, like complex trauma, applies not just to victims of war and genocide but also to marginalized groups in the United States, such as Indigenous, Black, Latinx, Asian, transgender, incarcerated, and disabled communities, who continue to suffer under historical injustices. Beyond the state and its immediate actors, ethical loneliness is compounded by what Stauffer identifies as the failure of "just-minded people to hear well."

I think of all my days in a white Catholic school—the fear, the isolation, the names I was called, the bad histories I was given. The days piled themselves on top of all the warnings and worries that occupied America, surrounding Black people like a second aura. There were days it felt impossible to learn.

Now, as an adult, the murders of Black people at the hands of the police populate my screens. There are days I swear I could weather away amidst the swell of state violence and the daily microaggressions that make me wonder how anything will ever change. Both my doctor and my therapist warn that my chronic pain cannot be separated from my stress, my memories, my current and inherited traumas.

We build monuments, watch Black names trend, while, year after year, our legislators increase the budgets of police departments, ICE, and the Department of Defense, meanwhile underfunding virtually

every social service that would render these violent institutions obsolete: education, food and housing assistance, mental/healthcare, disability services, programs in the arts, and employment benefits.

LOOKING OUT AT THE GRAND CANYON, I'M SUDDENLY AWARE, AND
in a new way, of the urgency to understand the difference between
stolen, lost, and gone, and all that is still there but which I have been
conditioned not to see.

Disability justice helps us to understand disability as it is experienced in tandem with other forms of oppression, such as race, class,
incarceration, citizenship, gender, and sexuality. Mia Mingus, one of
the developers of the framework and a Korean transracial/transna-
tional adoptee, says, "We must leave evidence. Evidence that we were
here, that we existed, that we survived and loved and ached. Evidence
of the wholeness we never felt and the immense sense of fullness we
gave to each other. Evidence of who we were, who we thought we
were, who we never should have been. Evidence for each other that
there are other ways to live—past survival; past isolation." We have to
be our *own* evidence.

Was this what my parents had been doing all along—leaving evidence? Now, in me and Stephanie's Brooklyn basement, Tupperware
after Tupperware holds family photo albums, hundreds of loose photographs, negatives, and home videos documenting Nigeria from the
1950s and beyond, next to scatterings of documents from my childhood, and from my parents' separate, then merged, pasts. Their insistence on documenting our lives in photographs, home videos, stories,
art, and the clothes on our bodies was a refusal to let any more of our
stories be lost.

"Like the transfer of trauma to descendants from Holocaust survivors," write Brave Heart and DeBruyn, "the genocide of American
Indians reverberates across generations." But then so does the resilience of their ancestors' legacies as they are taken up, collectively,
by the community. Together with students and their families, the
NADLC is fighting to have disability protections for students be ex-

panded to recognize the harmful effects of complex trauma and adverse childhood experiences on a child's developing brain and how they learn—including physical and sexual violence, addiction, poverty, incarceration, interactions with the welfare system, denial of educational access, and the real kicker: historical trauma. Their work is a countercartography, a map of state violence. Across communities of color, from Black to Indigenous, Asian, and Latinx communities, though our complex traumas vary, America ensures we have something in common: the trauma*tizers*.

WHEN I READ KIM NIELSEN'S *A DISABILITY HISTORY OF THE UNITED States*—where she'd written, "Most indigenous communities had no word or concept for what in American English we today call 'disability,'"—I thought of home. I don't remember any Black or African community I was a part of ever using the word. For us, like for Indigenous peoples, "'disability' occurred when someone lacked or had weak community relationships." And Black folks, well, we had our own names for that: *sell-out, no count, triflin', snitch, Uncle Tom, house nigger, Black Republican.* Beyond that, our bodies were just our bodies.

Physically, we'd been shaped by colonization and enslavement's legacies, by being of the South. Corporations were poisoning our land, our air, our waters. Our old folks had bodies that had spent a lifetime in physical labor. For some of us, history had left haints in our minds. Our backs, knees, and hips hurt. Decades of my grandmother cleaning a white woman's home got my father to college but left my grandmother with a body that ached all the time. There were days her hands hurt so bad she could barely make a fist.

Though it was a lesson I lost track of, the Black and African communities of my childhood were my first models of what disability justice could look like in practice. It was a love we left unnamed. We never threw anyone away. Those around us who ailed were cared for in their ailing, still valuable to everyone who surrounded them. There were times when there was so much tenderness for a body it softened the language and volume of our play as children. In the Black Period, we believed in what we owed to our ancestors.

In those days, disability was a word used to say a check had come, or one was late. All we knew was that it didn't hold our whole story, like how, when our bodies were too tired, too hurt, too harmed, too disassembled to meet the world, we were carried. When the folks who carried hurt from the carrying and couldn't carry anymore, it was enough just to be sat with for a while. If you couldn't work, someone fixed you a room in their house. Everyone fixed you a plate. Being Black meant, to get *in* the black, we had to pay it forward—and we had to pay it backward, too. In the Indigenous context, "healing is relational," writes Chicana and Apache scholar Natalie Avalos. "It must be facilitated in and through not only relationships with others, but also one's relationship with one's own wound. This kind of healing invites the process of feeling once again and is supported by being witnessed, having one's humanness and pain acknowledged by others."

The last years of my American grandmother's life, I watched our whole family change its orbit to be near her aching body. By then, she mainly reigned from her front-room sitting chair. Friends and family members circled, asking, *Madear, Madear,* wanting to know if anything they had was something she needed. As a child, I felt quieted by witnessing, by wanting to be a part of that tenderness, too. There were days God seemed constructed of only music, and you knew right then in your bones that tenderness was too holy for the Lord, our savior, to be a white man.

If we understood disability, it was as a moving line drawn by the ways the white world refused us. But having lived refused by America all along, no one around me knew disability was the word to use. It was simply our humanity spilling from us, we had so much of it. We were waterfalls. We were wind-tossed. Our parents made sure we knew that our humanity was pollinating a whole fucking country. To quote Mississippi writer Kiese Laymon, "This that black *abundance.*"

But before I found, again, that Black abundance the Black Period had drawn in me, my main companion was shame. In America, my mother, my origin story, was simply written as something Black that had fallen out of use. After she died, I lived in shame over her body's slow, then abrupt demise. What did a dead mother with an ailing, failing body say about mine? At home, what looked like taking care and making space the white world painted as weakness, painted a sick body—especially a Black one—as inconvenient, disruptive, poor. Was my shame the bruise of historical memory? Of forced sterilizations, bodies killed, sold, maimed, humiliated? Was it simply the work of *the Fall*?

Losing my mother so young is something I'll never completely understand. But there's been other work. I had to learn who, in her absence, I'd become. It would take me another decade to understand that my shame was a ghost story. I learned to say "I have a disability." My anxiety and chronic pain—though often invisible to others—means I have more than one.

NEXT TO ME, CAMILLE FLICKERS BENEATH THE SUN. SHE UNWRAPS a Clif Bar—a faint sound that beckons an overly domesticated squirrel, who approaches her begging aggressively. Because of man-made pollution, legislation protects the air quality that is the canyon's 160-mile sight line. A clear view is simply more profitable. A pandemic is coming, but the one called capitalism is already here.

I am torn between my back's crying, the start of time, a beautiful place, and marketing. In Supai, the cops who patrol the reservation and the cops who circle Havasupai Elementary are one and the same. There is about 1 cop for every 150 people, compared to Phoenix's 1 for every 500. And as with the teachers at Havasupai Elementary, as of 2017, none of the tribal police officers are from Supai. Instead, they are assigned by the BIA, though, in many Native communities beyond Supai, the police are staffed from inside the tribal communities. The BIA itself has Indigenous preference in hiring and many Native people, in search of steady employment, or in their desire to help Native people inside the broken U.S. federal government, work for the BIA. In a country that creates contradictions, this contradiction is not unique to Indigenous communities, but replicates in the form of Black police officers in Black neighborhoods and Mexican Americans/Chicanos who work for U.S. Border Patrol.

AS A CHILD, I'D WITNESSED BLACK PEOPLE IN CHURCH WAIL WITH the joy of having outrun something I could never understand but knew was American. And now the view ahead of me, again, asks history be taken in. At the Grand Canyon, like everywhere, knowing is a matter of both desire and looking.

Soon, and all over the world, Black Lives Matter protesters will, once again, flood streets. We'll be protesting our murder at the hands of the police, our state-enabled deaths by Covid-19, massive unemployment, a housing crisis, and our disposability as "essential workers." Fed up—traumatized—protesters will smash in the windows of AutoZones and Targets. The news, mistaking business and corporate shopping complexes for home, will tell us not to destroy "our own communities."

SHOULDER TO SHOULDER, WE ARE FOUR AND A HALF DIFFERENT kinds of citizens, including the unborn. It's as easy as it is hard to forget that at some point, history has declared each of us illegal in some way: miscegenation, queerness, gender, self-sovereignty, and immigration. We mark time by the way the sky changes.

Around us, children roam, looking like the people they've come from, and I feel okay missing my mother. Trees jut out from the canyon's rocks. Some grow sideways. Their invisible root systems make them appear as though they defy gravity. A root system is another way to say "I remember"—like how acorn, hickory, and beech trees, sudden synchronists, mast-fruit in unison. "If one tree fruits, they all fruit—there are no soloists," says Robin Wall Kimmerer, a botanist, a scientist, and a member of the Citizen Potawatomi Nation.

Seven months from now, come October 2020, and with the help of

Black and Latinx kids living in California's Compton School District, a judge will rule in the NADLC's and Havasupai Elementary students' favor. Two years before the NADLC suit, the Compton students had won their own for students with complex trauma—stemming from growing up in one of the county's most under-resourced cities—to qualify for disability protections, requiring the school and the federal government to finally start meeting their educational needs.

And though it is one thing to win and another altogether to get the government to act, the NADLC's suit, aided by the community of Compton, opens the possibility of changing education, not just for all forty-six thousand students under the BIE's control, but for students with complex trauma all over the country.

"Not one tree in a grove," Kimmerer says in *Braiding Sweetgrass*, "but the whole grove; not one grove in the forest, but every grove; across the county and all across the state. The trees act not as individuals, but somehow as a collective. Exactly how they do this, we don't yet know." From copse to orchard to entire woodlands, the genius of the community of mast-fruiting trees creates a symphony. The language of mast-fruiting communication is invisible to humans, but it reminds me that the work is global and collective.

IN A FEW HOURS, FROM THE FIELD OUTSIDE AN AIRBNB IN PAGE, Arizona, when day passes into moonless night, we'll hold Ursa Major's stars in our sights. By this time the Diné nation will be completely closed, and the next day, cutting short our trip, we'll rush back to New York trying to outrun a virus. But in that moment, we'll cling to stars.

In six months, Camille and Andrey will name the baby Nova, Latin for "new." In astronomy, novae—ascendant luminous stars— most frequently occur in the sky along the path of the Milky Way, which, other than Andromeda, holds every star we see from earth.

But for now, the viewpoint is full of language: Russian, Arabic, Korean, Chinese. Nothing but history can explain this canyon, this color, this string inside of us that it pulls. Below us, the Colorado River makes itself heard. Our bodies mixed up with the wind that pushes up the basin.

Book critic Parul Sehgal asks, "What would it look like to emerge from erasure?" Is it a world where we can safely fruit?

SIMULACRA

AGE II

IDENTITY WARS

CAN'T TELL YOU THE DAY OUR MOTHER EMBRACED THE FACT
that the state was not invested in saving her, but I can describe
the years.

She was a co-op shopper, bread maker, juicer, fresh fruit drier—a
woman of natural remedies. By the early 2000s, she'd veganed out
gallstones, tried out-walking hypertension, high blood pressure, her
father's uncertain death in Nigeria when she was four. It was like she
was trying to pull the lever of a railroad switch and change the direction of a train no one else could hear, but she knew was coming. As
my mother neared the end of her fifty-one revolutions around the
sun, I grew petrified for her body, which, by the time I'd become a
teenager, I could see was beginning to populate with gaps.

- 5'6"
- 115 pounds of metabolism
- Skin the color of home
- The most flexible adult I knew
- A Fulani woman raised in a British Hausaland

My older sister and I had been raised in America since the ages of
six and three, but our home life had been dominated by the country
we'd left. We ate jollof rice, tuwo shinkafa, kuka. Like a proper Nigerian, my mother could turn any food into a stew. Both of my parents,
even my American father, wore the intricately wax-printed clothes
they had custom tailored in Nigeria. My father's art leaned against and
hung on every wall: drawings of West Africa's landscapes and the oil
painted replications of people he'd lived with and taught among at
Ahmadu Bello University for seven years.

Nigeria is a country split between Islam and Christianity, which didn't bother my father. Once upon a time a believer, he'd spent most of his life surrounded by women renouncing idols—his mother, his old and new sisters, his brand-new wife. But during the seven years my father lived there with my mother—the years in which my sister and I came—he was a layman among Muslims. A Black American artist, he went from village to village, a witness to my mother's corner of the Muslim and African world.

IN 1987, THE YEAR WE MOVED TO AMERICA, EAZY-E RELEASED "Boyz-n-the-Hood," Toni Morrison, *Beloved,* and Rita Dove won the Pulitzer. Aretha Franklin, the "queen of soul," had just become the first woman to be inducted into the Rock & Roll Hall of Fame. *A Different World*—a sitcom about Black kids in college—premiered. On every stage, Black people were rearchitecting the straw man's version of American history.

We arrived in the United States and bounced from Dayton, Ohio, to Lynn, Massachusetts, to Kent, Ohio, before settling in Akron in 1991. In our American life, we were a kind of repository for my mother's friends and relatives who cycled in from Nigeria for months at a time: Uncle Abubakar; my auntie Mairo, my mother's eldest sister, who seemed to spend whole days making everyone laugh; later her daughters, my cousins Mimi and Baby, in their hijabs, and then again with their own small children in tow. Everywhere I looked in this childhood of mine, there was prayer. There were women cloaking themselves in their god's invisible sheen. Islam and Nigeria were the life-sized picture book we lived inside. Our mother's whole existence and my father's art instructed me and Jamila to question the truth of a map.

In Akron, Ohio, our three-story turn-of-the-century house occupied the corner plot of Cochran and Firestone. At 324 Cochran Avenue, our grass grew wild like a field that had been abandoned. Our grass grew to heights that made neighbors stop, look, talk. The kind of lengths that made me wonder, were we poor? The rhododendron bushes that hugged all sides of the house were overgrown, overactive bloomers, and all day you could hear the bees hanging their hives, the branches bending and smacking our French windows like switches twisting in the wind.

Firestone led to the streets where mostly poor and lower-middle-class Black people lived. It led to Bookman, the underfunded Black school my parents pulled Jamila out of after only three weeks of third grade, transferring her to the private school we both attended for most of our childhoods, St. Maria's Catholic School.

On the Cochran side, our street was racially diverse, but my playmates mostly Black. Segregation lived among us politely. Catty-corner to our front pine, Cochran dead-ended into the back of Bookman High School's football field. It was where Jamila learned to rollerblade but not come to a full stop. Come summers, we played red rover, catch, jacks, and four square. We listened to the air backlit by the sound of Bookman High School boys learning how to brutalize a body in the name of football and discipline. We taught each other *down, down, baby, I'll never let you go* and sang, with jiving hands, *rockin robin, tweet tweedly dee*, the rhythm undeniably Black.

With my American father and my Muslim Nigerian mother, our family stood on the edge of every line—money, homeland, ethnicity, religion. Jamila and I were something new. We were the water between two land masses. We were our parents' Halfricans.

Mornings after her Fajr, our mother folded her prayer mat away like her own private country. In the second-floor room where my sister and I bunked together before Jamila moved into the attic, our mother stretched, surrounded by boxes full of old tax records that, like her daughters, reached back to the eighties.

On the ground, her legs a V, she could touch her forehead to each knee. Could touch her forehead to the hollow space between her legs. Once limber enough, she performed ardha matsyendrāsana, paschimottanasana, halasana, and sarvangasana poses, her stomach concave, a perfect posture.

Thin wrists, long legs—but my mother was no ballerina. Still, her body could pirouette with laughter. And though she laughed constantly, it was like every laugh took her by surprise. Every part of her—shoulders, mouth, eyes, hips—contained an arch, a delicate fortress. All the arches of her gracefully crowded around the sound she shyly tried to stifle, but which always escaped. Where my father laughed like a man—wide-legged, echoing, and sure—my mother teeheed like a woman blushing into easy joy.

My mother was a woman who could be fiercely private. She didn't talk about her feelings, her childhood, our bodies. These things she left unsaid. They were a gap, a spreading lacuna. I followed in her image. Privacy became my fortress. Its walls I constructed thickly, until it became confinement. But my sister, born fearless, the constant talker, swam upstream in a different direction. Jamila: an open book to the world, like our father would become in his later years.

Though, in many ways, my mother was as mysterious to me as her history or our Nigeria, I knew her skin intimately, like a deep breath. She was always affectionate toward her daughters with her body. I remember weekends, me and my mother snuggled up in bed; her hands over mine as we baked bread in the kitchen; our shoulders touching in her garden as she showed me the proper depth to root a marigold. When my mother laughed, she couldn't help but reach for you. As much as her privacy habit, I inherited her love of touch. With Stephanie, and among friends, along with acts of service, touch is my most prized love language.

As a child, I tried to mirror my mother's image. In stretching and prayer, I mimicked her position, her watchful smile cutting neither her concentration nor the devotion mornings afforded her body. The skin of her legs, soles of her feet were an impossibly soft leather. She was a current of electricity that ran through me like the hum of a train through a town at night. We were the daughters she halfheartedly shooed away as she prayed. She was the woman who taught me the rak'ah, which I've long since forgotten. Decades later, Jamila would convert, eventually moving back to Africa in 2020 with her family, by way of Gambia. My nephews, Zayd, Nuh (*New-hah*), and Ibraheema, now the ones mimicking their own origin story's shadow—proof that my mother, gone before any of them were born—left something in her wake.

Akron winters, my mother woke early to warm every used car we ever owned before driving us to school. Decembers, she dragged us to Kwanzaa, doing her best to weave Africa to a Blackness she was a foreigner to. Saturday mornings, she taught African dance classes to me, my sister, and a small gaggle of her Black American friends' children. There, she assigned each of us poems by Langston Hughes, Gwendolyn Brooks, June Jordan, and Nikki Giovanni to memorize. They were poems that, along with our choreographed dance moves and the seven principles of Kwanzaa, we presented at the holiday's seemingly endless events and celebrations. My mother, the poet that Allah planted inside of me.

More than a religion, Islam was a landscape, simply another song she sung in the Black Period we were making. From my mother I learned to cook, learned how to tuck a laugh into my chin. Mornings, kneeling next to her, I mimicked the rituals her god required with all the earnestness my child-body could muster. She had us memorize the names of every African country, taught us to count to ten in Hausa—ɗaya, biyu, uku, huɗu, biyar, shida, bakwai, takwas, tara, goma—lost language that felt like a strange home on my tongue. But her religion she kept close to the chest. It was something Jamila and I mostly witnessed, but which she never fully invited us into.

But as much as we were a family of silences, we were also one of records—through paintings, photographs, home videos, food, our clothing and this made a detective and a watcher out of me. Gropingly, I reached for the histories my mother quieted. I flipped endlessly through her prayer books, counted every bead on her misbaha. Through photographs and videotapes that I spent hours watching and rewatching, I recognized faces from her world that I'd first seen in my father's paintings.

From our home in Akron, Ohio, over and over, I followed my parents to Kano's Galadima Market, where young girls sold cuts of goat and women pounded yams in gourds that were like the dozens upon dozens of gourds that scattered our house. I watched boys no older than fifteen ceremonially whipped as they transformed into men in a video taken in Jigawa State for the Sharo festival—my mother or my father holding the camera steady as one can in an excited crowd, and the boys chanting with the anticipation of proving the thing they'd come to prove.

When it came to Islam, Nigeria, and her children, was my mother's take that there was nothing to explain?

∞

As a child, I always wondered what it would be like to be from a place, a people, who knew what to say when asked, "Where were you when Kennedy was shot? When Martin and Malcolm were assassinated?" Instead, the people I came from seemed to have memories worn down by oppression's haze. *Where were you when—? Where were you when—?* Where were you those years when history was something heavy, unfolding around you like a drape, when history was something that could shift the air or the love in the room? *Workin, child, I was probably workin, where else.*

We were a people who were always working, though none among us could ever seem to get rich. History was neither a marvel nor a mile marker, it was something we made every day between our hands.

My people were people who remembered every detail and no details at all, which, for us, were simply different ways of remembering the same thing. They might forget where they were when the bullet spun through the minds of the men they hoped would change the world, but could remember: though they were short on grocery money, *Lord being able,* they'd managed to pay rent. Despite the gaps, my parents quilted their histories together to make Jamila and me something that was both a Black and African country—a tailor-fit Black Period.

The outside world was crafting false narratives, but inside the state of Ohio, my father spent most of his time working. He was either teaching art at the University of Akron, painting, or with my mother running Hikima Creations, the Black art gallery we owned on Copley Road. My father was the main breadwinner, though he'll tell you, whatever was made or brought in, he and my mother made together. What they lacked in money they made up in their love story. They'd gone on two dates and then gotten hitched. A fact they didn't flaunt. Neither Jamila nor I really understood the brevity of their origin story until after my mother was gone.

My mother was his second marriage. My father, thirty-one, was already the father of a young son, my half-brother, Gerald. My mother was twenty-four and, until my father, had never been more than a visitor to the United States. Before the stroke that took my mother's life found us, they'd been married for twenty-seven years. For most of me and Jamila's lives, they were always hustling miracles, pinching pennies to make the money work.

Neither my mother nor my father was the kind of parent to not know where their children were at all times, and with my father always working, this situated my mother as the main caregiver. We were either at school, its accompanying activities and friendships, or with her, which I didn't mind. I was an anxious child, and my mother was my safety blanket. Whenever she was around, I tended to wrap myself in her in search of relief from my worries, which grew in relation to my awareness of others' watching eyes.

At Hikima Creations, my mother handled the books and created an organizational and filing system that only she or another Nigerian could understand. She sourced new artists for the gallery to show and sent my father's work out to museums and galleries. She surveyed the side of America we could reach by car for the art fairs that encapsulated our weekends, school breaks, and summer vacations.

The gallery was the social center of our parents' lives. Beyond strangers stopping in for framing work or to peruse—but from what I could tell, seldom buy—their friends and other artists they knew were always popping by. It was a loud childhood filled with adults who were always mixing laughter with heated talking. I didn't always know what it meant, but it was clear that whatever was happening could only happen when Black folks were together. We hosted art openings that could last all night long and Kwanzaa events where African storytellers were hired to translate Black history for history's future storytellers—us.

Still, I want to know: where does a history start?

"MY FATHER TOLD EACH OF HIS CHILDREN THE DAY—THOUGH NOT the year—we'd die," says Auntie Mairo of my grandfather, Malam Adamu, whose portrait my father painted from the only photograph my mother ever had—a painting I now wear tattooed on my upper left arm.

"Alhamis," I imagine my grandfather saying to my mother, who at the time had just turned four—their shared Hausa pointing toward an unknowable Thursday, which for my mother was forty-seven years away.

"We're a bit psychic," Auntie Mairo continues, as she goes on to describe how my grandfather had a premonition of his own death.

Auntie Mairo speaks into the camera, translating between my grandmother Yaya, who sits in an armchair to her right, and my father, who asks questions from behind the camera. It's 1991. My father is on sabbatical from teaching at the University of Akron, and for the first and only time, he's in Nigeria without my mother.

My auntie Mairo removes her headwrap, as their father had on the day of his perishing. "He looked at Tini and patted his head," she says, calling my mother by her middle, most intimate name.

"He said, 'Come and rub your father's head, that is his gift to give you.' He had never done this," says Auntie Mairo with a serious pause, the way the faithful do when stunned by foresight.

My maternal grandfather died on my mother's fourth birthday, December 13, 1956—a Thursday. Auntie Mairo was home from boarding school. "His lips were purple," she says, describing how she could not wake their father from his nap. They sent for his best friend, who instructed: pour a drop of water into your father's mouth. When she did, his Adam's apple dropped. He was alive. Her signature scar, dark as her mouth, which is darker than the rest of her body, cuts jaggedly like a border from the right side of her bottom lip all the way down her chin.

"I remember it like it was yesterday," my auntie, who is dead now, too, says before describing how he died in Lagos a week before they moved to Kaduna. "Back then, they buried you where you died." And suddenly, I can locate my unknown grandfather in a city. Suddenly, I feel less guilty about my mother being buried in Confederate land.

"They poisoned him," says Auntie Mairo flatly, to a story that, until this rewatching, my memory has always recalled as a heart attack or a stroke. "Why?" asks my father from behind the camera—his voice so young it still has its highest melodies. Auntie Mairo traces her fingers around her lips as though her lips are her father's purpling ones.

"The whites were on bicycles and motorcycles, and my father was an African driving a car," she says, flatly but painfully, as if chiding my father: keep up.

She speaks of wars. Translates between her mother and the camera. "My uncle, my father's senior brother, was the emir of Kontagora. My father's father, my paternal grandfather, was made the emir of"— I lean in to hear her say "Wushishi." I'm unsure what to make of all of it.

On behalf of Yaya, she tells my father that all this history my mother—still alive and in Akron—doesn't know. She tells my father that theirs, Western educated, was expected to succeed his father as emir. But he turned it down and instead was transferred as a civil servant to Kaduna, where he'd later meet my grandmother. Yaya says, at the time, she was twelve. My grandfather, a grown man. I can't read the look on either of their faces, but this history, full of its darks and lights, spills from Yaya to my auntie to my father, across time and space to me in the present.

"Cold water," Auntie Mairo says of my mother, to which my father laughs. Off screen, I smile too, recognizing my mother, perpetually even keeled except for real anger or a good laugh. "She took everything from him, his demeanor, his face."

His cold-water calm, and the way they could cradle the quiet around them, was something my mother and her father also shared. "He loved blues and whites"—picked the color for his funeral attire—is the last thing Auntie Mairo says before the final twenty minutes of the audio drops, forever disappeared before a bluescreen splices time and space—

"I HAVE PICKED COTTON. I HAVE CUT SUGARCANE. I HAVE STRIPPED it. I have plowed mule."

My father now records from our Akron, Ohio, living room. It is still 1991. His mother is seventy-three in the video, younger than my father is today. "My mother's name is Lizzie Phillips. My father's name is Gus Phillips" says my American grandmother, Gussie Mae Simon. She tells the camera that she is the oldest of sixteen. She goes on to list her living siblings. She says her grandparents' names: John and Sue Della Daniels. "My great-grandmother's name was Martha. My father's father was Isaiah Phillips. His mother, Ollie Phillips."

My grandmother wears her classic red muumuu and a white barrette in her shoulder-length, pressed black hair. With that southern Black molasses of an "r," she says, "I am the mother of three children," before correcting herself. "Four. One died. His name was William Lewis Geter," she says, finishing her roll call. From the way she speaks, I know that my father—afraid he's not ready to hear what she's got in her to say—is no longer in the room.

She tells the camera that my great-grandparents were sharecroppers in Heard, Georgia. They worked for a white man named Thomas Powers for eighteen years, and they also lived on the farm.

"We canned everything we ate—peaches, apples, fruit, green beans. My father raised and killed hogs. We raised peanuts that we pulled up from the earth ourselves." She goes on in this way, gently retelling an iron-hard history.

She describes the railroad tracks she got her siblings across. Says, "I went to Tin Top Elementary." Forty students, one room, a single teacher. "That's what we had, but it was love. It was happiness in that one room," says the woman who had to leave school to sharecrop after fourth grade, and who, by fifteen, had already begun her lifelong career in domestic work.

She sits in the orange velvet chair that now occupies me and Stephanie's Brooklyn living room beneath a limited-edition print of

Charles White's *Mississippi*—that one where White declares Mississippi his *true* North.

Decades dead, my grandmother's kindness spills through the screen like water, splashes against me. "We all didn't finish high school, didn't all go to college, but our mother did what she could to keep us in school." And then, and for almost five full minutes, she sits in the quiet before the past disappears once again into blue screen. Is it her quiet that interests me most?

∞

Sometime near February 1, 1945, my father entered the world in Anniston, Alabama, the youngest of three living children. My father's birthdate is an approximation for a people who gave birth at home in the arms of elder women and midwives, who knew better than to risk the lives of their unborn by driving up to a whites-only hospital, and who had to get back to work faster than they could register the birth of a child. And though lynching, George Wallace, and Jim Crow were king, the women I come from ensured that there was still more than enough Black joy to turn a February day into something warm enough to be born into.

My father's father, Lewis, I've been told, oscillated between beating my grandmother, drinking, and leaving his children. The only picture I've ever seen of my paternal grandfather hangs in my office as a reminder of something I don't know but is my duty to hold. My grandfather wears a scowl and a three-piece suit. He holds a pocket watch, leans to his left with angry shoulders, and looks out from the photograph with skin as dark as my mother's—his face betraying none of my father's softness.

At fifteen—that age when hope truly begins to ripen—my father, with his sisters and my grandmother, fled to Dayton, Ohio, from Alabama at the tail end of the Great Migration. My grandmother fled first, following the wind as far as she could afford, to a relative in a state barely over the Mason-Dixon line. Heading North, she left my father, my aunt Liz, and my aunt Sarah with their grandma Lizzie and the man my father calls the meanest in Alabama, my middle-namesake and great-grandfather Gus.

My grandmother had gone first to investigate Ohio's conditions. It was the whiteness she knew, but in a different regional suit. While she saved up money, her children waited six months to run. Months that washed over them like a veil, so close to history they were, and in a world not much different from it. A world that inserted itself like a crowbar, that separated Black families with miles, daily humiliations, and violent endings. A world determined to give us no Edens, only Falls—though Edens we surely made and tended together like a public secret.

In Ohio, and for the remainder of her working life, my grand-mother cleaned the home of a white woman. Like millions of Black women before and after her, she helped raise her employer's children for low pay and occasional hand-me-downs, with no benefits and no social security. It was a denial of resources that my grandmother would strategically leverage to guilt the white woman into paying for my father's first year of college at Ohio University, where'd he'd also get his MFA in painting—only the second Black person at OU to do so, the first being his good friend, the artist Robert Peppers, who growing up we called Uncle Peppers, a man gentle and funny, who walked around with a gap between his two front teeth just like me. It was a single semester sat out at Ohio University trying to raise his sophomore year tuition that got my father drafted into the Việt Nam War. Though, thanks to that single year of college that my grand-mother had worked her whole life to secure for my father, he was drafted, not into combat but into Germany, where he was a munitions sergeant.

War, Ohio University, my mother, and Lindiwe Mabuza—the late South African poet, anti-apartheid activist, and member of South Africa's first democratically elected parliament, who'd helped arrange my parents very first (though supervised) date—radicalized my father into the global politics and struggle popularized by Angela Davis, Assata Shakur, the Soledad Brothers, and the legacy left behind by Fred

Hampton and the Black Panther Party—the politics that Jamila and I were parented in.

Ohio was a migration that would, for a time, last. After moving back to America from Nigeria, where, like our mother, Jamila and I were born—and after a brief stint in Lynn, Massachusetts—our parents would eventually return us to Ohio.

Ohio, a place that for my father, like everywhere in the United States, was a reminder that rescue could still leave you dry-drowning. I try to imagine my parents falling in love, my father explaining his country to his new wife and why, in America, Black meant *enemy*—explaining that her new country held only a simulacrum of freedom. "You've got to learn this, Tini," I imagine him saying. My father trying to prepare my mother for a fire in a country deep in a centuries-long burn.

ST. MARIA'S CATHOLIC SCHOOL WAS A PRIVATE PAROCHIAL SCHOOL just off Goodrich Street in Akron, Ohio. It was three miles from The Universalist Old Stone Church on High Street where Sojourner Truth gave her speech famously known as "Ain't I a Woman" at the second Woman's Rights Convention in 1851, though I don't remember it being a fact we were ever taught in school.

Ever since its inception, St. Maria's had been run by white nuns and sisters of the Dominican order. Each of its coed preschool, single-sex elementary, middle, and high school buildings sat segregated on a thirty-three-acre plot of lush greenery.

The student-teacher ratio, like the school's diversity, was low. The combined enrollment across grades never broke three hundred. The teachers were white, and over the course of my nine years there, all but one were women. Our school weeks were marked by religion classes, mass services, and school-wide assemblies in the gymnasium during the Catholic Holy Days.

Nuns and lay teachers quizzed us on God's mercy, the significance of a burning bush, and the generations spun into the Table of Nations. In music class we sung "On Eagle's Wings," "Hosanna in the Highest." We rang handbells up toward the sky wearing white gloves, the fullness of each octave carrying us closer to God.

Some of the white parents had intentionally picked St. Maria's for its parochial education, others because they believed in *you get what you pay for* more than they believed in the public-school system. But it was also the place for white parents at their wits' end. The only all-girls high school in the five-county area, it was the last resort for daughters they wanted to keep segregated from boys. For daughters who'd made themselves unwelcome in previous schools.

For the Black and brown students, though our universally strict parents also wanted the single-sex education, there seemed to be another common denominator: our parents wanted to maximize the return on our educations, to place us somewhere that might, in our futures, grant us a modicum of control. A place where we could learn how to secure for ourselves what white children expected and were given. In the nineties, for families of color, this was no small feat. In the face of redlining, housing discrimination, and the underfunded public schools that populated communities of color, Black and brown parents—trying to eke out an existence inside of America's racial capitalism—counted every penny. Like mine, they collected scholarships to send their children to the private schools that lived almost exclusively in whiter, richer communities.

By fourth grade, I could already sense that most of my teachers didn't see me as the same as my peers. I have memories of receiving harsher punishments for the same infractions as my white classmates: talking in class, not raising my hand. My jokes always treated as aggressive. And so, there was no one to tell when a white girl spit in my food, or when she sang the n-word at me under the guise of a rap song.

Teachers watched and did nothing for months while a white classmate bullied me mercilessly for being poorer, only to defend her when my parents, finally fed up, came in for a parent-teacher conference. I knew there was something racist to my classmate's teasing. There was the year my parents had to send a "medical" note to the teacher who refused me whenever I asked to use the bathroom despite permitting my white classmates. All around me, a world was being constructed in which I was to remain an object of suspicion.

I was surrounded by clues that reinforced that it was not okay to be an "other." My fourth-grade teacher, Mrs. Donna, who, like she was for me, was everyone's favorite, came to school every day with a smile, a gray streak down her dark hair, and an escalating case of multiple sclerosis. Rumor was, either the school wouldn't give Mrs. Donna a classroom on the first floor or, resisting the idea of special treatment, she herself had refused. There were days she trembled, called in sick, arrived with a cane, while we pretended nothing was happening. Her illness and the disability that came with it—we were supposed to behave like none of it was there. It was the "I don't see race" version of love. To make it work, we erased a part of her.

MY WHITE CLASSMATES WERE NOT SPECTACULAR IN THEIR CRUELties. They were seldom overtly racist. For the most part, when their cruelties did arise it didn't seem like anyone, including me, really understood what they were doing.

In *We Want to Do More Than Survive: Abolitionist Teaching and the Pursuit of Educational Freedom*, educator Bettina L. Love writes, "Many White teachers are by-products of White flight and White rage. They have grown up living and learning in communities created by their grandparents' or great-grandparents' hate and fear of darkness." My classmates' gazes were simply being architected by how the white adults around them held history, including the white teachers we all shared.

"The gaze" is an analytical framework that describes the power dynamics in society and in our personal and institutional relationships—how we enter these relationships, and who we get to be when we arrive. When white explorers and missionaries told the stories of Africa as a land of exotic savagery, they weaponized their god to help them justify the monstrous ways they exercised their power to objectify and subjugate African people. Still, my classmates and I were only children, and amidst all this inherited history, we formed friendships.

There were talent shows, band concerts, birthday parties, basketball, volleyball, and soccer games. There were sleepovers in Kerry's basement where we gulped Pepsis and pizzas, played pool, and I watched *The Sandlot* for the first time. How we all knew no one alive could beat Sophie at tetherball.

My childhood best friend, Catherine, was the sandy-haired child of two white South Africans, and the oldest of three. In Catherine's basement, we put up away messages, listened to Tupac and No Doubt, to Alanis Morrisette defining "woman" with "fed up." We counted our paperback *Goosebumps* by the dozens, made mix CDs and hundreds of prank phone calls. Together, we learned swans were vicious, could never keep our Tamagotchis alive. We mourned Princess Diana, Oklahoma City, spent whole weekends snapping slap bracelets and flashing our monkey-bar calluses toward the sky.

Catherine and her family were the only other place I felt like home. We shared our childhood secrets, traded dreams. I'd often spend whole weekends at their house in Bath, Ohio, where their acreage spread wide enough that we could stray far from home without ever feeling lost and there were endless days together where the moon inside me, finding peace, rose.

MY PARENTS WERE ALWAYS BUSY WITH THE WORK OF MAKING money and running the art gallery, where Jamila and I got trapped spending most of our weekends and after-school days, which meant that when it came to our lives at St. Maria's, our parents weren't the mingling sort. The rare relationships forged were with the few parents of color, who mine seemed to have more ease with in their bodies, histories, and conversation. The white parents they did interact with were limited to those with whom Jamila and I spent most of our time, or those whose houses, like Catherine's, had made the tiny list of those approved for sleepovers.

As an adult, I would ask my father, "Why were we so private?" I remember the slippery surprise of his laugh as he said, "Were we? I suppose we were." He still can't name why. Did it have to do with my mother's foreignness? That she was Muslim? My mother never wore a hijab and after sixteen years, never found herself a Muslim community in America. She prayed every day but seldom spoke to anyone beyond the other Muslim parents at school about the fact of her religion. In Ohio, people outside of our family and intimate network were seldom invited to our house.

I didn't realize my parents were simply doing what all Black people reflexively do in a world as violent to us as America: concocting a spell of protection. Instead, I asked myself over and over, What are we hiding? What are we afraid or ashamed of? I drove my mind up the walls trying to figure it out. I didn't know if it had something to do with where we lived and how police sometimes patrolled, not for our safety, but as if in search. Or if it had to do with our uncut grass, or how the outside of our house had given way almost completely to paint chips. We were so deeply private. It felt like our privacy could make a ghost shy.

In many ways, throughout my childhood, my mother remained a foreigner to me. We were always stopping at gas stations to buy calling cards, which seemed to go faster than food, and most days of her life, she spoke her language to a relative or friend on the phone. My eavesdropping was limited to listening to her laugh into the receiver in a tongue I couldn't understand. Unlike my friends and their mothers, I could comprehend maybe half of mine. I had no answers, and even fewer clues that could be gleaned.

Those long conversations across the Atlantic—the ones where the laughter of joy and the laughter over disillusionment for her country were indistinguishable—my mother spoke always and only Hausa. Language, by default, gave her a privacy curtain. When we lived in Akron and had family in from Nigeria, my mother disappeared almost completely into Hausa. It was the language she used to speak about the deepest reservoirs of her life. My father, Jamila, and I weren't lost in translation; we were exiled from it. We were relegated to the land of English, which seemed more barren without her.

Maybe my own need for privacy's protection starts there, in the fortress of a Muslim woman's language. Maybe, for ease, she wanted us to assimilate, and losing language was the quickest way to do it. But I'd heard her suck her teeth at this country enough to know she never believed in the "promise" of America in that way. Decades of guilt has my father saying it was his fault—he felt left out. But he's never been that kind of selfish. Even if he was, my mother would have laughed in his face. My mother, who wouldn't bow to the patriarchy of her religion, wouldn't have bowed to a living man, even if he was her husband.

Because my mother died when I was nineteen, we never got around to having the important conversations. I never got to grow up and hear her say the things she loved about me as a child, or be grown and hear someone gasp and tell her how much we looked alike. There were so many stories she didn't tell. So many questions I was too young to know to ask, and even more answers I didn't know to demand. Her politics I can only glean from the way she lived, and the people that, through her, Jamila and I have become. When I dream of my mother, most of the time, she speaks in a language I don't understand. Though, in the familiarity of her unintelligibility, there is a strange comfort, too.

BY LATE ELEMENTARY SCHOOL, I'D RECOGNIZED THAT BEYOND race, beyond religion, there was another part of me that wasn't like the others. Though I could not have named my queerness out loud, everywhere I looked, implicit and explicit messages told me queerness was not simply a sin—which, maybe, I could have lived with—but that it was an abomination. I'd looked up "abomination" and learned it meant: *something regarded with disgust or hatred*. More than anything, I didn't want to be disgusting.

I attended St. Maria's for first through ninth grades before we moved to South Carolina. By that time, I'd accumulated over nine thousand hours entrenched in a world that thought me disgusting, an abomination, a mistake. In the Muslim people that surrounded me, queerness was so invisible as not to even be an option of existence.

My burgeoning queerness was more than just my secret. Catholicism insisted that it was also supposed to be my shame. Queerness, as so many "origin" stories told it, made me a danger to anyone I loved.

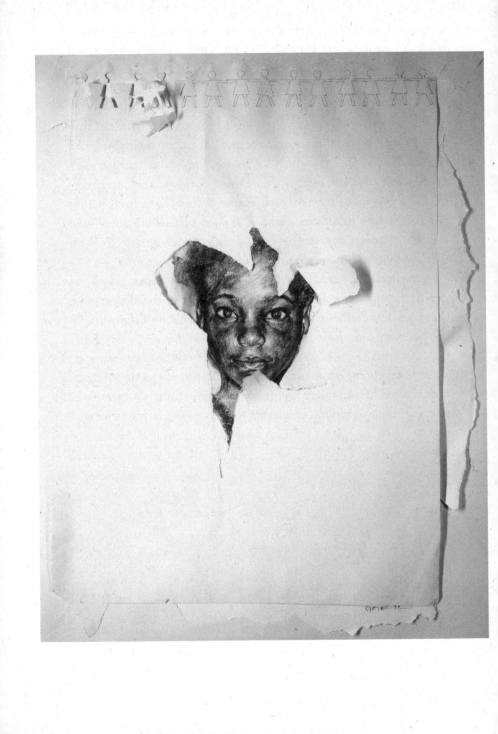

I CAN'T REMEMBER HER FACE, BUT I CAN REMEMBER THE WOMAN. She wasn't my teacher, but Ms. Evans taught the older girls at St. Maria's, and she was built like a trucker. Rumor up and down the halls had it she was a lesbian and lived with her partner, the two of them holed away in some secret life. Was it a small closet? Her office, I mean. She called me to it, sat me down in that office of hers that seemed so small as to be a slight from her colleagues, almost punishment.

Could she see how classmates gnawed at the bone of my difference? Could she see a girl who could not yet see herself? She said, It's okay. She said, It happens to me, too. She said, Sometimes when you're different people don't understand. I was in middle school. I didn't know what she saw, but it made me hot with fear to know she saw anything at all. It was a rare tenderness to run into from a white person. It knocked me off-kilter. I'd been trying to be so invisible, and yet there she was, telling me I didn't have to disappear.

Sometimes the loneliness and fears of those years make any kindness feel more coal-smudged dream than diamond-cut memory. Thinking of this kindness that I'd forgotten about until now makes me want to cry. It breaks me in two to know how long it's taken for me to understand that I should be loved like that, like the love Ms. Evans wanted me to have. But her offering was incongruous with the world she and I inhabited together, the one where everyone gossiped about the life she hid. She was a woman up for grabs, and that terrified me. She said, It's okay, I love you. That scared me even more. It was information I shut away. Safer to be accepted than loved, I thought. Every edge and border of me felt like a simulacrum.

A simulacrum is an imitation that fails to hold the weight or substance of the original. It's a replica, a forgery, a xerox of a xerox that's been xeroxed. It's like Civil War reenactments, or white people singing soul music. A simulacrum is the "United" States of America, an American, an American Dream. It's the version of freedom granted to Black people and it's what America has tried to make out of me. I was an unsatisfactory imitation of myself, and I couldn't bear the weight of my real image. When I speak of simulacra, I see that image of my lost self. I was falling, falling—gone.

St. Maria's confirmed what the world had already told me: my queerness was a fact to be hidden. But it was a lesson that couldn't keep to the boundaries of a queer shore. In my mind, connections were forming. Like queerness, anything that was not talked about—like my family, who talked about nothing—I took to be shameful. With that connection made, I doubled down on our family's privacy and secret-keeping. I connected the dots and, with the strength of Hercules, moved our entire household into shame's position.

There was something about my existence in the world that, outside of family, always seemed to require an explanation. At St. Maria's there were no Black Muslims. The Pakistani, Syrian, and Iranian girls wore their hijabs every day and wanted to know where, with a Muslim mother and an American father, my allegiances stood, or if God lived in my naming alone. An "other," I wanted to be invited into their otherness, too. Identity was complicated, but it didn't seem we were supposed to have more than one. I distinctly remember watching them, a spattering of hijabs scattered around our lunch tables—all of them as sure of Allah as our principal, Sister Rosemary, was of the Holy Spirit—me, young and jealous that when they went home, they got to return to a place populated by a singular god, instead of my many.

"Identities," writes the "godfather of multiculturism," Stuart Hall, "are the names we give to the different ways we are positioned by, and position ourselves within, the narratives of the past."

"Identity" was my mother calling the names of Allah. Sundays, it was my paternal grandmother pinching our thighs to keep us attentive to the Lord's word as we sat in the pews of Mount Zion Baptist, the church our parents made us accompany her to during the years she lived with us in Akron. It was Easter vacations with Aunt Sarah, being dragged to church morning, noon, and night. It was the women, middle-aged and old, and the way the spirit always seemed to catch them by surprise. They shot up from their pews like rockets. They spoke in tongues, driven to the ecstasy of the desperate, while the congregation stared on, satisfied, satiated by what witnessing could do. The preacher's whooping proselytizing, a salve across their want: for rest, a break or blessing, a reprieve, that their children never meet the State. Resources stretched so thin among the congregation that even their want they had to share.

On Holy Days at St. Maria's, "identity" was a forehead marking made of ash. It was the white girls lining up to take the eucharist. Mostly, Black and brown girls that sat watching from the floor as our white Christian classmates swallowed the grape juice blood and wafer body of Christ in a mini theatre where they received memory, love, and forgiveness. What did all that taste like? The queerest parts of me always wanted to know.

Identity happened at prayer circle, trying to decide what or on whose behalf to beg God's blessing for. How *what* you named was its own reveal. All were careful. Even the saddest among us (the ones the teachers looked at, suspicious they had something going on at homo) prayed for pets, for annoying siblings to get a grip, for sports games and good grades on tests, for abstract notions of world peace. But one day, Ashley West, a senior at St. Maria's: "I want to pray for people who can't locate Kosovo on a map." Around us, girls snickered. I opened my eyes. Saw others cracking their lids.

Ashley West was a white girl who walked around with an intensity that others took as weird. It was an intensity I liked. Her laugh was loud and defiant, too hard-won for a girl her age. By the time Ashley cast her prayer out into our dimly lit circle of uniformed girls, I was in ninth grade. Kosovo—a majority—Sunni Muslim country, which to this day still struggles to be fully recognized as a sovereign state—had often been on the nightly news or splashed across the morning headlines.

Maybe I understood people were dying. Maybe I was simply attracted to the tragedy. Impressed that a kid *I knew* walked around with a world-sized grief and outrage. The white girls at St. Maria's rarely talked about other countries, so I never talked about mine, or all the ways ours was a global family.

I knew some of our classmates thought my sister daring, a little curious, for studying abroad in the Philippines for her entire junior year of high school. After the Philippines, and a monthlong trip to Pakistan with her best friend, Iram, Jamila would become addicted to the world, eventually living in Thailand, the UK, Venezuela, Saudi Arabia, China, and the Gambia.

Where most siblings navigated their teens and twenties in a kind of physical, familial proximity, from the time I was fourteen, Jamila would be thousands of miles gone, leaving a permanent, unknowable gap between us. There was simply so much of each other that we hadn't been around to see. But still, the independence and fearlessness with which I watched Jamila travel did heavy lifting in expanding my notion of the world. *We* could go anywhere. Though, with all my anxieties to shoulder, it would take until my twenties to try.

ASHLEY'S NAMING OF KOSOVO WAS THE FIRST TIME I'D EVER HEARD anyone white speak with obligation to something that wasn't American. But even more, it was that Ashley's prayer was not specifically *for* Kosovo, it was for those who had failed to know, to keep track. It was a prayer for her disappointment and was most likely directed at a classmate whose apathy had, at some point in the week, disgusted her.

In Kosovo, in the eighteen months that marked the conflict, between 1998 and 1999, the army of the former Federal Republic of Yugoslavia vandalized or destroyed a third of the country's six hundred mosques along with Sufi tekkes, Islamic schools, and Islamic libraries. Rare books, manuscripts, and five hundred years of archives were eradicated like people. Of the 13,535 killed or gone missing during the war, 10,317 were civilians. NATO—this military coalition of Western and European whiteness which, on its side, reported no direct fatalities—was responsible for what some estimate was up to 5,700 civilian deaths.

No matter where in the world it happened, whenever Muslim people died, especially if they had been murdered, I took notice of how the world responded. When Ashley opened her mouth to pray for Kosovo, it was research I gathered in anticipation of the day I might need to protect my mother, whose body by then, even though her hypertension had yet to be named, seemed so fragile.

Nigeria was the language my mother spoke, but to me, Islam seemed to be the language of something that was bigger to her than her body. Her foreign tongues made it clear there was a whole other continent that it was our responsibility to love. Whatever love looked like, my mother's existence proved it was more than just what was in this country. If home is where the heart is, then our hearts, by her nature, were obliged to be global.

Even though in America, by the Kosovo War, the idea of Islam had transformed from Black American and African Muslims and disappeared behind a browner Arab face, if you were to ask Jamila and me then what a Muslim is, we'd have floated like butterflies, stung like Ali. We'd have said Malcolm X. "Have you heard of the Nation?" We'd tell you that in Arabic, our mother's first name means *Eve*. Her maiden, *Adam. Hauwa Adamu—there was a whole origin story written in your name.* The Eden she pictured in her prayers she derived from a creation myth where colonization hadn't painted Adam and Eve white.

In *Beginnings*, the Palestinian writer Edward Said writes, "Beginning is not only a kind of action; it is also a frame of mind, a kind of work, an attitude, a consciousness." Constructing a beginning requires us to "move from present to past and back again."

In social studies classes, white origin stories reigned. I'd been taught that the beginning was a white man. But at home, nothing came more natural to my parents than letting the Black Period show.

In the Black Period, beginnings could come in multiples. Beginnings were aunties, grandmas, the folklore of our bodies. Beginnings were Saturday mornings when my mother taught free African dance classes to the children of her Black American friends, who were endlessly in search of their roots. Missing roots they strategized on how to recover at art openings, while cooking rice in their kitchens, or in the elephant ear line at Juneteenth celebrations. At art festivals, rewriting our adopted nation's notion of beginnings, our mother resold Black Kens and Black Barbies that she'd redressed in the African clothes she'd stitched in her sewing room at night. No matter their birthplace, the Black adults I knew were after excavation, all of them convinced that whatever America had made of them, it was not their first truth. Beginnings, we learned, could begin in revision.

America might have wanted our heads underwater, but in our Black Period, we pulled that good feeling we made together across and into our bodies, pulled it so deep that in our collective exhale, the breath we made had its own sound, that deep *relief* that sung, *we*.

My Eve has been dead sixteen years. Though this beautiful Eden is plagued by weather, poverty, war, drought, my mother is a natural resource I protect in memory: the curve of her back, prostrate as she prayed. The freckles that lined the soles of her feet. The way she pushed down a bead of her misbaha for each of the ninety-nine names of Allah, one eye watching me watch her, the other on the task at hand. I didn't understand her god's details, but when I watched her watch me as she prayed, I understood Allah had something to do with the way she loved me. Her prayer lived between us like the string between two cans—she called: *Ar-Raheem,* Bestower of Mercy; *Al-Hakam,* Giver of Justice; *Ash-Shaheed,* the All- and Ever-Witnessing; *Al-Hafeedh,* the Preserver, All-Heedful and All-Protecting; *Al-Awwal,* the First; *Al-Aakhir*—the Last.

KUJICHAGULIA

AGE III

SELF-DETERMINATION

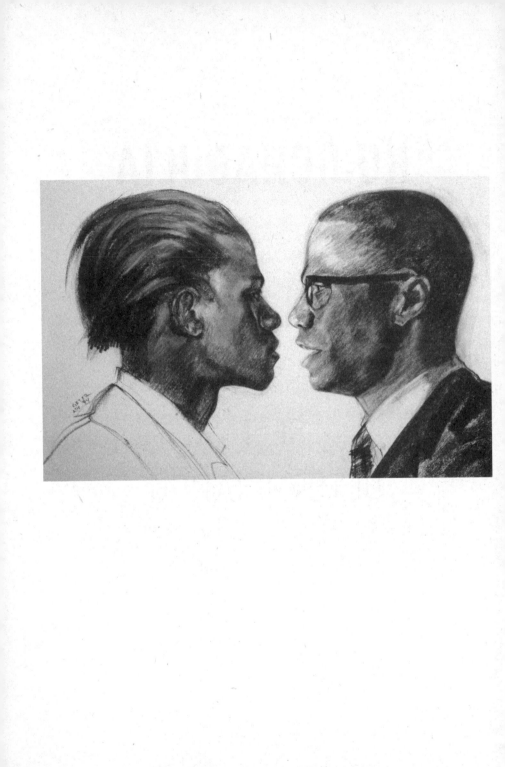

"I think you know what Tini means," my auntie Mairo says to my father in a nineties home video taken in Nigeria. "That God has remembered someone at last."

Auntie Mairo's wrists flutter, in the way women in my family's wrists can't help when speaking. It makes me miss her something bad. My auntie who, whenever she saw me, laughed so large the sound lifted me up and set me on her tall shoulders.

"God remembered my mother and gave her Tini," she says, speaking of the eleven years and four months between herself and my mother, who in the moment of this video is very much alive. On screen, next to Auntie Mairo, my grandmother, Yaya, sits in an armchair listening intently as her eldest daughter translates our histories into a language she doesn't understand.

"Hauwa is Tini's baptismal name," my auntie says, crossing over into information that we also know—this name that my mother has most people in America call her. It is only watching this video as an adult, my mother long dead, that I learn "Hauwa" was also my great-grandmother's name.

"We have many Hauwas." Auntie Mairo is speaking of Yaya's sisters, of her own cousins whom I don't know. She points at Yaya, who, in Hausa, rattles off a list of at least six:

Hauwa
Hauwa
Hauwa
Hauwa
Hauwa
Hauwa.
An incantation.

Y MOTHER FOUND KWANZAA AS THE WORLD was settling into the nineties. My parents' Black American friends wore their hair up in colorful wraps or down in dreads. African art and statues adorned their homes. They learned Swahili words and organized Black history events for us to go to throughout the year. Some performed African dances, while others hired African storytellers for us, or taught us how to make djembe drums. With longing, they spoke about "returning" to Africa, this place they'd never been but missed in their bones. They reminded us that we'd survived slavery and invented the stoplight and over three hundred uses for the peanut, too.

Through the Seven-fold Path of Blackness—a set of principles created by Black studies professor Maulana Karenga in the wake of the 1965 LA Watts Uprising—Kwanzaa reminded us: "Think Black, Talk Black, Act Black, Create Black, Buy Black, Vote Black, and Live Black." It was a way to create and maintain a collective Black consciousness in what Black people had been promised was a post–Civil Rights world. In Kwanzaa, origin story layered upon origin story like layers of the Grand Canyon's Precambrian rock.

"No geology is neutral," writes Kathryn Yusoff, a professor who studies the racialized origins of geological extraction, in her monograph, *A Billion Black Anthropocenes or None*. Kwanzaa was a geology that our parents mapped beneath another: the geology of Americanism—that brand of patriotism that fuses the nation to whiteness. In this context, Kwanzaa was our terrain. It was both new and ancestral. In Kwanzaa, it was revision all the adults seemed to be after. "Any effort at naming is an ungainly process, and begins with metaphor," writes Sehgal. We were the progeny of people in need of new names.

At Kwanzaa events, we were given front row seats from which we watched adults, in real time, create origin stories from the melted pot of the African diaspora. We ate collard greens with fried catfish, jollof rice, and plantains. Black parents sipped libations and in chorus shouted, *ashé!*— their voices thick with ancestors, ghosts, and Great Migration drawls.

WITH MY OWN IDENTITY WARS WAGING INSIDE ME, I FOUND KWANzaa's blatant expression of pride an affront and bully to my shame. But still, there was something about it that, despite my exterior resistances, I loved. At the Kwanzaa celebrations my mother dragged us to every year, Black hips fell into African dances. The whiteness of our school days at St. Maria's faded to the background.

Benedict Anderson, a political scientist and historian who studied language and power, defined nations as "imagined communities," and communities "by the style in which they are imagined." Kwanzaa was an exercise of diasporic style. At Kwanzaa celebrations, we adorned our bodies in the holiday's deep reds and greens, and because Black was something beautiful, it was a color we decorated with, too. We memorized words like "umoja" (unity), "imani" (faith), and "kujichagulia" (self-determination). Kujichagulia was how, individually, we might work together to determine our shared future against occupation, and toward peace. It pointed toward our right to name ourselves. In kujichagulia, what we determined for the "I" would manifest in community. As kids, we shouted the principles in unison, learning that the "self" could be nothing without community. Without a country to call our own, we made among us a country we called "We." Now, I call it—this antidote to America's complex traumas—the Black Period. Kwanzaa was simply one way my parents attempted to counteract the venom unleashed by America.

A decade after my childhood Kwanzaa celebrations, I learned that Kwanzaa had been created from a hornet's nest of trauma. In 1971, five years after his invention, Karenga would head to the California Men's Colony prison for a sentence of one to ten years for felony assault and false imprisonment. Karenga would be released after serving only four for the imprisonment of two women, Gail Davis and Deborah Jones, whom he had once gifted the Swahili title of an African queen. Karenga held the women against their will, beat them with a karate baton, and whipped them with electrical cords.

According to Davis's testimony, Karenga, tweaking under the weight of government surveillance and drug addiction, thought she and Jones were out to poison him. The women testified about an escapade of torture at the hands of Karenga and his estranged wife, Brenda. He tightened their big toes in vises. Branded them inside their mouths, then on their faces. He hit them with toasters and ran hoses in their mouths after gagging them with powdered laundry detergent.

In a world where home internet was still a new idea and where mainstream news seldom told our stories beyond crime statistics, information came slow, through dial-up, from gossip and libraries. If any of the adults around us knew these origin facts of our Black pride holiday, they never once let on. They were writing a new story. Revision was messy.

The hybrid stories written by the Black Americans my parents knew didn't seem, to me, anything like how I understood Nigeria to be in my own home. My mother seemed to be the sole African to be found in these roots-searching places full of Black folks, several of whom, wholly rejecting their birth narrative, gave themselves Swahili names: Kamili, Ayele, Musa, Johari, Koffi.

To my white counterparts, America was home, inheritance, and their right. Their entire lives they'd ridden shotgun as their parents, other adults, and all the media we consumed taught them how to steer. Among my ancestors, living and dead, no one had quite driven the roads that my sister and I now traversed. On both sides of my family, Jamila and I were part of the first generation to be so deeply emerged in a white world. A world we could participate in, not just tend to or clean.

I cycled between two extreme poles: the safety and comfort that home provided and the fear and violences given to me by the "American" story, which I could not name, but could see, sense, and had already begun to carry. I was a hypervisible apparition in my white world. I lived on adrenaline. I watched and watched and watched how the white people could at once surveil and not see me. At our sports games, band concerts, any event that necessitated a parent's presence, I was petrified for my mother. To them, with her accent, strange name, dark skin, and her Nigerian clothes, she was more for-eign than me. I never wanted anything to happen that might make her or me feel embarrassed. I never wanted her feelings to be hurt the way the world seemed to be constantly hurting mine. I teetered on the edge of fear so long. I fell from one world to the other.

But I knew I didn't want to be white. I'd never heard any white people laugh the way either side of my family laughed all the time. And white people didn't walk around their lives absentmindedly breaking into song like every Black adult I'd ever met.

Even if they couldn't have articulated it, our parents understood that without an intentional, alternative origin story, the only thing for us to buy into would be the lies written by white America. Kwanzaa was just one part of the system that they were building into our city of origin stories.

►

On an old home video, my mother videotapes. Me, Jamila, Kwame, Terrell, Mikaela, and Ayo—the children of my parents' friends—dance barefoot on a stage. Behind the camera, I hear my mother smiling. Jamila and I, twelve and nine, wear matching canvas-colored skirt-wraps and cropped short-sleeve tops adorned with green, red, black, and yellow threads, dime-sized mirrors, necklines scooped like half-moons, small carved canes across the backs of our necks, our arms up, wrists flopped over each edge, keeping the canes in place, our history being born through memory and the rhythm of our bodies. Where I dance shyly, unsure, Jamila grins like a ham, unafraid to be seen, to command any stage.

||

ONLY AS AN ADULT, HAVING EXPERIENCED THE CHAOS OF TRYING to dismantle one false origin story for something truer, can I comprehend the gift of being given these messy moments of revision to witness. Our parents scattered oral traditions, folk stories, laughter, remembering, gossip, and shit-talking around us like breadcrumbs. They let us stay up late eavesdropping on what was grown folks' business. All of it in service of giving us, as children, a way to recognize ourselves in a world that treated us as illegible.

Whether they knew it then or not, Kwanzaa's violent and complicated origin story was another lesson in how complicated origin stories could be. We were Black. We were human. And even though white supremacy meant that the Black Period was full of violence, even in our own pan-African origin stories, our parents were our reminder that violence didn't write us.

∞

Scientists say that fear sends the brain's amygdala into overaction, which lays down denser sets of memories. Maybe this has been my whole life?

My therapist, Dr. Lamb, pointed out to me that I tend to process an enormous amount of information daily. I never just people watch. I watch for defense. From body language to voice lilt to the way a set of eyes can look you up and down in pity, disregard, disgust, or confusion, for as long as I remember, I've studied people and my surroundings this way. How much I'm able to see, I've taken pride in and attributed to the perceptiveness of Black women. It's my superpower.

Dr. Lamb often tells me she worries about my stress levels. I'm always at a mild earthquake. Between us, we know I could weather away. Part of me blames the library childhood my mother encouraged. In libraries, I spent weekends, whole summers, reading books about human psychology and body language. All the books I read seemed to have one thing in common: beginnings. In psychology, beginnings were your mother, that primal scream of birth. In body language, it all stemmed from attraction, and so I snuck secretly into the other stacks in search of something queer.

Now I can understand that voracious reading as a manifestation of a child desperate to fit in to and understand her world. And if I couldn't fit in, at the very least I wanted to recognize white America before white America could recognize itself. Definitely before it could recognize me. Whatever was going on at school, I knew it was in some way related to the Black books that populated my parents' shelves next to my father's old collections of Lenin, Marx, and Stalin—he said we had to anticipate the oppressor's side. And then, I grew and grew. I was careful to never let on to anyone how closely I was watching. I was a girl determined to never get got.

I have lived all but the first three years of my life in a country that wages war, that hates, that legislates against every ingredient of the woman that made me. And I have lived more than half of that life in a post-9/11 world. Though the story of Islamophobia begins long before 2001, 9/11 stains my grief. For me, three weeks into sixteen on 9/11, it is the dividing marker between my childhood and my adulthood. And militarization, I suspect, is a defining element in my life.

HALFWAY BETWEEN THE UPSTATE AND THE LOWCOUNTRY, COLUM-
bia sits in the Midlands region of South Carolina. I had just turned
fifteen when my parents moved us to this military town for my father's
new job teaching painting and drawing at an HBCU, where he also
ran its art gallery. Up until then, the only thing I knew of the South
was my father's family who'd fled it, but who'd taken the South with
them in the migration from Alabama to Ohio. From their drawls to
their food, to their stories, to the way their bodies held you, my American side was southern, through and through.

What, after a decade in the American Midwest, did my father say
to my mother to prepare her for our move to South Carolina? Ours
would be an almost identical Great Migration, but in reverse, to his
own. Like his mother, my father left six months before us, while I,
Jamila—just back from her study-abroad year in the Philippines—and
my mother remained so Jamila could finish her senior year of high
school at St. Maria's. I was finishing fifteen when my feet first touched
down in the South Carolina soil. I arrived unprepared for all the ways
I'd fall in love with my southern inheritance.

It was a surprise, the slow knowing that, despite my family having
fled, despite all the Black blood, I could love a place so deeply. And
even though I was a new arrival in the land and landscapes that spread
out before me, it was like my body remembered an ancestral song. It
was like when my mother said "Allah" and the name arrived from her
belly instead of her throat. *This,* I thought, was beauty.

But, too, it was visual shock. In Ohio, by 2000, Black people hov-
ered at not quite 12 percent of the population. In South Carolina we
were almost 30. I couldn't understand why so many Black people had
stayed instead of fleeing like my father and his family.

We arrived in South Carolina the summer before my sophomore
year, and in that move, I'd tracked another kind of change in my parents. With my father's new job at his HBCU, more and more, my parents began inviting people over to our house. No longer was it just
family, or the same small cast of close friends popping by. Now, all
sorts of people streamed in—teachers, students, friends of friends. It
was like that scene in a movie when someone opens the windows of a

house that's been vacant too long. Air, color, and the loud sound of Black folks cackling rushed in.

No matter—I still felt hunted by worry.

Though I couldn't put it to words, I'd long been aware that a home life full of paintings, wax prints, and Kente cloths, and surrounded by a revolving door of Nigerians who sucked their teeth at America, and militant Black artists who still talked like they were in the revolution, made my Blackness something that my classmates—Black or otherwise—didn't often seem to recognize.

Catherine had transferred to public school the year before I moved. She didn't have to wear uniforms and there were boys. That pretty much was it for what I knew about the changes that awaited me—that and, in contrast to St. Maria's, my new high school was majority Black.

After nine years of fashion being defined by remixing aspects of our polyester uniforms, I had no clue what kids my age wore, or what the rules were with the opposite sex. I had yet to realize that my attractions spread vaster than the limits of gender—or that when it came to my own sexual fluidity, I didn't have to put a name on it beyond "queer." And so, I thought to myself hopefully, *maybe I'm not.* Maybe I'd just lived in single-sex segregation too long. I was excited, curious. I was terrified. Before I'd even stepped foot on my new high school campus, my hackles were up.

COLUMBIA IS THE STATE CAPITAL OF SOUTH CAROLINA AND SERVES as the site of Fort Jackson, the U.S. Army's largest training base. Fort Jackson holds the reputation for being the largest, most active training center of initial entry in the U.S. military. Here, the young transform into a single, uniform tactical expression. Fifty percent of male soldiers and 60 percent of female soldiers pass through Fort Jackson's gates every year. A city unto itself, it takes up a whopping two-thirds of the city. Fort Jackson is so big that neither civilian nor soldier can take in its size from its outskirts—it requires an aerial view.

In Columbia, Jamila began her freshman year in international studies at the University of South Carolina, and I entered the public-school system. Fort Pleasant High School is located just a ten-minute drive from Fort Jackson's training base and is the temporary home for military children whose families are passing through. All high schools in the county are affiliated with their own Junior Reserve Officers' Training Corps, aka JROTC, and at Fort Pleasant, we were affiliated with the Navy (NJROTC). I remember NJROTC being mostly populated by children of color, children of service people, white kids on the Blacker end of the class spectrum, and the boy I lost my virginity to.

At Fort Pleasant, the white girls of my youth—girls in oxford shirts and plaid polyester jumpers and skirts—were traded for teenagers in Abercrombie & Fitch, American Eagle, and Navy fatigues. It wasn't unusual to see NJROTC drill team cadets marching in lockstep formation preparing for competitions. At the beginning of football games, cadets carried the American and South Carolina flags stiffly onto the field. On NJROTC dress days, the school campus became dotted with our peers in military uniforms. Our classrooms under a sudden occupation of children like us, but who, with their parents' permission, were being groomed to follow orders, to kill.

None of this I connected to war. But still, even then, I found militarization curious. We weren't a family that entertained the idea of guns. My mother found the pairing of children and weapons crass; my father found it dangerous. We hadn't even been allowed to have Super Soaker water guns.

In South Carolina, the military is like a vellum over the state. It's everywhere, and with it comes its propaganda. I'd never been anywhere before where white people *loved* America like they did in the South. Knowing what I knew of history, I found it confusing. It was an overload of data I couldn't read.

If I am not a child of war, at the very least I am its heir. Its citizen. I have been alive for Operation El Dorado Canyon's Libya bombings, the Iran-Iraq War, and George H. W. Bush's invasion of Panama, dubbed Operation Just Cause. Was aware that my faraway, older half-brother, Gerald, was off fighting in the Gulf. In my lifetime, we have warred in Bosnia, Kosovo, Afghanistan. We have "intervened," have enabled human rights violations, in Pakistan, Somalia, Haiti, Chad, El Salvador, Nicaragua, Venezuela, Mexico, Palestine, Libya, Saudi Arabia, Congo, Cameroon, Rwanda, Thailand, Việt Nam, Yemen.

"Almost every dictator in history, at one time or another, has been propped up by the U.S.," my father, who in his Ohio University days was a Black radical and active member of the Youth Communist League, is always reminding me. As of 2017, the United States was providing military support to 73 percent of the world's dictators—our foreign policy, a suicide mission.

There is the trade war, the War on Crime, the War on Drugs, the War on Poverty, the War on Welfare, the War on Social Security, the War on the Middle Class, the Culture Wars, the Privacy Wars, the Border Wars, the so-called War on Christmas, the very real War on Truth. There are the wars we refuse to name: the War on Black people, the War on Indigenous peoples and Indigenous lands, and what some call World War III: the Climate Wars. But no war grips our modern imagination like the War on Muslims—disguised as the War on Terror. That war begins in language makes war the most dangerous metaphor of all.

Thanks to the technological advances of oppression in the modern world, for the average American, war is like magic. If we don't look for it—*poof*—it disappears. As Harsha Walia writes in *Border and Rule,* of the language used to describe America's border wars, the phrase "migrant crisis" depicts "migrants and refugees as the *cause* of an *imagined* crisis at the border, when, in fact, mass migration is the *outcome* of the *actual* crises of capitalism, conquest, and climate change." War—the act, the word, and the idea—is a tug (of war!) between simulacrum and semantic satiation. Semantic satiation, like being ten and saying a word over and over and over, till it gets so fuzzy on your tongue all meaning evaporates. *Iraq Iraq Iraq Iraq Iraq Iraq Iraq Iraq Iraq Iraq* and now I'm losing track of what Iraq really means.

In the fever pitch of the global War on Terror, Islamophobia is, itself, a simulacrum. "Instead of naming and fighting the forces of capitalism that break down social relations and deny humanity," writes

Vincent Lloyd, a professor of theology and religious studies, "Islamo-phobia offers an opiate, a simulacrum of collectivity that blocks efforts to realize genuine, democratic, humane collectivity."

In the War on Terror, when we say "Islam," it bears very little resemblance to the actual religion. It is simply fear and American capitalism, carved down to a single word. The political football of Islamophobia has come, in our collective imaginings, to replace the reality of Islam itself. But when I think of Islam, I know my mother is there. Her faith bespoke, but brightly burning. Her hair uncovered, unless in prayer. My mother's version of Islam, a world of possibility where she, a woman—Eve—could lead.

GOD'S COUNTRY

AGE IV

NARRATIVE

Many of the dead were Latino, or light-skinned black men, or Indian or Arab.

But now the Falling Man is falling through more than the blank blue sky. He is falling through the vast spaces of memory and picking up speed.

—TOM JUNOD, "The Falling Man"

F ABOVE ME EXISTS A HEAVEN, I MOSTLY BELIEVE IN A DEITY unmotivated by human belief. Though a habit in me still prays to all my childhood gods. One part of me takes the wafer, another dances the pews of my many minds speaking in tongues. The remainder of me kneels East. Every thread I pull leads me back to my mother. In my childhood, the ease of her insisted that faith wasn't the wave that overwhelmed you. It was the shore.

But then the towers came down in every American town. Even if you were out of earshot, collective memory and group trauma would forgive you for having thought you'd heard it. In Columbia, the World Trade Center came down on our classroom TVs—their bulbous bodies mounted to cinderblock walls or rolled in on carts for the occasion. A girl ran home crying because it was her birthday. In Mr. Roof's Juniors' Honors English class, we witnessed replays of ash crawling up the sky.

My classmates and I hadn't seen anything like this since the Oklahoma City bombings, which, minutes after, newscasters across the country attributed to Islamic terrorists instead of the two white army vets who, it was reported, didn't much like Black people. But even Oklahoma hadn't come close to all we watched on our shared screens be, newsreel after newsreel, so quickly decimated.

It was a wordless feeling. Like every last one of America's haints had come home. Even in the most "secure" country, those who did the getting could still get got. Before the school day ended, I'd heard classmates both in and out of ROTC say things like "They won't get away with this. We're going to blow up those terrorist motherfuckers."

To most Southerners my name was less Arabic than it was randomly foreign. That my mother was Muslim was not something my classmates at Fort Pleasant knew, outside of my close friends. I wasn't hiding the fact but wasn't leading with it, either. I was mainly relieved that it never came up, lest I would have to explain, and realize the person I'd thought was a friend was actually a danger to me.

I was used to white people asking me questions whenever a Black person did something bad on the news. I knew that as Black people we were forbidden our individuality and our imperfections. When one of us did something bad, the rest of us paid for it in one way or another. In 9/11, I received confirmation on what I'd long sensed, that when it came to my mother, her Muslim identity wrote her into a lower hierarchy even among Black people. I wondered what my mother was doing, thinking. What would she say?

By then, I was acutely aware of how much of Black life, as white people received it, was watered down to the fact that Rodney King had been beaten and O.J. acquitted. We were reduced to only our bruises. But in 9/11, I watched something twist. Fort Pleasant was a majority Black school, and in 9/11, many of my Black classmates were ready to string up my mother's god. I was terrified of what 9/11 would mean for our family and my mother, the Muslim woman who led it.

That day, my mother, who didn't live to see a Black president—let alone one with a Muslim and African name—didn't say much, but she did pick me up from school on time. This was a rare occurrence for a woman who, despite her years in America, could not shake her Nigerian tendency to tardiness. My mother could push lateness to absurdity. Like our father, Jamila and I had learned to lie anytime we wanted to arrive somewhere on time.

Despite the fact that all my friends drove and many had their own cars, my strict parents had yet to allow me to drive on my own. My mother gripped the steering wheel of our purple Chrysler Town & Country. Her knuckles taut, threatening to turn translucent. Her dimple-smile gone.

Though she had fear and a great sadness over so much death and her hijacked god, in front of her children she could only express difficult emotion through silence or anger. I'd never seen her cry. *Allahu Akbar.*

A low NPR voice crept from the car radio. Al-Qaeda. Thousands dead.

Say something—

I wanted my mother to say something.

In my memory, she only sucked her teeth.

Once home, she grabbed up her calling card. She dialed Kano. She dialed Zaria, Lagos, Abuja. Cradling the phone at her shoulder, her hands—two fighting birds—waved in a language calling toward a home that was no longer mine.

Again, and again, into the phone, my mother sucked her teeth. Her exasperation strong enough to pull a river through a straw. *Ah-ah! Kai!* The sounds of her trouble tugged at the receiver. Her language was no longer her language. It was a dirge.

Later, I watched the news with my parents—our family of four, temporarily three. Jamila, who loved the world and who was growing less and less interested in living in America, was off studying abroad in Thailand for her junior year of college. She was not yet a practicing Muslim. In my parents' silence, I was often all alone. On the couch, my mother wrung her hands. At bedtime, she whispered to my father behind their bedroom door.

The next morning, my mother, who only covered her head when she kneeled, who only kneeled two times a day with the cycle of the sun instead of the obligatory five, performed her wudu. She shook her prayer mat East, her body clean for Allah. Her body casual and relaxed inside her devotion. Or maybe that is the fiction I've overlaid on top of a too-hard-to-hold memory.

In this country, my mother mainly loved her god alone. In her loneliness she'd have mourned Allah alone, too. Whatever my mother was feeling about 9/11 and the new wave of Islamophobia that began before the dust from the towers had settled she kept to herself.

I didn't know what to do, and so I did what I'd always done around our family's silences. I chalked it up to shame. Like queerness, there were some things you just did not talk about. I didn't know if it was fear, frustration, or maybe it was simply that my parents had a much better understanding of America than I did. What America would do to bodies like ours it would do, and who was going to stop it or find us worth saving other than our own people?

Decades after 9/11, I learned, to see the future: rewind.

1996—

It was the year of the Atlanta Summer Olympics. The year mad cow disease arrived in Britain and NASA mapped Mars. Tupac was murdered. We'd cloned our first mammal, Dolly the sheep. It was the birth year of Pokémon. Of begging our parents for movie money to see *Space Jam, Independence Day,* and Leo in *Romeo + Juliet.* It was the year we Macarena'd, that Denzel became the first celebrity of color named a magazine's "Sexiest Man Alive" and Fox News made its debut. Internet usage was exploding. What we were still calling "global warming" had reached its all-time high. I was twelve and the world I'd eventually inherit was being created all around me— supposedly on my behalf.

In response to right-wing anti-immigrant sentiment, Bill Clinton— known comically as America's "first Black president" to Black folks who'd remixed Toni Morrison's reference to how Clinton demonstrated "every trope of blackness: single-parent household, born poor, working-class, saxophone-playing"—passed the Illegal Immigration Reform and Immigrant Responsibility Act (IIRIRA). IIRIRA made more people eligible for deportation, and made them easier to deport, while also making it much harder for "unauthorized" immigrants to seek legal status. IIRIRA unleashed an immigration enforcement policy whose damage, like chattel slavery, we'll never be able to fully quantify. Clinton passed the IIRIRA immediately after instituting his restrictive welfare reforms and two years after signing his disastrous crime bill—both of which disproportionately surveil, target, and police Black communities and poor communities, which are often also communities of color. Six years after the IIRIRA's passage, detentions had tripled. The number of women incarcerated in detention centers quadrupled, making the United States' immigration policy another brutal extension of gender violence.

The passage of the IIRIRA coincided with Congress and the Clinton administration's efforts to increase funding and the number of agents at the United States–Mexico border. By the time of IIRIRA, between 1995 and 1996, 145 Black churches across the South were set on fire in acts of domestic terrorism. But the infiltrator we were in search of was a brown-skinned foreigner.

Like anti-Blackness, Islamophobia is a nonpartisan political cause. Post-9/11 legislation hogtied immigration to criminalization and terrorism—terrorism being equated with my mother loving her god.

My mind repeats a childhood vision of my father, always showing me his broken heart. Defying what Susan Sontag thought possible, his body always folds "regarding the pain of others." His face knotted up in warning as he repeats a genocider's words, Stalin's: "If only one man dies of hunger, that is a tragedy. If millions die, that's only statistics." Each number, each date, each oppressive law, each death, reduced to hollow record. An eradicated archive. He is so close to a cry, he looks like a flood; who can feel a million deaths like this?

I am pinned between tragedy and statistic. Pinned between attention span and what minuscule impact my caring can have on people suffering so far away, who are strangers, people who are not mine. So *this* is how people are left to die, I think to myself of myself, feeling wholly American before my mind wanders to what offers immediate and simple pleasures—TV, Twitter. Empty rabbit hole after empty rabbit hole.

My parents taught me better than to set the world aside in this way, but for my own survival, I feel like sometimes I have to. I know forgetting is a power structure. But, too, I know forgetting can be a condition necessary for rest. How do I moralize it?

∞

In the month after 9/11, Tamir Rice was waiting to turn one. Hollywood screenwriters were meeting to figure out how to capitalize on and patriotize the moment. We were three months away from George W. Bush signing into law the No Child Left Behind Act, which would wreak havoc on marginalized students and lead to the Bureau of Indian Education taking control of Havasupai Elementary, to devastating results. We had no idea that Facebook, a Black president, Donald Trump, or a pandemic was coming. With fire still burning underground, with ash still in the sky, cancerous debris had just begun to take root in first responders' lungs. There were bodies still being recovered.

While the destruction was still revealing itself, George W.'s administration authored and passed the Patriot Act. It was legislation so broad and sweeping, the War on Terror slinked into our homes, both invisibly and with scarring violence.

In 2003, amidst protests from Muslim communities, legislative pushback from both Republican and Democratic senators, and opposition from states and cities like Hawaii, California, Chicago, Dallas, Attorney General John Ashcroft set off on a sixteen-city speaking tour, where, in front of invite-only crowds, he continued the Patriot Act's extensive propaganda campaign.

The Department of Homeland Security and Immigration and Customs Enforcement, better known as ICE, were created less than two years after 9/11, Homeland and ICE continued the American government's extensive work to execute our official immigration policy through a detention-and-security apparatus. Both departments imagine crime and policing along the lines of war and work in concert to arm police departments to the teeth with military equipment.

In all this, the foundation for what is our present-day human rights crisis at the borders was expanded. It would take more than a decade before we understood the wide-reaching consequences of what we had given away to the government in terms of personal privacy. We did not know then that the privacy rights of others that we enthusiastically sold in fear would contribute to a world where Facebook could sway the 2016 presidential election, the full cost of this barter only beginning to reveal itself at the start of a pandemic that was still years away. A pandemic where—while people go hungry, lose their homes, die—the profits of surveillance capitalist corporations like Facebook, Amazon, Google, and Zoom skyrocket.

By 2005, four years after the Patriot Act's passage, a Gallup poll reported that most Americans felt the act was appropriate or did not go far enough.

By 2014, thirteen years after 9/11, fueled by the Patriot Act, militarized equipment (machine guns, *literal* tanks) patrolled Ferguson's grief and outrage after the murder of eighteen-year-old Mike Brown by a white police officer. Though militarized policing had long been a constant of Black life, it would become the de facto government response to our insistent cry, *Black lives matter!*

WHILE OUR POST-9/11 WORLD WAS BEING BUILT ONE SURVEILLANCE mechanism at a time, I, too, was building my own secret police. It was plain as day someone was always watching, and my police force patrolled my body. With the combination of my Black skin, Islamic name, foreign birth, travel habits, and citizenships, I felt nervous in airports and began to count how often I was selected for the TSA's "random" screenings.

By the time Barack Obama came around, I was living in Chicago, about to start my final year of grad school for my poetry MFA. My mother had been dead six years from the stroke that killed her. My sister still had a year to go before she both became and married a Muslim. After her AmeriCorps year in Texas working with Vietnamese climate refugees who'd been displaced from New Orleans by Hurricane Katrina, Jamila had moved to Chicago.

Chicago would be the first and only time Jamila and I inhabited the same city since we'd left our parents' house. It is where her first child, my nephew Zayd, would be born and where Jamila would survive a marriage so terrible it scared us all, before she'd eventually meet her second husband, Alieu—a Gambian in America.

In Chicago, Jamila served as a case worker at the Cara Collective, a nonprofit that provides life and career training skills to individuals whose lives have been disrupted by the forces of the state: under/unemployment, incarceration, houselessness, child services, and/or debt.

On November 4, 2008, we'd managed to find each other amidst a crowd of 240,000 people as Obama delivered his presidential victory speech in Grant Park. Vendors hawked Obama T-shirts, party pipes, noisemakers, and glow sticks. Obama's voice seduced the crowd into louder and louder cheers as he reminded us to *be the change*. All around us, Black people of all ages, even children, wept. Electricity spun between Jamila and me, and it felt good to be together, Black, and alive, inside this moment that had rendered our father speechless, and which our mother did not live to see. It was day one, the past was written, but the future was yet to be decided. We were two motherless daughters—sisters. Whatever distance lived between us in that moment evaporated in the palatable atmosphere of a new history being born.

IN CHICAGO, I POURED MYSELF INTO POETRY AND LIVING LIFE AS A graduate student, which mainly meant late nights and drinking with my cohort. On weekends, with Brett, one of my best friends from South Carolina who'd moved to Chicago, too, a white queer—not out, but far more out than me. He and I frequented Boystown, Chicago's gentrified gayborhood, dominated by mainly white middle- and upper-class gays.

Walking around Boystown, I was still a decade away from the other side of my queer story. A decade away from knowing, as Mariame Kaba writes, "When we set about trying to transform society, we must remember that we ourselves will also need to transform." All I knew was that even in Boystown, I didn't fit. The anti-Blackness and misogynoir of the white queers, especially the men, were thinly veiled. In Boystown, white men mimicked their idea of Black vernacular. Without consent or warning, they touched my hair, groped my breasts, all with the casualness of a handshake.

In Boystown, the very first government-created neighborhood for queer people, there were tall rainbow totems to let you know you'd arrived. But with not even so much as a nod to the Black queers or Black trans women who had built the queer movements of America, I didn't know that Black people like me, who were queer, had our own history here, and one we'd written for ourselves.

I didn't know Marsha P. Johnson's and Sylvia Rivera's names, or how, in a world determined to keep transgender and queer people at the margins, something in the two of them said, If we build it, our people will come. And then they did it. Johnson—a Black, self-identified transvestite and drag queen—and Rivera—a Puerto Rican, Venezuelan, New York City–born trans woman—said, We can make a Black Period anywhere, even here, and they built STAR House, a shelter funded largely through sex work.

"STAR," Rivera said, "was for the street gay people, the street homeless people and anybody that needed help at that time." And though STAR House was open less than a year, Johnson and Rivera cut an opening through possibility's velum.

In Boystown, like everywhere, whites sassed my deep voice and interrogated my Islamic name. For the white queer women who dotted the neighborhood, the way I gendered was wrong. I was neither femme nor butch enough. My Blackness could be safe with Black folks, but having been raised in a community that had internalized Christianity's homophobia, my queerness always felt in danger.

In Boystown, queerness was offered refuge, but not Blackness. I saw Black queers and Black trans women hanging out on street corners of Boystown after having just come from some place, but I never had the courage to approach them and ask, from where and could I come, too?

I think of Eve, Eden, the lushness of a garden, her belly full of knowing and the punishment she suffered after her knowledge had been rebranded "the Fall." In Black spaces, I tried to de-queer myself. In Boystown, I tried not to be too Black. I was King Solomon's baby split in two. Between the two halves of me, I built a decontamination room for each half to pass through, but never touch.

I WAS STILL A DECADE AWAY FROM UNDERSTANDING THAT THE framework of abolition intends to get us free of more than just slavery. I was addicted to punishment, even if it was only my own.

Kaba writes that, "the PIC [prison-industrial complex] is linked in its logics and operations with all other systems—from how students are pushed out of schools when they don't perform as expected to how people with disabilities are excluded from our communities to the ways in which workers are treated as expendable in our capitalist system."

The PIC includes X-ray vans, social media monitoring, predictive policing software, TV police procedurals and the way they profit off turning state brutality into an entertainment genre, the criminalization of sex work instead of the protection of sex workers, surveillance-enabled lightbulbs that turn streetlights into cameras, police stationed on public-school campuses, and Havasupai Elementary students who suffer under the U.S. government's carceral neglect. And it includes how we respond to and interact with each other and ourselves.

If a closet is where shame hides, I was in America's closet and my own. America didn't want me, and I wasn't sure that I wanted me, either. The secret police force I'd constructed to keep myself in line was mastering the act of self-surveillance. Unbeknownst to myself, I'd been mimicking a country, and the exact thoughts and structures the state used to police Black, queer, and Black queer bodies. At the time, I had no idea of just how much Black queer people, especially Black transgender people, were targeted, brutalized, and physically and sexually assaulted by the police, but I was trying to make it redundant for any state force to ever police me.

Meanwhile, Obama had just begun expanding George W.'s Secure Communities program from 14 jurisdictions to its eventual 1,210. With Secure Communities, police departments, sheriff's offices, and jails become a front door for Homeland Security and ICE officers, but I knew nothing beyond the mirage of ecstasy at our first Black president. And anyway, I wouldn't have been able to see anything behind the queer secrets I was keeping. I felt like I hadn't taken a deep breath since my mother's death.

AS A CHILD, I HAD ALWAYS BEEN FASCINATED BY MY MOTHER'S documentation. I knew there was a world where mothers, separated by continents, were forced to love their children from afar. I knew my mother barely ever got to see her mother. My mother's documents, I understood, were the only thing that allowed her to be in America and to mother us in person.

She had her green card, proof of her vaccinations, one, and then—after her naturalization—two passports. A passport said *where* you belonged and *who* you belonged to. But more than that, a passport determined who would take you in. I wondered, of my countries, who, after seeing all of me, would still let me call home *home*.

There are seventy-five countries in the world where queerness is criminalized, and thirteen of them punish with death. My birth country of Nigeria creates the largest number of queer refugees after Bangladesh and Pakistan. Queerness casts the LGBTQ people of these countries with majority Muslim populations out of their homelands and into a world where Islam is made synonymous with terrorism. Religion, like queerness, once again names them as people who will be allowed no home.

Between her American and Nigerian passports, it seemed to me that all my mother's identities had a home. But I—a queer, a woman, African and Black, with this Islamic and Arabic name—am a permanent traveler. Boarding gate A will accept my American passport. And though there will be restrictions set—a big red warning stamp, to mark my Blackness and womanhood—I know I'll still get in. Boarding gate B says, Come on in, (straight) Nigerians! But there's no boarding gate that will accept a passport for my queerness, not when attached to my other identities.

In a world where oppressors fight for a monopoly on oppression, if I ever have to flee a home, where on earth will I go? Where can Stephanie and I be safely queer where Jamila and her family can be safely Muslim? When scholar and civil rights advocate Kimberlé Crenshaw coined the term "intersectionality," she meant double consciousness is not enough. I cannot protect myself without protecting my sister. I cannot protect my sister without protecting myself.

Even from behind the "safety" of American citizenship, I can't speak up for queer Muslims, queer immigrants, or queer refugees, if my biggest fear is being outed. I cannot care about one freedom—Blackness, womanhood, Islam, or queerness—without caring about the others.

"Shaming," writes bell hooks, "is one of the deepest tools of imperialist, white supremacist capitalist patriarchy because shame produces trauma and trauma often produces paralysis."

It's like the famous Holocaust poem by the German Lutheran pastor Martin Niemöller, finally having to face his own culpability: "Then they came for the Jews, and I did not speak out— / Because I was not a Jew." I could have added my own line: *Then they came for the queers, and I did not speak out— / Because I was one.* I learned, it was near impossible to fight for anyone from inside a closet, especially myself.

The War on Terror, like the "Border Wars," feeds the system that wages war on Black, Black LGBTQ, and LGBTQ bodies in a country that has already granted permission for bodies like ours—like mine—to be stolen, violated, and held unjustly behind bars.

Secure Communities was discontinued in 2014 after being declared in violation of the Fourth Amendment, which prohibits unlawful search or seizure. But it proved too good a blueprint and infrastructure to ignore, and to help provide bodies for his border war, former president Donald Trump restarted the program on January 25, 2017.

Trump, through executive order and in tandem with his administration, redefined "refugee" so that almost no one qualified for asylum. As Walia writes, the border crisis, "is more accurately described as crises of displacement and immobility, preventing both the freedom to stay and the freedom to move." Trump and his administration specifically targeted LGBTQ people through their anti-immigration policies, in addition to rolling back protections in the workplace and the military and putting restrictions on healthcare, education, family planning, housing, and representation—the ecstasy of a Black president having long since faded.

TO BE BLACK IN AMERICA MEANT A HOUSE FULL OF WARNINGS. MY parents, no fools, knew a threat could be anywhere, no matter the façade. We were warned of strangers, the list of friends' houses where we could sleep over kept impossibly short. We were warned of booze and drugs, boys and men, the sugary blood that coursed through our bodies—knew when to say "yes sir" or "yes ma'am" and had heard it repeated a thousand times that police and prison were the most dangerous things a Black person could encounter on earth. And my parents, who, in nineties Akron, chose to send their newly immigrated daughters to a Catholic school filled with mostly white children, warned me and Jamila constantly: white people have limits. "No matter how much you think they love you," my father would begin. "Not true," I'd reply, so-and-so "are my best friends." *Ah, ah,* my mother would interject, nodding at my father while sucking her teeth against my protestations.

Though my parents had white friends, including one of my father's best friends from Ohio University, my uncle George—whom I adored, and who always went out of his way to make us laugh—there seemed to be nothing they trusted less than white people. The British had owned my mother's country until 1960. She'd attended Queen of Apostles College in Kaduna, a boarding and secondary school run by Catholic nuns. Where my father had grown up under the shadow of colonization, my mother had grown up under its thumb. Both of my parents approached America with the skepticism and caution of people who had witnessed or been privy to a kind of destruction that made language inadequate.

Being, breathing, and sleeping inside the shadow a country made of you, my parents wanted their children to know, is to stare down the barrel of a gun. A barrel that has been, in perpetuity, cocked toward our intended extinction. History—that thing that white people had gotten to write, but *we* had to live—turned my parents soothsayers.

Twelve years after the 2002 passage of the Patriot Act, which must be renewed every five years (and was until it was finally allowed to expire in 2020), it was revealed that the government had been surveilling and collecting citizens' phone records and internet metadata. Beyond its National Security Letters provision, which allows the government to get phone records without seeking approval first, the Patriot Act's Section 213 makes it so that "sneak-and-peek" search warrants apply not just to terrorism but to any federal crime, whether felony or misdemeanor.

Sneak-and-peek warrants mean the government, on the grounds of suspicions of my name, phone habits, internet history, friends, family, associations, or on a neighbor's distrust can search my home, office, garage—any place I call mine—without informing me first. How can I protect myself or my family from the murderous American state when it's the state who's watching? Private as I still am, these daily invasions of privacy and home fill me with anxiety—like when you catch your phone listening to you via the internet ads that suspiciously match your in-person conversations.

In America, drug prosecutions are the engine of our federal government's law enforcement operations and capacity. Disguised as a war against terror, Islamophobia contributes to the spread of the most persistent and pernicious American poisons: prisons and policing. Though it's been proven that sneak-and-peek warrants have provided no meaningful information to the War on Terror, by 2013, sneak-and-peek warrant requests had already exceeded eleven thousand. Of those requests, only eleven were rejected. And of the more than eleven thousand requests, all but fifty-two of those warrants were for drugs, not terrorism.

You can draw a straight line from Islamophobia and xenophobia to anti-Blackness. In America, studies have long shown that the War on Drugs disproportionately, unethically, and intentionally targets communities of color, especially Black communities. Prisons and policing are two specters that hang perpetually over Black everyday life, and my parents made sure I lived in polite terror of them both.

While rounding up immigrants, exiles, asylum seekers, and refugees, the carceral state also targets Black and Indigenous LGBTQ people. For example, Black trans women are incarcerated at ten times the rate of the general population and both Black and Indigenous trans women are more susceptible to violence from guards and other inmates. Forty-seven percent of Black trans people have been incarcerated, and over 40 percent of the female population of America's prisons are bisexual women or lesbians. Through policies and social practices that allow discrimination, trans people who are unable to "pass" are locked out of mainstream work opportunities, only to be ensnared by laws that criminalize poverty, houselessness, and survival economies like sex work. By design the lives of LGBTQ people are made illegal. Illegalness, a form of erasure, too.

I've been policed by the state, by familial bonds, by white people, by Black people, by queers, by me. All this policing, over the years, constructed its own chains. I saw those chains and picked them up and I learned to get comfortable with them on. Even if I didn't hide myself well, seeing what the world did to Black people and to Muslims, in my queerness, I lived to never be found out.

Shame. America gives us its shame. I've worked my whole life to set it down. Brené Brown calls shame the "master emotion." Disability activist laura hélène calls it both social and interpersonal. Shame is a psychological colonization. hélène says being motivated by it can turn you into your own oppressor, and that shame "spawns the phenomenon of self-surveillance." For a time, shame had done just that in me. I'd forgotten the Black Period and, in the milieu of white America, shame surrounded me.

Now, as a grown woman, trying to trace the beginnings of all this erasure means I'm constantly swapping out one origin story to try on another. I take old memories, try them freshly on. In white America, a "secure community" requires police. But the Black folks that raised me lived with the attitude that a secure community was what, beyond white America's prying eyes and sabotage, we'd been patchwork-quilting together our whole lives.

I look back and there's an art gallery full of Black folks turning the room sweaty with laughter. There's summer and Ms. Asia's catfish fry. My father saying hold still as Jamila and I model for one of his children's books. There's my mother softly forking a thick glob of Blue

Magic grease onto a wide-tooth comb and parting the hair on my tender-headed scalp. I remember that, outside school and work, our lives were abundant with Black Periods.

THE FIRST TIME MY FATHER TRULY ENTERED THE WHITE WORLD, HE was eighteen. At the time, he was only the second person in the family to make it to college other than his aunt Linda, his grandmother Lizzie's last child, who—in a world where, without access to contraceptives, women gave birth across decades—was even younger than him.

With the United States barely desegregated, my father entered a white college where, with the other Black and African students, he carved out Black space. So far away from home for a Black boy who'd never been anywhere, he took up his inheritance. The lessons from home he carried forward. He remixed them across the diaspora and drew himself a Black Period of his own making. He joined the Black fraternity Alpha Phi Alpha. Working together and through student protests, Black and African students, brought together through dinners hosted by Lindiwe Mabuza—the South African activist who helped bring my parents together—forced Ohio University to create a Black studies program. And though, in my mother's Africa, the British loomed everywhere, it was a Black continent, and colonization was so visibly the blight.

Together, my parents were always making our Black Period—their version, one where, if not our bodies, then our minds could be free. Eventually, I would learn to render a Black Period of my own—the Black Period *I* needed, the one that could, once again, get me home, and I would create it using the two greatest gifts that I inherited from my parents: this hunger in my belly for knowledge, and an obligation to community.

In our everyday lives, though we were warned about white people, my parents mainly paid the white world no mind. It was more something that was in the way. To move it aside, they did so in ways that, by their careful design, appeared to me and Jamila an afterthought. To be raised by people who lived in and centered Blackness and art meant my sister and I were reared in a world that reflected our image—a world where Blackness was a world of possibility. Outside of our school days, we were surrounded by people who were constantly inspired.

"Inspire" comes from the Latin "inspirare," with "spirare" literally meaning "to breathe." Breath—this process that is, by definition, a reverberation of time, biology, memory, and ancestors—this thing that should be so simply, so obviously the body's right is what, all over the world, Black people fight for.

An adult now, I know how angry the white world must have made my parents, but as children, we never saw them overtaken by it. That, in front of their children, white supremacy could have nothing from them, not even their rage, set precedent, priorities, but most of all, it set the fact that where we lived was what was real, and what was real was the Black Period. What was real was home. What's real is my mother—forever alive in some dream—gesturing toward the front door.

I know it's summer by the way she says "in or out," our dogwood, pink and blooming, and how the fattest black ants travel the neighborhood to stalk it. By the way the Fugees push out from my sister's bedroom in the attic and Lauryn Hill's voice is rough as the inside of a whiskey barrel. *Ready or not, here I come / You can't hide / Gonna fiiiind you / And take it slow-ly* . . . With her hair done up in *Moesha* braids, Jamila, finally sixteen, sings "The Score." There's our whole family watching *Sister Act 2: Back in the Habit* for the millionth time, and the way Lauryn Hill stood at that piano—the entire song, keeping her voice, like God's eye, on the sparrow.

Years later in South Carolina, there's me, my turn at the wheel of sweet sixteen, my bare feet kicked up happily on the bed. In *The Miseducation of Lauryn Hill,* she rang a bell I'd still recognize anywhere. In the classroom she asked us what we thought about Black love. In the streets, we happily doo-wopped, with something in Lauryn's voice calling up the ghost of James Brown's "Black is beautiful!" In *Miseducation,* Lauryn sang us Black and proud once again. She sang at our

Blackness like *we* were the prize, her voice loving us giddy. And no matter how much our white friends loved the album, there was something in it only we could touch.

THE POET JACK GILBERT WRITES, "EVERYONE FORGETS THAT ICARUS also flew." That "everyone" included me. How lucky it is to me now, that no matter how far I might fall, my parents and my ancestors had given me everything I needed to rise from the ashes again. Though, in a country like America, when it came to truth, it was on me to find it.

Parul Sehgal, speaking of another kind of fall, asks in "The Profound Emptiness of 'Resilience,'" "Why rise from the ashes without asking why you had to burn?"

Only facts could solve this.

The poet in me cracked the gaps in America's stories open like a line break. You know what I found? Kiese Laymon's "Black abundance." Kujichagulia's "self-determination."

The Black Period was calling me home. But first, I'd have to remember the Blackest art.

The art of escape.

THEATRE OF FORGIVENESS

AGE V

BLACK RAGE

JUNE 17, 2015, TWO HOURS OUTSIDE MY HOMETOWN, a sandy-blond-haired Dylann Roof walked into Emanuel African Methodist Episcopal Church in Charleston, South Carolina. That night, Roof, surely looking like an injured wolf, someone already on fire, sat with an intimate group of churchgoers and, I have no doubt, was prayed for. If history repeats itself, so does religion: the twelve churchgoers like Jesus's twelve apostles in a twenty-first-century fable. Roof the Judas at this last supper. As we know, Roof would wait a full hour until heads were bowed in prayer and God had filled every corner of the room before reaching into his fanny pack.

By June 19, 2015, two narrow days beyond the shooting, there were reports of absolution. "I forgive you," Nadine Collier, the daughter of seventy-year-old victim Ethel Lance, said to Roof at his bond hearing. "I forgive you," said Felicia Sanders, mother of one of the nine dead, her son, Tywanza Sanders, twenty-six, not yet buried.

I have been held intimately by this wing of southern Black religiosity. My father is of Black Southern Baptists. At the church I attended with my Black American family, they were always praying to be gracious enough to receive forgiveness or humble enough to give it. A turn-the-other-cheek kind of church, it was full with products of the Great Migration, and they were always trying to survive white people.

As a child, though I could never quite name the offenses of white people, I could sense the wounds they had left all over the Black people who surrounded me. The wounds were in the lilt of Black women's voices, in the stiffened swagger of our men; it was there in the sometimes-ragged ways my boy cousins would be disciplined. The work of forgiving had left bruises on the women so deep it made their skin shine. In church, we prayed and forgave America like our prayers were the only thing between this country and damnation.

It's left me wondering: does forgiveness take advantage of my people?

∞

Being Black in America means having a *historical* relationship to forgiveness. If the law of Audre Lorde holds true and "the master's tools will never dismantle the master's house," Christian forgiveness was never built to tackle white supremacy, only pardon it. Christianity emerged from our enslavers. We were forbidden to read but could pray. In the face of this new, white god, our ancestors looked for solace and hope. Enslaved people were entitled to nothing, not even their anger over their enslavement. Performing forgiveness became a crucial aspect of enslaved people's lives. They buried their rage in negro spirituals and held forgiveness in their mouths as both salve and armor. But if Christianity is the master's tool, then surely white supremacy is its house, and the Christian ideal of forgiveness will never be able to address, dismantle, or truly forgive white supremacy. What happens when the performance of Black forgiveness gets repeated through several generations until it becomes ritualized and transformed into tradition, and where, in that case, does the Black Period go?

In the twenty-first century, how do we escape the theatre of forgiveness?

I am trying to trace the trickle-down effect of suppressing Black rage through forgiveness in my family. How my enslaved ancestors must have chewed on their rage like cud until it was unrecognizable enough to be called forgiveness. How that rage tumbled through our bloodstream, generation after generation. How it made some of the men mean and women the only thing America would possibly let them get away with breaking. How our women raised other people's children by themselves and arrived home too tired or too shattered to save their daughters from the grown men they themselves loved. How rage has sent us imploding. How rage grips us, turning us into tripwires, until both our traumas and our resilience are passed down from generation to generation.

∞

ACT 1: TRANSGRESSION

In 1990, I was standing in Aunt Sarah's basement, her linoleum-floor corners peeling beneath the damp, her basement a ghostly type of cold. Being in Aunt Sarah's basement often felt like being in a bunker. It always smelled wet like old snow resisting thaw, the ceiling low enough to give a tall man a backache. Thin layers of dust glimmered beneath the Morse code of flickering fluorescent lights, gripping the wood lacquer of the entertainment console.

Aunt Sarah's basement was filled with board games and decks of cards that neighborhood children would often come by to play with. These games were not for me. Aunt Sarah and I both knew it. The contract between Aunt Sarah and me consisted of only two agreements: I would remain silent and invisible in her house. Monopoly? Too vast in its pieces. The tiny colored discs of Connect Four? Too loud in their dropping clinks. Being six, I trusted myself enough to accurately consider risk, weigh all options. It was simple, though.

I knew the danger of the wrong game.

I don't know how cruelty finds us, but it was cruelty I incited in my aunt. It seemed that every little thing I did set her off. I the flint, she the firecracker. If I spoke, her eyes would beat me like a switch pulled from a backyard tree. If Aunt Sarah wanted to teach me anything in this world, it would be my place.

Easter breaks, when we were released from our Catholic school uniforms into the ether of our lives for two weeks, my parents would load Jamila and me in the car and drive to Dayton to drop us off at my aunt Sarah and uncle Rodge's. On those trips, I'd sit in the back, the synthetic velvet curtains of our Dodge Caravan windows splayed open as I considered escape routes, what it took to disappear, anxiously rubbing my fingers against the curtain's grain.

Throughout our childhood, these drives from Akron to Dayton were a regular occurrence. My father's mother and both his sisters lived there. Strife and the years my grandmother spent trying to get her children out of Alabama had banded the four of them together like cement. Both my father and my aunt Liz have testified to how the larger community around them included men who found relief in the bruises they left on women, who forwent water for whiskey, who worked but spent all but the rent money, who slid like lovers from the rooms of their granddaughters, nieces, nephews, sometimes their own children, zippers barely closed, pants sagging and unbuckled, their shadows leaving an oily grief slick.

On our visits to Dayton, I often looked from my aunt Sarah to my father, wondering when her love for him would translate to me. Aunt Sarah's anger for me was a confusing collision of worlds. I didn't understand it. If home was where the heart was and where the Black Period showed its face, then why was there so much cruelty between us?

∞

After word of Charleston broke, my father called me in Brooklyn to say, "Best stay in the house," afraid, despite the hundreds of miles that protected me. Charleston rose like a sickness in my father's throat, the old rages crawling out. Having lived seven decades, my father is disgusted by the institution of whiteness. Born in Anniston, Alabama, quite possibly one of the most dangerous places to live in under the reign of George Wallace, my father entered the world in the mouth of U.S. racism. My father's disgust, so old, so precise, he could balance it on the head of a pin.

"I don't want to hear anyone talking about forgiveness," he says sucking his teeth. "Black people need to spend time on something else." Clearing his throat, he prepares for his lecture, and I imagine being a student in one of his life drawing classes. "Child, be careful with forgiveness," he warns me. I know forgiveness cannot always be two-sided, the person you are trying to forgive sometimes being dead or unable or unwilling to participate in repair. But for my father, part of being Black and free means being able to withhold the forgiveness given to white people without it being a mortal or spiritual offense.

My father is convinced that our legacy of trauma has altered the kind of justice Black people have come to expect. How else, in the absence of justice or true racial reform, could we forgive our oppressors with their boots still on our necks, he asks, expecting me to fill the silence—but I can't answer his question.

∞

Having finally settled on the safest game, I slowly inched out a deck of Old Maid cards. I don't know if it was the penny taste of the blood warning in my stomach or if it was Aunt Sarah's footsteps that came first. But I do know that quite suddenly she was upon me, her eyes cutting like razors, her mouth a snake's hiss, her black hair in tight Medusa curls. A thin but sturdy woman, Aunt Sarah was a mountain that blocked all sun and her sudden approach enough to set my fear on fire. Her nearing footsteps like a sizzle warning a bomb's lit fuse. My fear sending cards flying to every corner of the room. I looked around, suddenly overwhelmed by the small enormity of my situation. I had made a mess and messes made me visible, heard. A mess broke Aunt Sarah's and my agreement.

Aunt Sarah looked at the cards flayed around me like a can of red paint had exploded in a white room. Her rage true, compact, when she said, "You come upstairs, and I'll beat you blind." Beyond the spill, what upset Aunt Sarah most was that I had dared to play, that I had dared to touch in a house where she had made it clear nothing belonged to me. Eventually, like always, night fell. Jamila coaxed me back upstairs, to the guarantee of a clear coast.

Years of terror-filled days with my aunt, and this is the one I return to. The simplicity of it. How, young as I was, I realized then, whatever my aunt and I were inside of, I would never get clear. How her fury for me could be both spectacular *and* plain—how every single cell in my tiny body seemed to make her feel robbed of something: the look on my face, how I ate my food at her table. Any love or positive attention I received from another adult was enough to send her into deep, sorrowful rages. With my parents around, her anger simmered like collards. As a child, it seemed to me she found pleasure in the wait—that moment my parents' minivan would disappear from her driveway and her contempt would surface unabashedly like a belly from a belt after a big meal. There was something primal in Aunt Sarah's need to be listened to—like she had spent her entire life saying "no," only to find again and again that her agency didn't matter. How many people had crossed Aunt Sarah's line?

For much of my childhood, my school years were demarcated by when and for how long we had to see Aunt Sarah. I could never, as the poet Galway Kinnell advised, "trust the hours," but with Aunt Sarah they felt mighty long.

Like a righteous woman who glows in the labor of punishing sinners, the moment my parents left, Aunt Sarah found her joy in shaming me; loved to look me in the eyes as she told her church friends that she'd have to keep her thumb on this one. Her deep-voiced niece who didn't know how to sit or behave like a lady. My Aunt Sarah's disgust for me is the first secret my body ever kept.

∞

On TV, in news articles and think pieces, I followed as white media marveled at Black forgiveness like children dancing in the sun, the sugar rush of absolution. The Theatre of Forgiveness is one of white America's favorite projects.

Act 1 is transgression. It is Roof's bullets through the air and the culture required to make the man who loaded the gun. Act 2, the culture of fear that forbids, vilifies, and punishes the victim for anything other than submission. Inside act 2 is the compulsive requirement to forgive. Act 3 is the forced complicity of the victim coerced into forgiving before the transgression has been given voice or name. Act 4 is the fatal finale, which is all the internalized rage that follows.

Perhaps there is no greater example of what psychology calls repetition compulsion—the habit of repeating traumatic events in order to cope with them—than the relationship between Black forgiveness and white America. After centuries spent learning how to make a home inside the unmerciful and unrelenting terror of white supremacy, the act of repetition compulsion is a defense mechanism against the past.

In an unconscious attempt to rewrite history, the injured resist the fullness of their predicament, necessitating the burying of well-earned rage, sadness, and despair. In act 3, Black people, condemned for marching in the streets, kneeling in a ball field, or daring to publicly declare our lives matter, are forced by white culture to wear forgiveness as a kind of Blackface, forced to paint conciliatory smiles on centuries-sized pain. In act 4 we bury our dead, leash our rage, never able to satisfactorily prove to white America that we are worthy of the long-awaited recognition of our humanity. Act 4 is what I do to myself when my anger has nowhere to go but me.

EVEN THOUGH I WANT TO UNDERSTAND FORGIVENESS, WANT TO believe it balms even the deepest wounds, I have to wonder, has forgiving whiteness ever set a Black soul free? In Christianity, forgiveness is supposed to follow, *not precede*, repentance. Repentance, step one. Forgiveness, two.

In different ways, I have been told not to hold on to my anger—to forgive—by well-meaning white friends and church-going Black friends. Each of them concerned for my soul. As a writer, as a queer Black woman, I have a double-double consciousness for the soul. My craft tries to find it. My people try to save it in the absence of our daily bodily autonomy. And, yes, in my life, I have been deeply forgiven in nourishing ways. It is in this forgiveness I've seen that my responsibility is to look not just at the injury but, too, to look at, honor, and acknowledge the history in the pain.

ACT 2: SUBMISSION

The many ways Aunt Sarah's house was suffocating made my head spin. From the moment the garage door opened, potpourri flushed every corner. It stained the plastic covers on her couch yellow, wrapped around my sister's and my polyester sneakers. Potpourri drenched the bed sheets, the blankets, the stench so blaring you couldn't sleep at night. It seeped into her porcelain Jesus and his porcelain white apostles. Decades later, when Aunt Sarah's mind would start to go, we'd sadly wonder if, all these years, the potpourri chemicals had been poisoning her.

A pious woman, Aunt Sarah had a fever for Jesus. On our visits, I would watch her eyes light up as she taught Sunday school to a room of children not much older than me, who weren't kin. In God's house, my aunt looked like a woman who'd stepped into baptismal waters one toe at a time. She could appear so full of light and kindness, though underneath, she wore the impatient desperation of someone always a hairsbreadth away from salvation.

Decades later, my father would draw an image of a Black woman stretching her arms out wide and call it *Flight*. The woman's dress, a robe of collaged, torn paper. Her face wearing the delight of someone who, after a long chase, has finally caught the spirit. At the top of the woman's head, another head, then another. Each head shape-shifting, until the very top of her transforms into an eagle's wings outstretched in flight. Aunt Sarah could be like this. How, in church, I'd watch her kindness spill out over the congregation before we returned to her house, where she stockpiled bags of scent-dipped flowers like someone anticipating the end of times but determined to mask the smell of it.

From all my years spent with Aunt Sarah, I've learned that people often mistake anger for rage. Anger is wind thin; rage roots you. Where anger is the pinprick, rage is the thousand needles in your haystack. While anger makes you see red, every rage I've known is Black like me. When I try to imagine the amount of rage Black people of my father's and aunts' generation and the generations before them have accumulated, it's breathtaking. I can see it everywhere, even in the whites of their eyes.

At family reunions, my father's living uncles slap him on the back, wrapping their arms around his shoulders, holding him close as they laugh, retelling the same memories. My father recalls sneaking onto whites-only golf courses as a boy to play rounds with his uncles and friends, and the groundskeepers who would cock their loaded shotguns at them, pulling the trigger, over and over again. Their aim not a warning shot, their desire to hit their target deep and precise. Whenever they tell these stories my father and my great-uncles belly-laugh before staring off into some abyss that is both in the distance and inside of them. "Grown men shooting at children. This is how much they hate us," one of them inevitably says, my father and great-uncles sucking their teeth like they're trying to suck poison from a snakebite. I didn't yet know that beyond my great-grandfather, we had other snakes in the grass, too.

∞

"We were enslaved and then we were sharecroppers, which was the same brand of life under a different name," my father says, reminding me what the early days were like. "The white men that were our slave masters became the landlords, and they kept after the children and the women."

I know that along with guilt, self-loathing, anger, helplessness, shame and fear, one impact of complex trauma is that victims sometimes mirror their abusers. But still, I can't stop myself from asking my father how any Black person could see that kind of abuse and repeat it—a new rage being born in my throat.

Wanting to know more of what my father thinks about this business of forgiving and the heritability of rage, I am prodding him for our origin stories. As a visual artist, he has spent his life carefully considering his people and his surroundings, carefully insisting his daughters see context.

There were the genocides of Indigenous peoples. There were the hundreds of years of slavery, the decades that followed disguised as sharecropping, the near century of Jim Crow, and the Black Lives Matter protesters that flood the streets today. Since the beginning of whiteness, the one thing that all African and Black people have had in common is living under the constant threat of annihilation.

My father reminds me that, from slavery to Jim Crow to today, America requires that we prepare Black children to hold their tongues in the face of abuse, fear, and exploitation; it has meant teaching our children to not be subsumed when white America tries to deny the dignity of our lives. And it has also meant the psychological trauma of witnessing the daily humiliations and degradations of their parents' physical, spiritual, and sexual exploitation on plantations, in share-cropping fields, and in white people's homes.

"After slavery, some fathers and grandfathers became the slave masters of the house," my father says so matter-of-factly it becomes the perfect snapshot of what history has unleashed in my blood. Was it watching their wives and children be assaulted over and over through the generations and not being able to stop it that rooted inside our men? Did they so deeply internalize their helplessness that when they were freed, they mimicked the only version of "master of the house" they had ever seen? Or do some men simply come into the world mean?

One day, during the time she lived with us in Ohio, my grand-mother, the age my father is now, began transmitting her life to my father, whom she'd cast into the role of family witness and griot. I think of what it must have felt like to confess to her youngest child, her only son, that she'd been raped by her own father. Was it a wild feeling in her body, that need for someone else to know? Was she try-ing to emerge from erasure? By telling, was she setting down a shame that was never hers to carry? Or maybe it was just that she understood how stories of the past could guard the future.

She had a kindness about her that could make you cry, and would spend her life being harmed by husbands who claimed to love her. Any strength my grandmother had left she saved and summoned to give her own children access to a different kind of story, even if it meant leaving her own self to the wolves she knew so well.

What my grandmother lived through rains and weeps like a willow tree in my body. Weeping willows are one of the most flexible trees in the world, able to bend in what should be impossible poses without snapping. I have no framework for understanding how the women I come from survived inside the heart of the unimaginable. Were my grandmother still alive, she would find a glimmer of God, a solace, in what I can't imagine.

"BECAUSE YOU COULDN'T STOP OR PUNISH THE SLAVE MASTER FOR anything, we talked about and performed forgiveness," my father says, speaking from the hole painful memories have gutted in him. "We performed forgiveness without naming, repentance, or justice for so long that we ended up repeating the slave master's crimes in our own family." He says "we" as though we're still there, trapped in the wrong century.

"Eventually, you have generation after generation who grow up watching Black girls and women get raped by white men, including their white fathers," mine says, reminding me of the way American history works and the lightness of our skin.

My father reminds me that even if a child escapes incest and rape, it is simply enough to be surrounded by it—history teaches being assaulted is simply the lot for Black women and children.

My father warns: rage, it can be inherited.

∞

Aunt Sarah relished the Black auntie's leeway in wringing your arm from its socket, and though, beyond that, she never laid a hand on me, when I think of her rage, I imagine it man-shaped. A whip in hand. The winding up. The snap down. *Snap, snap.* Again, again. The exhaustion from the beating given, welcomed, waited for.

I don't know how else to describe it: the way Aunt Sarah hated me cleaned her. The older I get, the more I've wondered, had she the freedom to hit me, if it might have healed something deep within her. When I share this thought with Camille over text, she simply says,

"No, it wouldn't have." When I tell Dr. Lamb, I feel like *I* am the saddest thought in the world. That nothing could have taken away my aunt's pain, not even my own, injures me like a blade. A rage like Aunt Sarah's, do only Black people have it?

Oddly, Aunt Sarah happened to be married to the sweetest man I've ever known outside of my father. Uncle Rodge's skin was dark and thick as tire. The kind of man who would laugh from his belly and let us tug at his bristled face. His laugh was something you could swim through, a laugh that connected the dots. And even though we weren't related by blood, we had the same pinky toes.

My uncle could sense my persistent shyness, and the fear and isolation laced through my aunt's and my dynamic. Uncle Rodge stayed in his lane, but he always made it clear that he loved me deeply, much to my aunt's chagrin. That he lived in that house with Aunt Sarah every day truly baffled me. That a kind man could love a cruel woman made me pay attention.

One Easter visit, when I was still young enough to practice keeping my lettering balanced between a paper's ruled beams, I bounded into my uncle's arms upon arrival. A big man, Uncle Rodge loved to pick us up and twirl us in the air before bouncing us on his lap. When my parents left, I remember the shape of my aunt's words, then her fingers yanking me off his lap, her grip tight like she was grabbing something slick.

As an adult, I've often returned to this incident. The dirtiness that stayed with me for so long after. It occurs to me that beyond fear, both her own and mine, Aunt Sarah bequeathed me her shame.

ACT 3: COMPLICITY

Perhaps Aunt Sarah truly could not control herself and the accusa-
tions in her eyes, but there she was, her eyes snatching my child body
as I giddily laughed on Uncle Rodge's lap. Her face accusing me of
some dark seduction. Or was it that the hurt hidden in her had acti-
vated, crawled out to save me. Her lost girlhood, warning me the best
it could, "Never sit on a man's lap," even if that man happened to be
my uncle.

Even though I was far too young to name it, what I felt was shame,
and the shame had everything to do with my body and what it might
incite in a grown man. "Don't you know better?" her face always
seemed to say. After that, I knew exactly what Aunt Sarah meant
when she told her church friends, "This one doesn't know how to be
a lady."

As a child and through college, the lines of gender always seemed
to me so arbitrary and so terrifyingly precise. I often found it difficult
and confusing to be a girl. Now I know that I identify as a cisgender
woman, but back then, who I was inside didn't feel like what I'd been
told girls felt like. It didn't match the white girls I went to elementary
and middle school with who seemed to wear our girlhood without
question.

I felt like and behaved like a cop all over my own body. It only
took a small slip, too much bass in the hips, to fuck the whole performance up. White America defines terrorism as something that happens to a nation, solely because they've been able to spend their lives
protected from the state terrorism that targets virtually every aspect
of the private lives and bedrooms of non-white, nonheterosexual,
non-able-bodied, non-gender-conforming lives.

On dress-down days when we didn't have to wear our plaid polyester uniforms, I was a deep tomboy in baggy JCPenney jeans. I had a
low-pitched voice and a confusing attraction to the same sex. I wondered, had God taken a left when they should have veered right? Had
I been born in the wrong body? As a preteen, sometimes white strangers in the mall called me *him*. Had I been meant to be a boy?

Nothing about the way I was a girl seemed to match what the world, my body, or Aunt Sarah was constantly telling me. I wore my baggy jeans and grew hot in the face with confusion, shame, and anger at what I recognized as irrational unfairness. Whenever my father scolded me about walking around with my hands in my pockets, it made me furious. Through his scolding I was being told, without it ever being said, that this simple gesture, this resting of hands, was reserved for men.

Only now do I realize that maybe my queerness was something Aunt Sarah could see. Did she suspect me of being not like all the rest? The god my aunt believed in would have had no patience for my queerness. My whole life, I'd been trying to pass unbothered through the rigid rules of other people's worlds. I didn't realize that to pass was to live inside a constant performance.

No one could tell me why I always walked around feeling like a spectacle, but I felt deep down that it had to do with more than being Black in so many white spaces—it was also about my attractions. I snuck around the early internet world looking for femme versions of queerness, not because femme came naturally but because, if I had to be queer, the femmes could teach me how to pass, undetected.

By the time I moved to New York, my body was screaming from behind the bars of my own policing. The armor I wore for protection had also become my most intimate cage. In New York, I found the gay mecca that had been built for white men. But still, the city was filled with Black queers. I saw myself everywhere. I saw Black people who lived gender on every spectrum. All over Manhattan and Brooklyn, I saw Black queers and Black trans women walking around looking like music—I saw my kin.

∞

As an adult, I think of my time with Aunt Sarah with increasing frequency. My aunt is old, my uncle long dead, and her mind slipping so much I fear she might not have enough of it left to remember the things my uncle loved about her. This moment on my uncle's lap often plays in a loop in my head. Without meaning to, I am trying to bring my forgiveness home.

Some holidays when my father and I are together, he hangs his head weepily at the distance I still keep from his dying sister. And sometimes he tries to apologize for the cold Easters he delivered me to by saying, "Your sister just looked so much like your Aunt Sarah." And I wonder if, perhaps, this means I might look too much like a man who harmed her deeply. Or maybe my father is wrong completely. Did I remind Aunt Sarah of herself? And in doing so was I a constant reminder of a deep shame? Or was it my queerness shaming her?

Nothing can ever truly explain the ways we are broken into or the ways our wounds convince us only another sharp edge will leave us clean. But the story of me and my aunt Sarah is now a shame my father carries. I hear it in his voice, his embarrassment that he can come up with neither an explanation nor a solution. I sometimes wonder, what shame tugs at him most? That he did not protect his child, or that the injurer was his sister? And now I wear the shame of my father's shame, of being the one to lift the veil off his sister.

By sixth grade I couldn't take it anymore. I wore a grown woman's anxiety. At some point Aunt Sarah had convinced me that I had earned her shapeless contempt. Surely, there was an evil in me. I was eleven and beginning to be aware of my body, a body I could not separate from Aunt Sarah's cutting look as she yanked me from Uncle Rodge's lap. My anxieties were compounding like pennies in a jar. Every time I heard Aunt Sarah's name, another coin inside me dropped.

Because I could not give my rage for Aunt Sarah directly to her, as the years passed, I delivered my rage both inwardly toward myself and outwardly, unleashing it like a broken and cornered animal upon my family. A shy, sensitive child, my sensitivities grew their own insecurities and their own temper. Even though Aunt Sarah's treatment of me was my secret, and a shame I'd accepted I was wholly responsible for, I thought, *didn't my parents have eyes?*

My big sister, who witnessed virtually every verbal and emotional lashing, was vividly loved and adored by Aunt Sarah. I felt like the only victim in a category-five storm, Jamila watching from the edges, calling my name, but neither of us understanding we could call for help. Outside of Aunt Sarah's house, I became the quiet of the storm's eye—the loneliness of my anger a danger perpetually looming inside me. I would rage and rage and rage. And like Aunt Sarah, my rage would be specific to the wrong people in our family. Like my Aunt Sarah's, my anger would be my only agency, and it would have a hair trigger. With my feet planted in my shame, I'd forgotten the lessons of my mother—the gardener of my life: what I planted would root.

∞

ACT 4: INTERNALIZED RAGE

At fourteen, a family reunion took me to my father's birthplace for the first time, where inevitably, the talk would circle back to my great-grandfather. A hundred or so Geters, Phillipses, and Simons, spread across five generations. Collards, ham hocks, cornbread, and not a drop of liquor for any man to find. I'd eavesdrop, listening to see who could tell the meanest Gus Phillips story. When the reunion programs started, the relative in charge of the reunion committee would begin the family tradition of going through a roll call of whom we sprung from. When the program arrived at Gus Phillips, they always said something like "He was mean, but he brought us here, and being family means we love him."

As a child, I did not know that my middle name, Augustus, was the heirloom passed down from a mean and damaged man. That though I might have been named after my grandmother, Gussie Mae, my grandmother was named after the father who raped her. I did not know I was sitting in rooms where people fetched plates for abusers, and were taught not to flinch. Was it easier to make forgiveness the story of Gus Phillips than assess the damage he'd done? Or is the work ahead for me to forgive him, too?

MARCH OF SIXTH GRADE, A WEEK BEFORE EASTER BREAK, ONE EVE-
ning Jamila and I congregated in my parents' bedroom. The two of us
leaning against their waterbed, still in our plaid polyester uniforms,
intoxicated by our parents' full attention. When, finally, Jamila and I
had grown tongue-tired from recalling our days, our parents told us
we'd be leaving the following weekend to be dropped off in Dayton.

The moment I heard the words "Easter" and "Dayton," I burst into
tears. Wails the length of sirens. My parents stared, truly confused. I
managed to sneak out "She hates me" before throwing my head into
their mattress, the waves of the waterbed rocking out my shame and
tears. Jamila stared at the ruffles on her socks before looking up and
saying, "Yeah, she really does. Aunt Sarah is really mean to her. I don't
know why"—the truth spilling like caramel from chocolate eggs.
Though I felt too old for this type of tears, I folded into my body like
I had seen women at church do when, after so long, they finally had
the spirit in their hands.

The details of what happened after are fuzzy. We were in bed
shortly after. The weekend came and went. No luggage was packed in
our Caravan. Jamila and I would never again get dropped off at Aunt
Sarah's. We still made family trips there, and sure enough, Aunt Sarah
still seemed to hate me, maybe even more now, but my parents would
never again leave me alone with her—though, after my confession, we
would never speak of it again.

I think this is how shame works: it makes everyone else's stories
about you the only ones you believe and know how to tell. After years
of holding my breath in Dayton, years spent listening to her whisper
admonishments, building my fear with never-fulfilled threats, I suspected Aunt Sarah was right about whatever she saw in me. As children, it had been ingrained in us that family was everything, and I had
done something girls are never supposed to do: I told—told my father
that the woman who'd protected him from monsters was mine.

I will never know what it was that made Aunt Sarah resent me so
much, or what kind of ghosts make a grown woman psychologically

target or emotionally assault a child. Even though my time with Aunt Sarah still sometimes spins my head, I try to imagine not the woman whose eyes wailed in the basement over spilt cards but the woman fierce and willing to rip my arm from my socket to save me. Even if I was the wrong girl, my uncle the wrong man. Was this the closest to the Black Period that, together, Aunt Sarah and I would ever get?

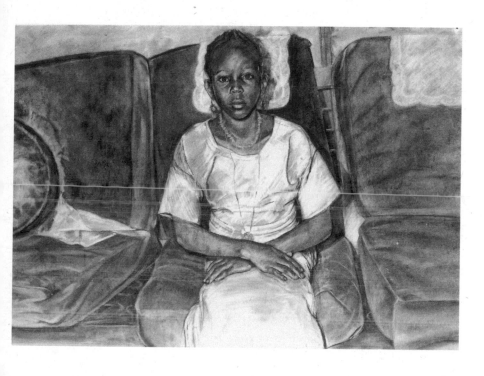

ENCORE

As proof that Aunt Sarah loves me, my father likes to tell the story of when we first moved to the U.S. I was three, Jamila six, my father taking his wife and children to the "New World." Deciding we'd been through one coup too many, my parents determined it was time to go. We'd fled Nigeria in the midst of the Kafanchan crisis of 1987, in which violence had broken out between Muslims and Christians and left nineteen dead as well as churches and mosques burned.

We arrived in the U.S., no work. My father sent my mother, my sister, and me to Dayton, the plan for us to stay with my grandmother and her third no-good husband, my father's stepfather Henry. My father says the moment my aunts found out, my aunt Sarah drove over. With the wolf already in the house, she waited outside her mother's door for us to arrive. According to my father, my aunt looked at my mother and said, "No one is sleeping here."

This is how my father found out that his stepfather was constantly going after my aunts, who fled their mother's house the first moment they were able—that when the women in my family leave, it's because they are trying to outrun a man. That they build their lives while under constant attack. In his seventies, when my father tells this story, he is still able to slip, so easily, into the fears of his past. He never actually says, "*See*, Aunt Sarah loves you." He believes stories can be proof enough.

∞

I think often about the families of Clementa Pinckney, Tywanza Sanders, Cynthia Hurd, Rev. Sharonda Coleman-Singleton, Myra Thompson, Ethel Lance, Rev. Daniel Simmons, Rev. DePayne Middleton-Doctor, and Susie Jackson, all of whom were murdered by twenty-two-year-old Dylann Roof. I think about how Roof, being one product of America, became exactly the person he was supposed to be: our slave masters' legacy. It is not lost on me that while the victims' families offered forgiveness to Roof, they stood in an American courtroom, a place that continues to be merciless and unforgiving toward the lives and futures of our living Black children.

Knowing the little I do of Aunt Sarah's history, it's almost unbearable to imagine all the times she must have had to be docile and compliant in the face of vicious authority, whether it was whiteness or another man. Her life about suppressing anger, her god insisting on forgiveness.

More and more, I'm coming to understand my aunt Sarah as a child gotten to by the specific nature of Black poverty and the Alabama South, the threat of men's unrelenting hands, and a turn-the-other-cheek, forgiveness-without-repentance religious philosophy. I am old enough to understand the number of times my aunt must have had to stand in a room laughing at jokes told by family members who were also their abusers.

The older I get, the more removed I am from those Easter vacations and the more my rage toward Aunt Sarah extinguishes, but how clearly I can see the rope of rage that leads from my enslaved ancestors to my great-grandfather to my aunt Sarah to me.

I do not know what it does to a child to be raised in a house of intimate violence, a world so deeply defined by women who will never have the resources to fully protect themselves or their children, but knowing my aunt Sarah, I know one version of the woman that child becomes.

∞

The other day my father called me, more scared than he's ever been. He'd just gotten off the phone with my aunt, her mind slipping so hard it'd almost left her body.

"I know it's Friday night and you're busy," he says. His voice betrays his desperation to talk to someone. "I just got off the phone with your aunt Sarah. She isn't making any sense. She keeps talking in a high-pitched baby voice. It creeped me out," he says, imitating her voice in a way that makes my skin crawl, the strangeness of my father using the phrase "creeped out."

"What is she saying?" I have to ask repeatedly, my voice grabbing him by the shoulders through the phone line.

"It was nonsense. Talking about men breaking in. It's so strange, talking in this baby voice, talking about men trying to get her. Either that or she's telling your cousin Regi—you know he's checking on her—that she's going to marry him and have a baby. It's nonsense," he says, as though he truly believes he can outrun this heartbreak. "She's doing this more and more, you know. Her mind slipping like this. Either it's men trying to get at her or she's asking about you. She's always asking about you. *Hafizah this, Hafizah that.* That's that guilt coming up, because she knows what she's done."

Aunt Sarah is reliving her trauma.

When I say this to my father, he takes what sounds like the longest pause of his life.

Of course, Aunt Sarah's cruelty does not equal the assault of white supremacy, but her pain *is* historical.

In *Freedom Is a Constant Struggle,* Angela Davis writes, "We oftentimes do the work of the state in and through our interior lives. What we often assume belongs most intimately to ourselves and to our emotional life has been produced elsewhere and has been recruited to do the work of racism and repression."

Aunt Sarah's hurt is a complex trauma, its root knotted up by the bloody soil of white supremacy, the violence wrought by the men in her and my grandmother's lives, and the centuries of internalized pain of Black people in a viciously white world.

As an adult, I've found my love for my aunt inside the context of her life. Her Black, Black life. Ringing in my ears I hear all the hurt she has been forced to endure and forgive. Beyond that, if I leave my eyes open through the beatings, the whiskey, the rape, the seething anger, I see a line of Black men roaming the cotton-king South, their heads sweeping the floor because it's lethal to look whiteness in the eye. I see their humiliations stacked higher than the little bit of money America allowed them to accumulate in their pockets. I see men bringing this humiliation home until—as psychologist Nanette C. Auerhahn and psychoanalyst Dori Laub write, speaking of intergenerational memory and the Holocaust—they all but conjured up the "rage of the perpetrator, whose victims they came to be."

No, we should not abandon the work of forgiveness, but I do believe we should reevaluate and honor our forgiveness by centering the cost of it. I do not want to live with a hard heart, but I want limits on turning the other cheek. "In white culture, forgiveness is synonymous with letting go," writes Terese Marie Mailhot in her memoir, *Heart Berries*. "It's dangerous," she warns, "to let go of a transgression when the transgressor is not contrite." I want to stop offering our injurers unconditional salvation. I want us to reject white supremacy's concept of justice.

One of the numerous traumas of slavery was having to seek in oneself the daily forgiveness and graciousness enslaved people were expected to grant our captors. Even our dirges had to be coded into negro spirituals and uplift songs. It is inhuman to dispossess an entire group of people of their rage, and the performance of forgiveness is one way Black people are continually dispossessed of it.

A true exchange of forgiveness and repentance requires that the offender and the offended agree on the sin. Until then, I want us to remember, our rage at the injustices we suffer is justified. That surely a people strong enough to survive centuries of enslavement are strong enough to hold our anger at our oppressions and our oppressors while keeping our souls intact. I want us to remind each other that we can hold on to our anger without being destroyed by it.

I want us to make white salvation, *and* the violence wrought by white supremacy, whiteness's responsibility. I want us to channel our justified anger into community and collective. I want us to stop forgiving institutions that can't rise to the challenge of restitution and reparations, and instead, dismantle and divest from every one of them—from the courts to the cops to the way we shoulder white redemption. I want us to exit this theatre of forgiveness—to forget everything white supremacy has taught us about it. When forgiveness enters the conversation—which I know, with true restitution, it most likely will—I want it to be a forgiveness that, like an abolitionist framework, builds.

∞

On January 11, 2017, I watched Roof sentenced to death while, in the same country that produced him, "the police in the United States kill three people a day every day—which is to say every eight hours, or if we think of it another way, all in a day's work," notes geographer and prison abolitionist Ruth Wilson Gilmore. Roof's death is confirmation that the state claims the monopoly on violence. But what is the legacy of the United States in a family?

Is it enslaved men born too powerless to protect themselves, their wives, their children? Was it the work of America that told women and children that it didn't matter if they were on the master's plantation, in their landlord's sharecropping fields, or freed and asleep in their father's house, that abuse was both their lot and family heirloom? What of agency? How do we—*how did we*—stop?

I asked Aunt Liz this once over the phone. "School," she said. "We went to school."

Aunt Liz—who taught me not to fear the quiet; who, my whole childhood, loved me proudly and unconditionally; who made me feel safe; who, along with Auntie Mairo, was one of the favorite adults that orbited my world; and who was always reading books she never talked about—said at school they learned they had a right to their own bodies, had teachers to confide in.

They were children who lived in a world where they couldn't stop the harm they experienced, but in classrooms—surrounded by the hope that is new knowing—they saw: the past was written, but the future was theirs to make.

Aunt Liz's answer was so simple, it seemed impossible. It was also incomplete. The history between us making it unnecessary to say my grandmother Gussie Mae Simon's beloved name—*Madear*.

Madear who knew that if she wanted a chance at saving her children, they'd have to flee inside that terrifyingly uncertain journey which history would remember as the Great Migration. The mother who, and long before Francisco Goya's Black Paintings, showed my father how to draw light into the darkness.

I want to tell my aunt Sarah I'm sorry that her rage was swallowed instead of heard. Though I did not deserve her vitriol, my aunt's pain deserved a proper witness. I want to travel back in time to all my father's fathers, from enslaved to freed men, beg them not to make our women wear their pain. I want to travel back in time to each of the women in my family's youth, grab them by the shoulders, look them in the eyes, and tell them that their bodies are theirs. Their lives are theirs. And if I cannot find them before the ruin, I want to meet them directly after it. To tell them to hold on to their anger, to let their rage draw their line, but to have that line be drawn in the appropriate direction.

I want to tell Aunt Sarah, freshly out of one of her episodes, that she did not make an angry woman out of me. I have become a woman who draws unerasable lines. I understand there must be a limit on how much forgiveness will cost me. I know the direction my anger should go.

∞

Two years after the fact, I arrive at the doors of Emanuel AME. Its white façade stretches high as a woman yawning, stretches long like legs in early morning. It is a blue day for the sky. Were there clouds, I imagine the white steeple of the church would bleed indistinguishably into the heavens. The church is different than I expected, but still familiar in that way all Black churches are to anyone who's spent time under their graces.

It takes three pushes at three doors before I find my way inside. Immediately, in the foyer of the church, two Black women sit in shadows, their faces lined like rings of a tree. Dressed in black, my abrupt entrance does not startle them. They look so tired, with a grief that extends beyond this new one that, now, they are women immune to surprise. Looking ahead, beyond the pews, the stained glass, the ornateness of God, I see the half-moon of a Black man's body peeking from a casket.

God help me.

I am the third to arrive at a stranger's wake.

I have not been in the room with a deceased since putting my mother in the ground. The suddenness snatches my breath and I pray they cannot see the whites of my eyes growing big enough to illuminate their private shadows. Though the women do not flinch at my presence, sure as they feel history in every bone, they know why I am here.

Even though South Carolina has long been a kind of home for me, I cannot help but feel conflicted for needing to see this, for needing to stand in this moment. This place where, now, everything that could have possibly happened has happened. Though Black women are deceptive agers, I know these women have arrived on the other side of ninety. I want to ask them, who have they forgiven and what did it cost them? And now that they've arrived so close to the other side that they can peer in, does forgiving the unrepentant get us anywhere?

Behind them, in the shadows, I can practically see my aunt Sarah standing in the pews—neither of us knowing she will be dead in just one year. But in this moment, I know, were she here, she would pray for this stranger's afterlife so earnestly it would come out in song.

And here is Aunt Sarah again, leaning against my mind's eye, her dusty Buick behind her, waiting for my young mother to arrive with me and Jamila—three and six—one on each hip. Aunt Sarah is listening for the huff and puff of her stepfather blowing her mother's house down from the inside.

I see Aunt Sarah patiently waiting to save us from a danger so great we will never be able to adequately thank her. Aunt Sarah making for us what she, Aunt Liz, and my father never had: our very own narrow escape. And I see her, all those years later, watching me on my uncle's lap. I think of how, despite all the damage and hurt that laid claim on their lives, my father's and aunts' generation fought for the future of our family with their teeth bared.

While we shared this earth, Aunt Sarah and I existed with each other inside a cruel history—one we had no shared language to name. I watched her wear her rage like a sandbag around her neck. Still, even if Aunt Sarah would fail me in so many ways to come, she was determined to stop the beatings, the molestations, the rape. My father says, in our family, the job of every generation is to take the whole lot further.

Kaba reminds that one purpose of organizing and community is to aid us in identifying who is responsible for the conditions we're trying to change. The work isn't to put our rage away but to see it in context, to honor it. And in doing so—by pointing our rage in the right direction—in community, transform it into justice.

All Aunt Sarah and I missed together reminds me, heartbreak is a political condition. But in the last years of her life, after Aunt Sarah couldn't drive and Uncle Rodge was long dead, my cousins Qjuan and Regi brought her groceries. Their mother, my first cousin Sissy, took her to church. Their love drew Aunt Sarah into the Black Period.

Rushing back outside through the doors of Emanuel AME, my eyes search for air. I imagine all the Black souls that have entered quivering from the fields, their bodies holding hundreds of years. Their rage coded in a slave's song for freedom, a hum so low, so strong it would cling to generations, so that when Aunt Sarah opened her mouth in song, not even she could stop herself from singing its beautiful, rageful freedom melody back to me.

The song of our inheritance whispering in every note she sang, "Go, child, go get free." I think of her cruelty. I sing my forgiveness back.

A POLITICAL CONDITION

AGE VI

LUCK

LOVE STORY CAN MAKE YOU AFRAID. IN THIS one, my parents have glanced at one another in an Ohio University stairwell. My mother was visiting my auntie Mairo, who was getting her graduate degree in education. My father, having finished his Germany-stationed draft service during the Việt Nam War, asked around about the woman in the stairwell until Mabuza vouched for him with my auntie Mairo. My parents went on two dates, then got married. They spent those first months intimate strangers, inhabiting two different continents. In a world without internet or cellphones, they swung letters from Athens, Ohio, to Kaduna, Nigeria, until my mother could get a green card. Years later, my father packed his bag. He gave my half-brother, Gerald, a "see you soon" kiss while his ex-wife looked coolly on.

Dark skin, a button nose, olive-shaped eyes that smiled and—when needed, or when she was tired or fed up—admonished. I can still hear her laughing like a child stifling a giggle at the back of a classroom. In pictures of my mother before children, she is disconcertingly beautiful. A decade later, my father will paint her as a Black Madonna in a long blue dress, her profile, finally pregnant—nine months wide. But back when they were still new to each other. My father, a handsome, sensitive, stubborn man of thirty, somehow still growing into his ears, must have felt incredibly lucky.

Culture and tradition being what it was, at twenty, my mother should have been already married or, at the very least, promised off. But looking around, feeling as strong and capable as any man, my mother wanted a different life. This I learned in Seattle on a work trip in 2018 when Bobo, a childhood friend of my mother, picked me up for dinner. Bobo was not so lucky. Her mother was Nigerian, but she bears the light skin of her Irish father, which, she told me, in Nigeria curried her no favors. I was too young to remember the last time I saw Bobo and am surprised at first, not having expected to be picked up by a Nigerian woman lighter than me.

Though she and my mother—and their mothers—were born on the same land, Bobo tells me she was often considered too light-skinned to be a "real" Nigerian. The wrinkles around Bobo's eyes were a field of spreading crows' wings as she spoke. I sat next to her in the passenger's seat not knowing what to feel, as she spun the image of my mother into Janus's two heads. Eventually, I settled on *alarm!* Quieted by the fact of how long a pain can follow you. We are pain in the root system.

It was fall. Bobo drove me the long way from Seattle to the burbs, where we met her daughter Ann Marie—the two of us born together in the same Zaria hospital on the same day. A parasite biologist, Bobo studies the gut. Wanted to show me that there, the trees are beautiful. Like my mother, she carved herself her very own creation story. Fate, theirs to make. The Allah my mother fashioned agreed that women would be the inheritors of the earth.

I imagine, though I never asked Bobo, that my mother felt lucky, too. To find a man she could, in an instant, if not love, see the shadow of a possible love in, behind the blaring sunlight of faith and attraction. A man who would borrow, starve, get a second job pumping gas, to save enough money so that they could return to my mother's homeland to live. In 1979, all the money a Black man could save would never be enough to fund a dream so big. Luckily for Jamila and me, luck struck. Months before, after stretching his last dollar and still coming up short, my father would be the first Black artist to receive a grant from the Boston Cultural Council. The grant— along with Uncle Peppers's encouragement that my father should go to Africa and not come back—was enough money to get them gone.

What luck! My father would think on the long plane ride to his new adopted country, unaware it was a leaving that would estrange him from his first child. Shrinking below him was a country still wet from the work of a Civil Rights Act that would change everything and nothing at all. He was saying goodbye to a country in the heat of a labor that would birth prisons and merge the War on Drugs with the war on Black people.

My father was a man ready to go. His leaving would allow him, my mother, and the daughters they would have a narrow escape from the devastating effects of 1980s America on Black life. It was a time when white supremacy was updating and camouflaging its technologies of oppression. The homicide rate for young Black males doubled. The crack epidemic ran cheap and wild. Fetal death rates, weapons arrests, and the number of Black children in foster care skyrocketed.

A period referred to by economists as "deindustrialization" would result in the disappearance of millions of jobs to overseas markets and the virtual extinction of Black farmers. Factories closed. Unions declined. And setting off a domino effect, local governments—suddenly without tax revenue—reduced spending for social services, including schools, hospitals, parks, libraries, public universities, and public housing. It was a loss that would hit Black communities—still reeling from the impact of centuries of slavery, a disingenuous claim of Reconstruction, and Jim Crow—the hardest.

Born in Nigeria in 1981 and 1984, Jamila and I, through our mother's return and our father's expatriation, spent the first years of our lives shielded from the white backlash to the Civil Rights Movement, as well as the Ku Klux Klan's recommitment to a reign of terror that included drive-by shootings of Black people and the firebombings of Black churches. By the time Jamila was two years old, the prison population of the United States had reached one million, half of them Black. With a feeling that Black people had gotten too much, had made it too far, were too undeserving—too lucky—white resentment swelled (see Affirmative Action).

Black communities were plagued by state-designed poverty, job discrimination, predatory lending practices, and media that presented all crime in Blackface. With the rise of prisons and our overincarceration came the loss of eligibility for better-paying jobs. All the while, through gerrymandering and overpolicing, we were becoming irreparably disenfranchised from weighing in on our political representation. Black women, historically one of the lowest paid groups of workers, found themselves trying to raise children alone.

SOON, MY FATHER, WHO OBSESSIVELY TIMES HIS ARRIVAL SO AS TO never have to wait or park, will pick me up from the Charlotte airport. Standing outside of baggage claim, the weather is balmy. I twist back and forth—hips, neck, shoulders—making a small scene as I try to push pain out and crack my spine into a more accommodating alignment. In the South, the rules I wish were stricter relax. Around me white people smoke in front of no-smoking signs.

When my father first moved us from Ohio to South Carolina, it was hard to understand why he'd risk untying the knot of his own Great Migration. Now I love the South—crave it, miss it. Having taken up my inheritance, I, too, am a Southerner now.

I can tell just by looking who is and isn't from here. Though I've always been made most curious by those who flaunt their belonging with Confederate gear and slogan T-shirts that tell the person looking to go back to where they come from, or dare you—*just try it, just try*—to take their guns. These are our fellow Southerners that make my father laugh the most.

There is a way that my father looks picking me up from the airport, so happy to see me that it heals the soft wound made when I see adult mother-and-daughter pairs on the train in New York. *Oh*, the joy of looking like someone. I relish these rare moments when, so clearly, so quickly, I can be recognized by any stranger as someone's child.

When he arrives, exiting the car, he casts his arms wide, as though he is saying, I love you *this* much, I love you the size of the whole world. He grins with his chin tucked into his chest and envelops me like the soft bear he is. A young-looking seventy-something, his only-now-graying beard tickles my face.

Once in the car, he leans into the steering wheel of his silver Ford pickup and stares up at the sky like someone steadying themselves against a miracle. There's been the prediction of rain, but the clouds don't know it. Their bodies, though plump, remain bright and white. "If we're lucky, we'll miss it," he says and then goes on to ask one of his favorite questions: "Do you know how hard it is to paint the sky?"

The drive from the Charlotte airport to Elgin, South Carolina, will punch us through a color palette—the expanse in the windshield before us shifting from blue skies, clouds of varying whites, and into a sunset that looks born beneath my father's brushstrokes—oranges self-immolating into reds, the purple ember of a bruise.

"It's in the white-point," he says. And though it's been years since I've sketched anything, I remember, *don't lose the light.* My father's instructions over my shoulder: depth on a flat page requires shadows, and shadows require light.

My father drums the steering wheel with one hand. "See the way the light holds the blues," he says, taking a break from his Motown humming. Despite the distance loss has taken him from his childhood god, he still believes in the mystery of creation. Believes in the way the sun can pull the string on a color, believes in the moon in the afternoon, the red clay earth, and the way the pine trees in his yard unabashedly toss their scent. He believes in what he's made with his hands: his paintings, Jamila, me.

"You could spend your whole life and never master a cloud," he says, his singsong voice failing to keep up with his aging, his seventy-plus years. I'm listening, but I'm also measuring his belly with my eyes. Trying to assess if his grief has left him any time to tend to his diabetes. His fifteen-year-old triple bypass. His two titanium hips that stiffen from not enough exercise and a lack of stretching.

He's been lucky. He's always had good health insurance. His surgeries amount to little debt. They can mainly be added up in the days that turned into weeks, sometimes months, of the two of us holed up in a house that had become a stranger to everything and everyone we'd lost. But in this new house that he's occupied since my sophomore year of college—just as with the old one where my mother died—my father, surgery after surgery, bled.

On Christmas breaks, summer vacations, on emergency family leaves from college, sometimes three times a day, I pulled gauze from a post-bypass wound—a gaping sliver in his chest that I cleaned over and over like a smudge on a window. Later, twenty-one years old, I fetched bedpans, scrubbed the blood from his mattress, turned stoic and sharp at the embarrassment of our exposure, replacing the bandages on one stitched hip, then eventually the other. I wept, I swept, cooked, cleaned puss, did dishes, my queerness tucked away like an airplane's black box.

My father shifts gears from Motown to Garth Brooks. Floods with Earth, Wind & Fire's "September." *The thunder rolls* from a hum in his throat. *The lightning strikes* in his eyes as he goes in and out of humming and complaining about the president, the two of us lucky: home before nightfall, not a drop of rain despite the warning of it in our achy joints.

KNOWING THAT I WAS COMING, MY FATHER HAS CUT THE GRASS. The hedges pared back to evict the bees. Driftwood, antique toys, and unidentifiable turn-of-the-century instruments litter the front porch of this white two-story house, waiting for my father to repurpose their second lives into art.

Inside, the house is what I worry it to be. The heat too low, laundry stacking. Cabinets in the kitchen wide open. Steel nails, razor blades, turpentine-washed paintbrushes, and forgotten nubs of charcoal pencil scatter the house: on tables, the floors, every bathroom sink. The recycling piling up. Too many items in the fridge on the verge of letting go.

Even happy to see me, my father, mind always in a painting, heads straight to his second-floor art studio, but calls my name to follow, halfway into some half-story. Upstairs, he's been making the sky.

When my father bought the house, he converted the entire top floor into his art studio. The right half houses printers, giant computer screens, and framing equipment. The left half he uses for drawing, painting, and sculpture. Remnants of collage litter the floor. The corners of the room piled with flat files, his illustrations from children's books, and sculptures that look like an internal haunting come alive. My father has fashioned a large piece of plywood that reaches from the slanted ceilings to the floor, runs the long length of a wall. To this larger-than-life easel he affixes massive canvases and sheets of paper. He steps back, a figure painter, creating life.

"Clouds," my father says, almost cockily. His palms spread out across his painted kingdom. A young Black girl swings from an expanse of pillowy white. In another painting, a Black boy stands, hands at his waist, looking off the canvas, his body enveloped in soft whites and the blues that gives them illumination.

"You know, it was just luck. I wasn't supposed to be there," my father says. It is a sentence he's said to friends, colleagues, old acquaintances, but for now, he is only speaking to me, standing there in his studio, imagining my mother stroking out.

MY FATHER LIVES IN A HOUSE STOCKED FULL OF OUR DUPLICATIONS—
our likeness filling the stacks of paintings, drawings, and children's
books he's illustrated: me, ten and eating breakfast with my mother
and grandmother; me, eight, sulking outside a doorway waiting for
Jamila's dance class to end; four years old, trying to tie his enormous
shoes onto my feet; Jamila and me, seven and four, standing on our old
front porch in Lynn, Massachusetts, leaning against our mother's hips,
new to my father's America.

"At the last minute, I wanted to have lunch at home," he says in a
voice both concrete and feather. If he notices me flinch, he never lets
on. But having approached the subject, my father is a man committed
to seeing it through: lunchtime, and he walks home under clear October South Carolina skies, my mother just off the phone with a cousin
in Nigeria. In the bedroom, while my parents talk, my mother's mind
will burst into aneurism. Her body will trail to its knees, her back
against the bedpost. The house silent, save the sound of a groan. A
barely discernible wind signaling a body hollowing itself out—
impossible to know where the sound comes from, my mother or my
father.

While he speaks, my father's body puckers into itself. A losing
boxer, his shoulders round forward into memory's sucker punch. He
could topple over at any moment, but instead, he sways, wading into
the waters where his luck and his misfortune are one. That he cannot
reconcile their simultaneous existence is a fact that still cleaves at him.

Listening, but denying him eye contact, I shift uncomfortably from
one hip to another trying to dodge this pain that haunts me with its
clear story of loss, while the chronic pain in my body wanders, name-
less. "Do you understand the luck of me coming home at exactly the
right time?" he asks, trying to make me a witness to a moment I don't
want to see.

MY FATHER THINKS I AM INNATELY LUCKY. EVEN IN OUR GRIEVING, he's believed me to be a queen in the land of the damned, a winning lottery ticket in a field of beggars. In this arrangement, it's hard to know what's been won. The luck couldn't buy me a car. It couldn't fix my current one—its sudden refusal to start, glaring against a never-ending string of New York no-parking rules. My luck is child's play. It's a few raffles won on the summer vacations and winter holidays when we roamed the roads of the U.S., our Dodge Caravan packed to the brim with my father's art.

On those trips, we pressed pause on our roots and became no-mads. We took the Black Period on the road. While my St. Maria's classmates attended summer camps or lolled their days away playing four square till dusk, our parents set up shop, one Black art fair at a time. Under white tents, we filled booths with my father's paintings and drawings and his cheaper stacks of prints. Sometimes the fairs were outside in the blistering Georgia or Florida heat. Other times, we sat for hours under the looming industrial ceilings and fluorescent lights of convention centers in Michigan or Indiana where Black peo-ple perused Black art, crafts, handmade clothes, like it was perpetu-ally Juneteenth. It was where we watched R & B singers like Brian McKnight perform before making it big. The children of the artists, we were stuck there all day. We wandered in search of the one or two booths that served as our entertainment, always promising at least a raffle or a carnival game.

Even when I'm in Brooklyn, through the distance that spans from New York to South Carolina, I can feel my father's grief in the trees surrounding me. The daughter of Eve, I am also my father's child, the daughter of a griot who is also the patron saint of ghosts.

The year my mother died, my parents were still living down the street from the HBCU my father retired from. At impromptu gather-ings at our faculty house on Haskell Road, my father and his friends told loud stories of the college, which constantly vexed and baffled them with its chaos. That day, my father was tired. Jamila was in En-gland at the University of Leeds. I was a sophomore in college, double majoring in English and economics. My parents were beginning to lean into their empty nest.

If a sudden death has mercy, it waits till everyone is asleep. In the story my father tells, he is a lone cowboy galloping across a highway to fetch his youngest child to her dying mother's bedside. In reality, he sat in the back of our purple minivan, a friend of his at our helm. That he and I sat in the back of the van, holding hands, the two of us sobbing, drowning the repetition of his apologies, is a part that my father always leaves out of the story.

"I'm sorry, I'm sorry, I'm *so* sorry," he cried.

It was the first time I'd ever heard an apology begged.

I wept with shock. I wept in utter terror of what was coming next. I wept into the echo that was Jamila's absence. I wept with shame that we were people who could lose so much. I wept until I thought I'd throw up, until I was sure I'd soured. Until I convinced myself, *hadn't I been this unlucky all along?*

Six weeks later, my father had an emergency triple heart bypass and, with Jamila, at his insistence, having returned to the UK to finish a masters in African human sustainable development, I put school on pause to help him recover. We spent a semester wound up like barbed wire in each other's grief. He was as scared and sad as I was, and I'd begun to resent him and his sadness for how much grief space they both seemed to monopolize, and how they leaned on me instead of carrying me.

It didn't seem fair. I was the youngest child. Between my father and Jamila, I'd had the least amount of time with my mother, and yet it felt like I'd been tasked to carry so much in her aftermath. I was nineteen when she died. I had just arrived at the crucial crossing from girlhood to woman. I'd been waiting for someone to show up and carry me through my grief. My sister was gone, and my father and I were both grieving in our own insatiable ways. The anger had begun to swirl, but the only safe place to put it was inside myself. It was easy to do in a nation where I had so much in common with the enemy's face America painted—African/Black, queer, a woman, child of a Muslim mother.

Now, more than fifteen years later, the corpses of hornets scatter the windows of a different house, but the familiar smell of turpentine steadies me. Staring at what he's made, my father says tightly, still unbelieving that any of this has happened at all, "You got to see her one last time." His voice leaps into a whisper, bows to take a knee.

"You got to say goodbye, you don't know how lucky that is. Your sister didn't." He chews his lip, a grasping man pulling the shortest straw. My father, the loneliest of the lonesome, so lonely he could die. It's the quiver of his voice that tosses me back—

Inside my mother's hospital room, a nurse gingerly hands me a cup of ice chips. My mother's lips dry and cracked in the absence of her mind. My father waiting outside while I listened to the machine that gave her heart its beat. Another that inhaled and exhaled on her behalf. Its wide and white accordion tube encased in glass and heavy sighs. My mother a machine of a woman. My mother at her wits' end. Me, scarcely more than a child, trying to figure out how to say goodbye. But the machines were preserving her organs. And wasn't this lucky?

Someone somewhere was waiting to be called up on the transplant line: the luck of new eyes, lungs that had never smoked, skin ready to be grafted. They were lucky and I, the luckiest daughter, was a daughter stunned. For my father, I sense that my luck hinges on this one thing: what he calls my luckiest goodbye.

"Your mother looked no different from any other day," he says, walking around his studio, pointing at the drawings he's done since the last time I was home. In his whole life, my father's never painted an image like this, of his wife disappearing before his very eyes. My mother's stroke became the picture that stalked not his paintbrush but his vocabulary, which turns alight with his grief. His mind spins topsy-turvy at his presence, allowing him to nurse my mother's sudden vanishing act—the luck of it all. He forgets, an alive woman is not the last woman I saw.

Sept 2016

I AM IN SOUTH CAROLINA FOR A WEEK, WHERE THE AIR IS SO DE-
ceptively fresh compared to New York. Daniel, knowing I'm in Columbia, texts from LA. It's one of those iPhone-generated slideshows
with pictures of us from the present day reaching back to our college
years. Brash baroque music plays in the background of us dancing
sweatily in South Carolina, then later in Hell's Kitchen, at SantaCon
wearing red and big wigs, and the message "I'm the past you've been
running from!"

Daniel and I have been inseparable since meeting our senior year
at Clemson, where, instead of sprinting to graduate on time, we
stretched our senior year into a summer and an extra semester, having
finally found, in a conservative territory, someone on the same side of
the aisle to laugh with. Daniel and I have senses of humor that are
carbon copies of each other, and he is a rare white face with whom I
let my guard down. In the time we've been known to each other, he's
yet to require I "prove" my experience as a Black, queer woman in the
world. Instead, Daniel, my white whale, takes me at my word *and* is
open to me correcting him, two things that, for a Black woman, are
rare occurrences from any white friend. He believes in what I see,
even when what I name is not apparent to him, believing the world is
defined by how it responds not just to him as a gay man, but to me—to
Black women.

Next, he sends a video of him kissing his cats, Wolfgang Fireball
and Purrtricia Ourcat. He groans over text that someone from Clemson has posted a picture of themselves eating Chick-fil-A (a chain
known for their homophobia) as an act of "freedom of speech." I laugh
out loud before putting my phone away, thankful for the reprieve.

All this, I suppose, my generation's rendition of the home videos of
our past. All this time, without knowing it, I've been making my own
record, though, for so long, I'd been afraid to look most any evidence
in the eye.

||

*There was that moment when my father—my mother so barely dead we
could still smell her all over the house—turned to me and, in his grieving*

anger, said, "You lost your mother, but I lost my wife, do you know what that means." I stared at him, still as a hurricane's eye, but in me, rain.

His teeth were a flash of lightning as he thundered. His newly triple-bypassed heart beat beneath the stapled incision at his chest, which was fighting infection after infection. Finally, his cardiologist turned to me and said, "We'll have to leave it open."

Nineteen-year-old me on bereavement leave from college, and there my father was, a gaping wound for me to clean. It was a horrifying intimacy, and we shared it three times a day—Jamila back in grad school in England, my father vibrating between two poles: weeping beneath my hands or refusing to look me in the eye as I irrigated what would eventually scar.

There was the strangeness of a ghost begging me to die. Then, finally, the miracle of having kept each other alive and all the years that came after for me to understand: yes, there was a difference in what we'd lost.

▶

IN MY FATHER'S SILVER FOUR-DOOR PICKUP TRUCK, I DRIVE WITH one arm out the window and one eye always at the mirror, attentive for cops, old ghosts. I breathe in with so much of my younger self to remember. I've never felt lucky here, in this place my parents turned into my hometown. But then, there lies grief's trick.

For a decade, it was like grief had thrown an inkblot of amnesia on every picture. This state is haunted by the black-headed dot of me trying to outrun grief, my difference, trying to be the right kind of Black, no kind of queer. This place where a Muslim woman could die and people wouldn't care. This place where I had so much knowledge of the fragileness of our bodies.

Other families always seemed so healthy, had mine done something wrong? There was something about illness that felt dangerous even beyond the fact of the illness itself. It was the impatient and pitied way white people looked at Black folks when our bodies were sick or didn't wholly work. The way they tightened their lips as though afraid our bodies would get in their mouths.

No one in my life had the language of disability justice—especially for the invisible ones that grab me in the present day. Disability, we were taught, was defined by wheelchairs or noticeable physical or mental impairments. And if someone was disabled, growing up, my teachers at St. Maria's made it clear it was rude to say so. Disabled people always seemed to be relegated to charity, inspirational posters, or the visiting hours of able-bodied society. The sympathy I saw disabled people offered in the U.S. looked more like pity with sharp teeth. Raised amid violence, poverty, and collapsing infrastructure—all those remnants of colonization and war, which had filled the country with hurting minds and bodies—my mother never used the word "disability." For her, a single moniker was enough: compatriot.

Even if I had been told, I wouldn't have wanted to believe that my mother's chronic fatigue and hypertension, my father's limping hips, heart disease, and diabetes, the chronic, often debilitating pain that was always creeping up my back, or the anxieties running down my throat cast any of us into a category of disability. Instead, I worried and carried shame about the unlucky bodies I'd come from. Shame was my colonizer's capital, and it made sure fear kept me at an arm's length from giving our bodies the exchange of tenderness we all deserved.

Between a mother dead of a stroke and a father with a fresh triple bypass and a broken heart, none of my origin stories seemed to have bodies that could take it. I didn't understand the arc of racism that reached into the diagnoses doctors offered, the treatment they withheld, or if, in their medical care, they would believe or recognize that we felt pain. And I definitely didn't understand what I carried with shame, I'd never be able to properly love or properly grieve. Shame was my psychic death sentence, and every day it threatened to string me up from its gallows.

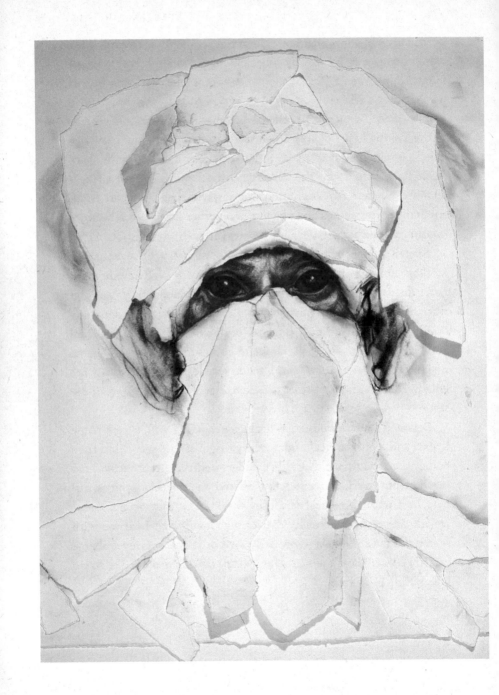

WHEN I'D RETURNED TO COLLEGE AFTER MY MOTHER DIED AND after my father, post-triple-bypass, could be left alone, I wore my grief like a tuxedo. Like an emperor parading their new clothes about town. I cried sober, I cried drunk. I cried in the morning, in the shower, and behind the wheel of my midnight-blue Saturn.

My father and I were of equally different messes. Jamila was back in England. At the beginning of my father's surgery, Aunt Sarah had come to help for what was the longest three weeks of my life. Not even my mother's death had been able to soften her toward me. While my father convalesced, she walked around me, oscillating between constant corrections or fury and quiet, as though I'd brought on what had befallen us. The rest of my family lived in Dayton or Nigeria. Whatever I was going through, I was sailing the river alone. I've never been so scared in my entire life as I was for the months that turned into years after my mother died.

The woman I loved more than anything in this world was dead, and everywhere I turned when I returned to my mostly white college, her death seemed to be met with indifference. A girl from student government, who up until that point I'd considered a friend, called me three weeks after my mother's death to tell me that I was making the choice not to move on. There were hard nights of partying that blacked out into grieving, and white friends who'd never lost their mothers let me know that they resented me still missing mine. It was eeriness inside my bones. Even some teachers were reluctant to be accommodating, instead wanting to hold a hard line with me so as, one put it, to teach me a "character lesson."

One night, during a weekend I'd returned to Columbia to check on my father, I sat on the balcony of Jude's mother's new apartment near the Kroger where I did my father's grocery shopping. Jude had been one of my best friends since high school. At the time, his parents had just gotten divorced, and my mother hadn't been dead a year. Like most every white person in this Carolina town, Jude had been raised Christian and up through high school had been made to go to church, but by the time we were nineteen, he wasn't all that religious. I remember it was still summer, but the weather was fading into fall. We alternated between sips from Pabst Blue Ribbon cans and his mother's sweet tea.

I don't know why he said what he said. But I remember his words clear as day. He apologized first, as though sorry to be put in the position to say what was coming. "I'm sorry, Hafz," he said. "Your mother is not in heaven." He told me that as a Christian, he wasn't allowed to believe Muslims go there. Even for Jude, who'd known my mother for years, her death was less loss than an ideological conversation. I stayed on that porch for three more hours that felt like years. In shock, I told him it was okay he felt the way he did. That I understood. On that balcony, I constructed my own little theatre of forgiveness. Immediately after, I returned to the work of resenting my father for being sick and having a body that needed me. Shame. I felt deeply unlucky, and ashamed that my unluckiness lived in broad daylight for everyone to see.

My shame moved in all directions. I could've salted every threshold like the old folks used to do and I still would not have been able to keep the haints of my shame out of the house. I was grieving from inside a closet. I was ashamed to have a dead mother, ashamed to have one whose body stroked out. Now Jude was repeating to me what the world was telling me every day, that I should be ashamed to have a Muslim mother.

It was only two years after 9/11 and I had yet to see any Muslim person be lucky enough to get away from the U.S. safely, not even through death. Though my high school English and yearbook teachers and a good friend who'd driven from Florida surprised me by coming to the wake at our home, when the imam prayed as he laid my mother to rest, none of my friends were at her funeral. I hadn't known to invite any. If I had thought of it, I probably wouldn't have. I would have been ashamed, afraid no one would have come. And then, for years, there was the shame of that regret following me around like a kicked dog. *All* of this can be attached to a body. Both living and deceased. It was still another fourteen years before I walked away from my friendship with Jude. Shame.

All of it pushed me further into my insistence on privacy. Never tell anyone nothing, I repeated to myself over and over again, until I couldn't hear my own whispers behind the iron bars of my brain. What I knew about a dead Muslim woman was that she didn't garner sympathy. I was ashamed to grieve, in public, a woman that the world outside of my immediate circle refused to. In America, my grief didn't mean all that much. I felt terribly unlucky.

∞

After my mother was *gone* gone, dead as a doornail—after I had waited, cried, begged, prayed hard and long enough to be sure she was never ever coming back—I spent the following decade terrified of my own death. By logic alone, it was the surest thing coming. Along with my mother, both of my grandmothers suffered from strokes. My blood carries the sickle cell trait so common to Nigerians a normally benign trait when recessive, but one that U.S. police departments will list as cause of death on autopsy reports when they kill us through excessive force. Between a family legacy of diabetes and bad hips, my body is haunted by the looming inheritances of the ailments of being Black in America.

If my father's childhood could be translated into today, he'd most likely have lived in the very kind of community, like Flint, that corporations and governments seek out to dump their toxins in. The same Black and poor neighborhoods where corporations tell us to recycle, while—without conscience, consent, or oversight—turning our streams into sewers. Where elected officials build us city parks on old industrial-waste dumps and turn our neighborhoods into sourcing grounds for American prisons, and where, after natural or man-made disaster, no government will help us rebuild. And where, beneath the laughter of Black, brown, and poor children, the ground is filled with arsenic and lead. A nation changes a body, and state violence is a disability issue.

From stories he's told me of his childhood, I imagine luck was in the rarity of a weekend where no wages were lost to drinking or a dice game. Luck was when the bruise on his grandmother's or mother's face faded quickly instead of deeply purpling. It was in the rare moments *no* was taken for *no*. In being in front of a white person and surviving a little talking back. The luck of not facing combat in the white man's war, but not escaping his draft.

DON'T WE ALL NEED SOMETHING IN THIS LIFE TO BE A LITTLE EAS-
ier? For most of my visit to Columbia, like all of my visits, my time is
spent cooking for my father and trying to organize his life and tidy up.
We spend our days on the computer, with Rachel Maddow and Joy
Reid blaring in the background, or else we're upstairs talking about
art in his studio. I take out the trash, drag him around his neighborhood for walks while he tells his jokes, slightly out of breath. How
lucky I've been to have a father who can make me laugh and who's
spent most of his life trying to coax me to. I freeze him packets of food,
trying to make this visit into something that can last, even if only for a
little longer, after I leave.

I want to pull the rug out from under luck. Because luck isn't in
the weather, or the crops. It's in a bank loan. Does it come through? Is
the loan approval intentionally not enough? Will more than six hundred thousand Black farmers in my father's lifetime be robbed of their
land? What the U.S. often names luck is actually a deck intentionally
stacked against Black people. It's America's design.

I want to pull the rug out from under "luck," because language
does more than express our feelings, it plays a vital role in shaping
them. And in language, whiteness wove anti-Blackness with its finest
thread: *black sheep, blacklist, black market, black plague, black magic,
blackmail, slave* instead of "enslaved people" or "men/women/
children/human beings in captivity," *victory* instead of "massacre,"
slave rebellion over "freedom fight." From *nekros* in Greek, meaning
death. *Negro*, meaning neither African nor American. *Civilizing,
Christianizing, thug, welfare queen, boy, Black as sin, articulate, well-
spoken, lazy, angry. Them.*

Selfishly, if I can pull the rug out from under "luck," then maybe I
can give my father a more precise word for the way my mother, guilt,
shame, powerlessness, and the exposure his body has had to endure
stands between us.

THE LAST DAY OF MY VISIT, MY FATHER AND I EAT BREAKFAST WITH bills marked *paid* and his paintbrushes strewn across his kitchen table. In a few hours it will be time for us to make the ninety-minute drive back to Charlotte. Having already tried to ask him about luck directly, I find myself flustered, taken aback, annoyed, and slightly gaslit when my father looks up and says, like it's the most obvious thing of all, "There isn't a Black person on this earth that believes in luck." His voice is almost indignant. "You've never heard me credit anything to luck!" My father's no stranger to a well-positioned plot twist. He floats like a butterfly, stings like a bee, having mastered one of the Blackest arts: living inside the contradictions.

What, in the past, my father's been calling luck—my mother, their meeting, their survival, and their goodbye—he's now calling fate. I think of all the other words. All the other fraternal twins of luck: chance, chaos, randomness, fortune, blessings, grace, privilege, white ness, supremacy. What's "luck" to whiteness is actually the organizational design of white supremacy, which enables white people to avoid living on the receiving side of racial oppression. What's "luck" for Black people is all the work we've put in to weather America's storms together.

"It's learning to live in a culture that hates your guts," my father says. "I've never felt the presence of 'luck' in my life. Everything that's happened to me I can trace back." Confronted with his contradictory usages of the word "luck," my father shrugs. At the kitchen table, his breath rises and drops as he peels an orange, satisfied to have the floor. "You can't tell a Black child they can be president. Obama barely changed that. But you can teach one to fight like hell," he says.

If, for Black folks, this idea of "luck" is in survival, in the act of living to breathe another day, then part of how we've learned to survive is by maneuvering our dignity in public space—in this world that seldom lets Black people live, let alone die, with dignity. Dignity, this thing I've spent my whole life chasing and desiring for me, for him, for my mother, for Black people, and everyone I love. "Every day of my childhood was a lesson in how not to get killed. Every good thing that's happened to me, I can give you the name of the person who sacrificed," he says. And then, "But you flip the coin, and it works the other way, too."

"When I was starting out," my father continues, sipping his watered-down coffee, "I'd send letters and queries to New York galleries who loved, just loved, my work. But inevitably, they'd find out I was Black"—and I remember just then the name Tyrone used to be white. My grandmother named him after *The Mark of Zorro* actor Tyrone Power, who himself was descended from a line of white English and Irish Tyrones, all the way to the 1700s. My father, a part of the pioneering generation of babies who would turn the name permanently Black.

"The honest ones would come right out and say, 'No one's going to buy work like this when they know you're Black.' The others, well, they'd just disappear." Now I understand what he means when taking the shortcut; he says: "I haven't had as much luck as I'd like."

Prolonging our goodbye, we talk about Eric Garner, Sandra Bland. Shuffle through our Rolodex of Black people who've been murdered at the hands of the state. My father says when Black folks are killed by police, it's not unlucky. And it's not a failure of our survival mechanisms. "It's the culminating point of racism," he says. Black dignity versus white supremacy. An unstoppable force meets an immovable object.

WHEN *I* THINK OF LUCK, I THINK OF JAMILA, BACK IN GRADUATE school in Leeds, six weeks after our mother died, her clean escape from our father's misfiring body—out of reach of his grief. But this is me absentmindedly falling into the trap of our colonizer's lexicon, which has always aimed to define Black people in opposition to humanity. This is me forgetting my sister's grief by envying what she might not even consider "escape." To invest in any language of oppression is to invest in the system of capitalism that's designed to leave us poorer for one another.

For the longest time I wondered, how could my father consider me the lucky one? In my mind, I hold that last image of my mother, thankful Jamila doesn't have to and resentful that my father doesn't recognize *that* as lucky, and—if I am honest—a vague feeling of emotional superiority for what Jamila doesn't have to hold.

I have longed for my sister's eyes: still clean from a memory I can never unsee. In this way, envy enters the lexicon of luck. Because what my father calls goodbye, I call an already dead mother. In that moment of gazing at my mother in her hospital room—tubes coming out of her every which way—it felt less like goodbye and more like gaping, for the first time, into the mouth of death. She wasn't dying. She was already dead, tubed up, turning *dead* into a verb. And why could no one see that made me terribly unlucky?

I forgot about Jamila's desires. For one last look, one last goodbye, for familiar arms to grieve in when the news came through to her flat's telephone line. How, while my father and I wept in the back of our minivan, she heaved across continents, alone.

I understand now what my father meant by luck. That no matter how destitute we were in our hurts, our griefs still had one irreplaceable thing: each other. Even in our mourning we could be a community, a melancholia of two.

WHILE HISTORY CIRCLES BACK ON ITSELF, MY FATHER CARVES AN-other furrow in his brow as he drives me back to the Charlotte airport. His fear for his children's and grandchildren's uncertain futures is at odds with the possibilities that white supremacy's current form has taken up in our present. This new-same world where Black people are freer than he or anyone who raised him expected to be in their own lifetimes. Knowing this, they plowed toward freedom anyway. My father lives straddling awe for the future and all the hopes he's inherited from the past. He lives and breathes unbelieving of the lives his children have made, considering the road behind our bloodline. At the same time, he warns us of the dangers of this life that we've been given.

My father has always worked hard. But then, so did everyone he knew. Every mother, every father who stayed, every sibling old enough to bring in money, every drinking uncle. If, as white America likes to say, luck is made through hard work, then why aren't Black people the luckiest folks alive?

Tapping the steering wheel once again, this time he sings B. B. King, "5 Long Years." *Lord, have you ever been mistreated.* My father's Blues is my reminder we don't have to accept the premise of this nation, nor its false freedom myth. My father warns me to watch for that low feeling reserved for Black folks reaching up. The heavens surely crowded with mothers, fathers, brothers and sisters, aunties and uncles, lives filled with coded hopes, centuries-long dreams, with beatings and humiliations trying to make our stories smaller and smaller.

At the airport, my father smiles slyly. He says, "If luck exists, then America is the luckiest country alive and Black people the most patriotic." He lets out a laugh of disgust mixed with disbelief.

"If Black people didn't believe in the possibility of America, we would have long burned this place to the ground."

He gives me a tight hug, laughs, and waves me off, trying to hide the mist in his eyes. He loves me in that urgent way Black people love our children and love freedom. I'm okay if this is the only luck that exists in America at all.

2

4

6

THE WAY
LIGHT HOLDS
THE BLUES

AGE VII

QUEER

THE SUMMER AFTER MY JUNIOR YEAR OF COLLEGE, I studied abroad in Florence. It was 2005. The two-year-old wound my mother's grave made in the earth still felt fresh, and I was happy to be out of America. It was my first time in Europe, and my first time being abroad alone. I occupied a large old house near where the Arno River met the Ponte Vecchio, with eight white girls from all over the U.S. Fifteen years have passed since that summer abroad and so many of the memories are hazy, like a smell that lights a memory in your brain but dissipates before you can catch it. But in Florence's museums, I found the actual paintings and statues that filled my father's art books.

My father graduated high school in 1963, two years before the legal end of Jim Crow. Up until then, neither his time growing up in Anniston, Alabama, or Dayton, Ohio, had seen fit to introduce a Black boy to the likes of Leonardo da Vinci or Michelangelo Buonarroti, but two art majors at Ohio University would. When Walter Isaacson released his massive biography, *Leonardo da Vinci,* in 2017, for months, this gay, vegetarian painter and polymath was all my father could talk about.

That year, when I visited him in South Carolina, on the hour-and-a-half drives to and from the Charlotte airport, he'd play the audiobook through the speaker of his purple minivan, dubbing his own narration and wonder over Isaacson's story. Even now, when I hear my father talk about da Vinci, his voice time-travels. Suddenly, he's that college boy, falling in love in an instant. I can see my father there, so young, so handsome, inside that moment when a single piece of knowledge abruptly makes your whole life different. I imagine it was like being in middle school at St. Maria's and learning about the Holocaust. Suddenly, I was filled with the knowledge that Black people were not alone in what history had done to us. Often the only Black girl in a room of white peers, knowing that it was whiteness to blame for these cruelties—and that these cruelties were specific to whiteness, not us—chipped away a little of the shame. It was a cold knowledge but one that, nonetheless, summoned a little more color back into the tiny world I knew.

Or maybe, for my father, finding da Vinci and Michelangelo was like when my fourth-grade music teacher introduced us to Beethoven. My parents played classical music on the radio, Tchaikovsky, Chopin, and Bach on vinyl, but I was never paying attention. In music class, when we studied Beethoven, for the first time I understood the way his every note was consumed with fury from loving the thing he was making. I decided: *I want to be a maker like that.*

By the time I got to Florence, I had long absorbed my father's love for da Vinci, and his love for Michelangelo, too. Though both could render the body precisely, I loved how they always made the souls of their subjects feel boundless. I spent large swaths of my childhood studying my father's huge art books filled with their work. I practiced my own figure drawings—trying to understand something about sex—by mimicking their anatomy studies. At twelve, I'd tried and failed to wade through my father's battered copy of Irving Stone's biographical novel of Michelangelo, *The Agony and the Ecstasy.* Over two decades later, when the Met had its 2018 Michelangelo exhibit, *Divine Draftsman and Designer,* Stephanie and I waited outside in the early morning rain in an admission line that stretched blocks. Once in, like I always do at museums, I took picture after picture and via text sent my father the whole show.

In Florence, the first time I saw Michelangelo's *David* in person, it went through me like a battering ram. At seventeen feet, I wasn't prepared for its size, or for anything that had been made from chipping away to be that smooth. Seeing the statue, I was practically the same age as my father was when he discovered both Michelangelo and da Vinci. It spun my mind in reverse to see the original of what I'd only known through thousands of reproductions. This was the beginning of every mimic, none of whom had been able to tell *David*'s story like this.

From Ohio to South Carolina, my friends' parents worked in banks, law firms, or in sales. They were military men and women, beauticians, assistants, or they fixed things with their hands. They were people whose work had clear-cut utility. They didn't spend their nights and weekends in galleries. I'd always struggled to know how to tell them that my father was an artist, or what exactly that meant. To our family, and to the Black and African people in our family circle, a commitment to our people necessitated art. To them, my father was a different version of what we all were: story keepers. That he was so talented made them proud, turned his "me" into an "us." The responses from adults beyond our immediate family and friends circle always seemed to be a mixture of confusion or pity that I had a father who didn't take his responsibilities to us more seriously.

The Galleria dell'Accademia di Firenze, which holds Michelangelo's masterpiece, and the Uffizi, one of the first modern museums in the world, were both within walking distance of my study-abroad housing, and I visited both almost once a week. By this time, I'd turned into habit the practice of keeping private my familial roots to art. When my housemates asked where I went during the days, I said, *Errands, just walking around*. I was from a place where art seemed to be only hobby or academic.

But in Italy, and everywhere in Europe I backpacked that summer, was a world where art was more than just art. It was memory and documentation. Even when history was frightening, everywhere art was, something could be beautiful—like my father marveling at light in Goya's Black Paintings. Alone, and in my now automatic mode of unconscious secrecy, that study-abroad summer I oscillated between the halls of the Galleria and the Uffizi.

The Uffizi, which first opened to visitors in the sixteenth century, holds Sandro Botticelli's *Birth of Venus* and his *Adoration of the Magi*. It holds Michelangelo's *The Holy Family* and da Vinci's *The Annunciation*. In the museums, galleries, and streets of Florence, the entire world was painted and sculpted. It was the whole Bible and the underworld. There was Caravaggio's *Medusa*, the world of myth made, too.

In Florence, my mornings were filled with language classes, my afternoons buried in the familiar warm and conversational silences of art that reminded me of my childhood. The evenings comprised of bars where all summer my housemates and I drank only fresh-minted mojitos. There were the Italian men who waited for us thirstily. I kissed them in bars, on the backs of scooters, and went back to their apartments, too young to be calling whatever I was greedily enjoying with these older men affairs.

In Europe, no one knew me or my housemates. We barely knew each other. Without the sexual mores that constrained us in America, in Florence, anonymity gave my housemates and me access to the kind of freedom that could ruin a girl back home. It was the freedom of the boys I went to college with, and there was no one to stop me from embracing it. I'd spent the first fifteen years of my life in a white, single-sex education with little or no interaction with the opposite sex outside of family, Black art, and Kwanzaa events. I was from a family that never ever talked about sex beyond warnings and dangers. In Florence, there was no one around who mattered to me to witness my escapades. When I walked out of a man's apartment, for the first time in my life I could do so without shame. Or at the very least, I could pretend I hadn't brought any shame there.

In America, as a Black girl in white spaces, it so often meant I was relegated to sleeping with or dating who would sleep with or date me. It was an isolating way to inhabit my own body. In Italy, compared to the small, old South ways of Clemson, when I had sex with low-melanin men, the sex felt a little safer than it did back home with those same-looking low-melanin men. And even a little more safety, even if only an inch, any Black woman can tell you is nothing to snub your nose at.

In Clemson, in the whole South—this region that was the only place my adult body knew—when I hooked up with white men, there was always the violence of American history and the way that shadow exhaled in and out in the present. No matter who they were, history spilled out between us. It was the elephant in the room, but only I could see it. We were only four generations away from slavery, and in the bodies of the white boys at Clemson (as well as mine) was the memory that I was a some*thing* that their great-great-grandfather had owned.

In Florence, the cobblestone roads were older than any of this history. The roads were older than anyone I knew, and older than the oldest person my great-grandma Lizzie could have ever known. The homes and architecture seemed to be made out of history, and one even further back than the history that draped the plantation homes in Charleston, South Carolina. In Florence, the squares were filled with large marble statues chipped by weather and from bearing witness to the city for hundreds of years. Not a single one of them paid homage to a Confederate soldier. Italy had its own violences, but I didn't know them.

Everywhere I looked, even if I couldn't name it, was proof enslavement was no beginning. I wasn't thinking of fascism or the Roman Empire. It didn't occur to me that Europe had its own Indigenous populations who were facing oppression, too. I wasn't thinking of how the U.S. was seeded from this continent. I was twenty. At the time, I only knew that in Florence was a temporary reprieve from the nation I wore everywhere, even to bed—both mine and the beds of others. But still, I'd heard enough said by both my continents to know neither was too keen on queers.

In Florence, there was the brunette that I'd drunkenly kissed, her bubble-gum tongue. The Turk—a bouncer, I think—my fling with him lasting almost the entire summer, and being wholly absorbed in the delight of an intimacy intended to go nowhere, but terrified and unsure what it meant that—between the brunette and the Turk—I'd wanted them both.

AFTER A SUMMER IN FLORENCE, I BACKPACKED TO GERMANY, France, Poland, the Netherlands, and Spain. A childhood in Catholic churches had reinforced in me my father's love of frescoes. From Rome to Paris to Versailles to Berlin to Munich to Amsterdam to the Vatican, I rode trains from cathedral to cathedral. I saw the finger of Michelangelo's white god reach out to touch Adam's hand. Up until that moment I hadn't known that art and history could collide to make you feel so giddy. History was a physical space you could stand in. And, too, there was the astonishment of being surrounded by countries that decorated themselves in art and cathedrals.

As structures, cathedrals generally have extremely high ceilings, and extremely hard floors of stone, concrete, or wood. The resulting combination of high room volumes and hard surfaces is why most cathedrals have very long reverberation times, and why when sound happens inside a cathedral it's like an echo that's changed its mind. By way of hundreds and thousands of small reflections that enter the ear, reverberation is the persistence of sound after that sound is first produced. Or to put it another way, it's how long our stories last.

To me, the way cathedrals hold sound has always felt like breath. On the one hand there's the voice that's making the music, and on the other, the whole room that holds you is breathing out. A cathedral did to music what I had, growing up, only ever heard come from B. B. King and his guitar. When I was a kid, my father played *Live in Cook County Jail* and *Guess Who* on vinyl. Later, he played "The Thrill Is Gone" and "Lucille" on CD.

B. B. King wasn't a breathy singer, no. But he opened his mouth, and inside him a whole cathedral fell out. Even his guitar, Lucille, had an exhale. He sang like a man who didn't take breathing lightly, which is not to say breathing weighed him down. In the way B. B. King could make even baby me rock my shoulders, as a kid, I loved the way the architecture of cathedrals turned sound so otherworldly it made the priest's voice sound like a breathy guitar. As children, cathedrals negotiated a reverence from us that turned our shouts into voluntary whispers. The Blues, like cathedrals, held history in every breath, every exhale, until time itself felt like something that had no meaningful borders.

The Blues is first documented as coming on the scene post-emancipation. Standing in those cathedrals across Europe, I had yet to connect that, while places like St. Peter's Basilica in the Vatican were being built, Africans like my mother were being enslaved and forcibly kidnapped to work stolen land that was drenched in genocide. I hadn't yet understood that, in white America, you could draw a straight line between their white god, destruction, and Black skin. In white cosmology, the three were born together.

While enslavement was turning Africans Black, Europe was getting rich on the other side. Which means, when the cathedrals of Europe were being built, the Blues was already in the making. Many scholars, including Angela Davis, argue that the Blues is inseparable from Black people's newly found freedom. Post-enslavement, for the first time in our history of America, our marriages, wombs, reproduction, gender and sexualities, were no longer under the whip of a white master.

We'd had the blues for centuries of enslavement, but before *the* Blues, no one had sung our blues into color yet. I don't imagine there was any plantation owner in the New World who wanted their cruelties sung at them. In those days, our blues converted themselves into spirituals and coded themselves directly to heaven. Emancipation meant our blues could stay on earth. We still could not speak our minds, but freedom meant, finally, we could sing them. Freedom meant no one could whip you for singing your saddest or freest song.

Emancipated, did Black folks rub their chests with the feeling actual chains had come off their lungs? We could travel, sit down, not dance when we didn't want to dance, and reserve making love for when it felt right. Lord, there was of course the violence, a world where nothing had changed in white people but their ledgers, and there was the whole of the country doubling down. But emancipation meant we could put our spirituals away, or at the very least, give them damn things a rest.

The Blues arrived during a period when Black people, for the first time, had physical and sexual sovereignty. Like my father's art, and the art and artists that surrounded my childhood, the Blues was as much witness as testimony. Testimony, any church-going Black folk will tell you, is its own kind of freedom. I try to picture what the earth I'd been simultaneously chained to and denied would have been like in our finally free hands. The exhilaration and glee, occupying the same body as the anger, the shame, the horror. All of this alongside the guilt, the fear, held by those who were the first generation born free, and having that lifetime born from and overlap with those who'd come into this world and been informed they were property.

There is so much history, so much Blues between the world of then and where I stand, queerly, now. You could line up every cathedral in the world between those two points. The first Blues note would go in, and on the other end, I would come out. And that, too, I loved about the Renaissance art that filled European museums and the sun-lit stained-glass windows and painted walls and ceilings of their cathedrals, how so often—church or not—these painted worlds were just so gay. Even the "heterosexual" depictions seemed queer to me. Bodies were always bare and dripping over one another. Men's faces glistened with painted passion whenever they looked at each other. Women's faces flushed with secrets. Here, heaven seemed like a lazily veiled metaphor for orgy. So often the faces looked at the edge of edging. Even on the ceiling of the Sistine Chapel, when I looked up to see God's finger and Adam's hand reach for each other, there was a desire undeniably and palpably homosexual.

∞

In Paris, I was an ant underneath arches from the Arc de Triomphe to the Eiffel Tower. There was the holiness at my knees as I stood in front of the Louvre. All this art my father had studied, dreamed of, but never, not once, in person seen. There was the Palace of Versailles, its sheer size and ornateness signaling death, raising questions as to how long a nation had to be starved to make something this gilded, this gold. In the Cathédrale Notre-Dame, my heart bowed like a Blues note. I hadn't remembered the note was inside of me, then a cathedral hulled it out.

In Rome, the city was as filthy as my future home of New York. But from the Colosseum to the Roman Forum to Palatine Hill, I stood in ruins and breathed in and out. I saw that some things could stand forever, even after a fall.

In Amsterdam, I smoked a joint purchased from a coffee shop, sipped a cocktail nervous and terrified at a ladies-only bar and didn't say a word. I watched women dance in windows in the De Wallen red-light district and returned to my hostel feeling lonely, impenetrably sad.

But from museum to cathedral, art proved what nothing else in my world would say: queerness, naturally, was everywhere. And, too, in the way each museum, each holy place opened its lungs, I saw that museums, cathedrals, and song were the same kind of structures. In all, I found confirmation of what home had already taught me: sound could make a place sacred.

THE SOUNDS OF WHAT WAS SACRED CAME FROM LIVING ROOMS. IT gathered out back in someone's yard or around the kitchen or dining table. It could happen outside, an hour into saying goodbye standing next to someone's car. It happened at family reunions, Kwanzaa, and it happened at art galleries. It was more than shit-talking, more than laughter, and it was more than what happened when those two things got together.

That sacred sound was the way my mother said *ah-ah!* or *kai!* in frustration to someone on the phone, and the laughter that came when whoever in Nigeria she was talking to said it back. Even 5,857 miles apart, that sacred sound let everyone know we were in it together.

That sacred sound was the way, at openings at our art gallery in Ohio, adults stomped their feet and clapped their hands with their chins pushed into their chests as they laughed into news of who was still trifling. The way I could see, plain as day—*and because goddamn, no one was trying to hide it*—how, together, the weight of their blues was redistributed. Heat came off the fact of them being together. As kids, we watched how collective could loosen your armor, and right before that armor turned itself into a prison.

That sacred sound was *smch*, the way both of my continents could suck their teeth so hard it sounded like Velcro unclasping. *Smch*, they said in the morning. *Smch*, they said at night, and you had to be listening oh so carefully to know if *smch* meant they were fed up or if it meant the world was upside down but we were all right.

When you were lower than you had ever been, B. B. King's voice could be like a field of teeth sucking, and all of it, on your side. Blues was music that invited Jesus to the nightclub and told him to pull up a seat at the bar. It was Blues that, like Jesus, remembered the drunks, the lepers, the sex workers. And Blues, like Jesus, recognized sin as a socially and politically defined position. It was the Blues that remembered the people I never wanted to forget. The Blues queered music with its ache.

When the Blues was born, it was led by Black women who were transgender, gender nonconforming, lesbians, bisexuals—all-out queers. In the twenties and thirties, and with Black people having not even been free that long, Bessie Smith, Ma Rainey, and Lucille Bogan, "the big three of the Blues," sang about and lived their queerness openly as they could. Gladys Bentley dressed in tuxedos and men's clothing and performed backed by a chorus line of drag queens. Across the newly free cities of the U.S., queer women like Bentley, Rainey, Josephine Baker, Alberta Hunter, Ethel Waters, and Billie Holiday sang Black and white folks into the queer night.

Ma Rainey, in 1928, three years after being arrested for participating in an orgy with multiple women, flaunted her queerness with her Blues hit "Prove It on Me." "Went out last night with a crowd of my friends. They must've been women, 'cause I don't like no men. It's true I wear a collar and a tie . . . Talk to the gals just like any old man."

Blues singer Lucille Bogan sang a freedom song for every Black bull-dagger (BD) butch into 1935: "Comin' a time, BD women they ain't going to need no men." We were old as time, natural as nature.

In the early 1900s, a time when my paternal grandmother still felt new in the world, there were Blues women preparing the world for me. After four centuries of physical, reproductive, and sexual enslavement—of the "United States" growing rich in the fertile soil of Black and Indigenous peoples' Black Periods—nothing could be a greater reverberation or insistence of freedom than these Blues women kicking open their closet doors to live and love their queerness best they could.

Even before I could really hear their songs, queerness, unbeknownst to all of us, was flooding my parents' house. There was the way my father's voice became a proud song when he spoke of how much Angela Davis—a queer woman, though I didn't know it then—loved us. Queerness rode in on the backs of my father's Blues women, never mind that for the longest time, when they sang, I heard nothing.

AS A CHILD, I NEVER UNDERSTOOD WHY THEY CALLED IT THE BLUES. I knew nothing about its hypnotic repetitions, its blue notes and how they came at you lower than you'd ever been conditioned to expect from music. Yeah, the notes came for you from the bottom up. Flooded you feet to hips to heart to lips. But, too, the lyrics my father sang through our house winked. The lyrics always had a bit of sass, a little jive talking, like if there was anything Blue there, then dammit, it better come with a sound that made you close your eyes before you moved your hips.

Even as a child, spending most of my childhood carefully watching—exhausted by all that self-surveillance, by being overly seen and never seen at all—B.B.'s voice could get me high. There was just so much oxygen to it. It reminded you that breathing was a constant conversation with the fact of life.

The Blues was gaudy, crass, full of drinking and lust. It had lyrics that, as a child, I didn't understand but nonetheless made me blush. When our parents sang the Blues, it made us hotly suspicious that outside of us, they might have other lives. The Blues I heard had the kind of lyrics that made Black folks point to a friend and say, with knee slaps, a smirk, or shimmied shoulders, *Hey, now!*

Where Motown could lift you up, spin you round, make you put your hand on your girl's waist or your best friend's shoulder, in the Blues, sadness could make you laugh, and it could set you free. Blues music was a celebration of a feeling finally named in the light. With so much left silent or unexplained in my family and in the world, naming meant everything to me.

In the Blues, there was the million acres between your body being stolen by enslavement every single day and the freedom to pick, to point, to say: *you*. In the Blues, forever captured was that hairsbreadth of a second post-emancipation, when the freedom we felt in our bodies could be summarized by choosing and by saying, *no*. And even when it was bad love, even when, in reality, "no" didn't always or often matter, it was not nothing that "no" might finally be said.

The Blues sang that instantaneous, if ever-fleeting, moment where *please* turned into the open want for another's body, instead of a beg for mercy for your child's, your sister's, your mother's, your own. The Blues reverberated with a freedom—a queerness—that, for the longest time, I didn't recognize, one it would take years to understand that I could simultaneously claim and live through.

∞

In Europe, on a Eurail train pass, I went to Munich and the small towns of Germany. Though I remember the lederhosen, the lagers that poured from the keg taps ice-cold, and the half-timbered Fachwerkhäuser that made all the dwellings look like a page from one of my childhood books, all the towns' names I've forgotten. But I remember walking around those German towns mainly thinking about my upcoming trip to Poland, with the specter of U.S. empire feeling closer to me than it had in months.

After a week in Germany, I took an overnight train to Kraków where, confused and scared, I'd been made to surrender my passport to train attendants who spoke no English. No one I knew wanted to go to Poland, or was it that I wanted to go alone? I was sure I was the only Black person I'd seen for days. I imagined the people I'd learned about in school being train shipped to concentration camps. I was in the middle of someone else's Middle Passage.

Like most middle-schoolers, back in sixth grade we began to learn about the Holocaust, though, on my own, I'd already been reading library books about it for years. At St. Maria's, we read *The Diary of Anne Frank*, Lois Lowry's *Number the Stars*, and Elie Wiesel's *Night*. We took our middle school field trip to the Holocaust Memorial Museum in D.C. where it was less horror that I felt than connection, though horror was there, too.

I didn't yet comprehend the deep kinship between Black and Indigenous folks in America at the time. It was in the Holocaust that I understood that what happened to Black people had happened at least twice. I remember the newness of the knowing. It stuck to my ribs like the rice my mother sometimes used to make the sticky balls for tuwo shinkafa.

People's humanity was being stolen all over the world and all the time. I checked out book after book from the library about Adolf Hitler and the Holocaust, wanting to know who these Jewish people were whose tormentors were like ours. And even though it pained me to know there was nothing I could do about it, I realized then, our histories didn't have to live alone in the world. Our histories were connected. We could help carry each other.

Once in Poland, I took the hour-and-a-half bus ride from Kraków to Oświęcim. Maybe it was just what I was carrying inside me, but everywhere I looked, the city of Oświęcim seemed depressed by history, like the whole town was trying to tell me it couldn't take it anymore. The place looked as sad as I thought America should.

The photos of my trip are buried, lost to a hard drive and time. Still, even without pictures, and over a decade later, I see the gray sky clearly. In Oświęcim, Auschwitz spread out in front of me, an intricate complex. I walked the bunkers, the gas chambers, through rooms piled high with eyeglasses, gold fillings, shoes, suitcases. I was twenty and didn't yet fully comprehend the price of failing to weep for strangers, or how a place so full of ghosts could feel so empty.

There was the surprise of seeing the physical site of Auschwitz, this place where, in my U.S. history books, so many people were turned into afterthoughts. Even in real life, the place looked like a black-and-white photo. As if no color could exist in tandem with so much blood and tragedy.

In the history books at St. Maria's, at Fort Pleasant High School, at Clemson, and at all my local libraries, they documented the Jewish people systematically eradicated in the Holocaust. But even then, the violence I'd read about seemed sugarcoated against the reality. I didn't yet understand how hiding and obscuring the truth is its own kind of weapon.

No books I was given or had access to recorded the Afro-German children forcibly sterilized without their parent's knowledge, or the Roma people (almost the entire Eastern European Romani population) eradicated for not being Aryan enough. No classroom I'd sat in talked about the people with disabilities labeled "unworthy of life," who'd been "mercy-killed" by the Nazis. No one ever told me that the methodology of Hitler's Final Solution had been streamlined and perfected on people with mental and physical disabilities, who were gassed under the banner of Operation T-4. Genocide was a many-tentacled thing, though my history books never made it a point to tell me.

In the world history written by white supremacy, I wasn't supposed to know the various systems that oppressed us were connected. If the books I read ever mentioned these additional losses, it was always with all those stolen lives crowding a single sentence, their murders never counted beyond "some," or "also." No books I read in my youth mentioned the more than a hundred thousand gay men arrested in Nazi Germany. Nazis found male homosexuality particularly offensive and regularly conducted medical experiments on camp prisoners in search of a "cure" for gayness. Others were simply castrated as punishment. In concentration camps, gay men were used for target practice by SS guards and sodomized with wood. They were beaten to death, sometimes by guards, other times by their fellow prisoners, who, even in the midst of their own eradication, found queerness intolerable.

Along with Jewish women, the Third Reich forced lesbians into German camp brothels where gay men were made to perform sex acts on women who had already been turned into sex slaves. These women were subjected to forced sterilizations and abortions that often proved fatal. My books never mentioned why, of the lesbians, bisexual women, and transgender people arrested or sent to the camps, no one had even bothered to keep count of how many went in, or how many did not come out. Queer people were systematically eradicated and there didn't even seem to be a historical record. More than just our bodies, even the memory of us had been relegated to a single grave labeled *some, also.*

My breathing echoed into the buildings where prisoners were bunked. My breath reverberated into the incinerators where bodies turned into the ash of snow that blanketed the German sky with peoples' remains as white Germans went on with their lives. There was both nothing and everything here.

The semester before my study abroad, I'd taken a class on the Holocaust where we'd spent most of the term studying the ordinariness of evil. We never once talked about all these concurrent genocides. That silence, I can see now, was a branch of that evil, too. I knew that Hitler had looked to Americans for guidance and had found inspiration. In the United States' genocide against Indigenous peoples, its segregating use of reservations, and the control of Black communities through terror and lynchings, America had written a blueprint.

From Germany to Poland, I was in the United States once again. Wherever genocide was, my nation was there, too. Genocide could come for you by way of disease, displacement, murder, kidnapping, rape, cultural and linguistic assassinations. It could be a gas chamber or a rope swinging from a tree.

In the Holocaust, there were disabled people, lesbians, bisexual women, and transgender people, simply gone. With six million Jewish lives murdered, it was wild, terrifying, and utterly silencing to me that after losing so many, there were still certain kinds of people whose disappearances the books I was taught from didn't count. During enslavement, the machine of white supremacy worked to ensure that the lives of Black people vanished with no account of us beyond economics' widgets. That machine of erasure was a similarity I recognized in the Holocaust. It was one I would later recognize in "Manifest Destiny."

Genocide is what happens in the days, years, and generations it takes for a nation to confess. It's a padded room were the stories of the dead, the murdered, the raped, the stolen, the starved, the beaten, the suffocated don't reverberate.

I was years away from recognizing all the shapes resistance could take: from the way my father depicted us to Kwanzaa to the Havsuw 'Baaja tribe fighting the goliath of U.S empire on behalf of their children. I was lonely for the dead, the tortured, the missing, the forgotten, the survivors, the lost. I was twenty and trying to find my place in the world. All my searching seemed to keep leading to bafflingly violent intersections. Standing in Auschwitz, the gray sky crying its grayness down, the sight of genocide reverberated through my bones along with the thought, This could still happen anywhere.

In Auschwitz, I searched for all my childhood gods. Everywhere, there was silence.

I thought, If this isn't the Blues, what else could be?

ON HAINTS

AGE VIII

TRANSFORMATION

Fear is the cheapest room in the house.

ΠΑΓΙΣ

1.

Leaf-peeping season.

A weekend feeling, hidden inside an afternoon. People congregate at the Prospect Park trees. A single, enormous oak provides a grand, cinematic backdrop. Catnip for New Yorkers who recognize a deal when they see one, the tree simultaneously provides a backdrop for a wedding photo, an engagement announcement, three sets of head-shots, two wide-lensed nature photographers, selfie after selfie, and a group of Hasidic women who, in wigs and uniforms of modesty, gather nine small children in front of a camera while another Hasidic woman kneels, her large circular reflector bouncing fall light onto their boy-children's payot curls.

The sound of leaves and decay crunches below children's feet as they run. It is a chorus of endings, and the trees are full. Altos of thick greens hold tight to branches despite the prior week's rain. Golds tenor into flaxen. Reds soprano. Older children loop Prospect Park astride leash-led horses. Runners smile behind scrunched noses, avoiding piles of manure. Black men with tights under their shorts, their dreads tied back, nod to the older Black women powerwalking, controlling their breath into gossip.

Nodding at the Black folks I pass, none of us are who we used to be: donning shirts that read BLACKNIFICENT, ANGELA & GLORIA & AUDRE & ALICE & BELL, BLACK BY POPULAR DEMAND, and ASSATA TAUGHT ME, we are mobilized. In our heart pockets, a list of other people's children: Kyam Livingston, Trayvon Martin, Eric Garner, John Crawford, Korryn Gaines, Michael Brown, Rekia Boyd, Sandra Bland, Akai Gurley, Tamir Rice, Walter Scott, Freddie Gray, Breonna Taylor. A list of names so long that even in winter, I rarely walk around with my hands in my pockets, lest I run into a cop in search of ex-cuses.

The late-thirties white women of Brooklyn give their nannies the morning off. They push their three-wheeled strollers on the smooth pavement loop, their infants wrapped like caterpillars in rent-priced down sleeping bags, ready to cocoon into butterflies.

In this sanctuary city, I see the jaw of white supremacy everywhere. Groups of Mexican men fire meat on the park's community grills, their life belongings stacked high in shopping carts half-circled around them. It is still the pre-Covid version of this world and there's not yet a face mask in sight. Houseless Black men with matted afros mutter in and out of the fringes of the park's long, winding trails, ravaged by drugs, booze, streets, oppression, American indifference. Police jeeps. Police sedans. Police covered go-carts. Police floodlights. Police on foot every three-quarter mile. Every Black person in the park looking their way behind a barely perceptible side-eye. Fall brandishes its reminders about time. How it runs out. How it passes. How it can be lost, snatched, taken: by nature, cop, or as Dr. Lamb constantly warns me, worry.

Among all this, I can't remember when my body first began to feel like a fading tree, when my back began to feel like a grandmother clock gone rickety with rust. I run with each vertebra feeling heavier than Stonehenge's stones. Where was the first fracture? Was it a misstep or a fall? Had I stepped on one too many sidewalk cracks, and too often tested the boundaries of superstition, until, with a dead mother, there was no back to break but my own?

I can't remember my first back-hurt or my second, but sometime around the fifteenth stab of pain that ran from my shoulders to my sacrum to my sciatic nerve, I accepted it would always be this way. Pain cemented into me.

FOUR MILES INTO AN EIGHT-MILE RUN, AND I PUSH MY BODY INTO AN exaggeratedly legible look of being hurt free. Around me, Black and brown people gather in all the old Black and brown ways. They host family reunions, anniversary parties, and no-reason get-togethers full of music. Barely noon and an accordion-drenched conjunto blasts from speakers where cowboy-hatted Mexican couples dance. There's a quinceañera, a retirement party, a fifth and eightieth birthday where the able fetch plates for those whose bodies seek rest. It's hard to know which child belongs to whom the way everyone watches. Even the fourteen-year-olds, playing at grown, yell for the younger children not to roam so far off. Everyone who comes brings a little something, even if all the something they can afford is themselves.

Black folks sit on blankets, toss footballs, and have brought just enough chairs for the bodies that need elevated sitting. Above dueling music, Black people play the dozens like dice. Across the way, queers congregate from the beginning to end of the gender spectrum, and we are all either under- or overdressed for the still-warm fall weather.

For the first time, I notice how quiet the white people are. They gather and their laughs barely make a sound. I realize how rare it is I ever see generations of white people coming together in public outside of the formal structures of weddings, funerals, Republican conventions, and church, or photographs like KKK meetings and historical postcards of lynchings.

Language whirls past—men and women who cackle, purse their lips into English, Russian, Hindi, Yiddish, Chinese, and Tagalog. All of us the products of a leaving or an arrival. I was the product of a migration lore, too. Like so many migration lores, mine originated in escape.

IN 1987, MY MOTHER WAS A SECRETARY AT AHMADU BELLO UNIVERsity, where my father also worked, teaching art. All around them, Nigeria was failing, and by now, even my mother was scared. There were massive country-wide strikes. The value of the naira plummeted. The university stopped paying employees, and my parents worried that soon they wouldn't be able to get money out of the country, and then leaving would no longer be a possibility.

From our home of Zaria, they'd dropped Jamila, who was six, an hour and half away at Bobo's in Kaduna and took me, three, to Lagos to get my mother's travel papers. While they were in the air coming back to Zaria, a disagreement erupted between the Christian and Muslim students at Kafanchan Teachers' College. The disagreement spilled over into neighboring towns—Zaria and Kaduna—unearthing age-old resentments between the Hausa-Fulani who ran the region and its predominantly Christian inhabitants.

It was only when they'd landed that the news of the violence swept over them. Churches had been burned; teachers killed. Seized with panic and afraid, with ten other passengers, my parents bribed a bus driver to take them from the Kaduna airport into the city, where they were pulled over by military police, who ordered everyone off the bus.

This is one of my father's favorite stories, and one he always tells with a smile that shows me how much he misses my mother, who, my father always says laughing, cut him a vicious look, which said, "Don't you dare say a word." With blank faces, the soldiers lined my parents up against the side of the bus. My mother held me in her arms. One soldier looked barely old enough to shave. He kept his hand pressed into the bus driver's chest, pinning him against the vehicle.

"We will be up and down this street in ten minutes. If we see any of you, there will be trouble," the commander shouted in our direction. "Now," my mother whispered in a hushed but urgent tone, as she took off with me on her hip. My father says he'd thought the commander was exaggerating until he felt the wind of my mother gone with me in her arms. My father, who still had enough Alabama blood in him to know better than to hesitate when someone colored said run, took off behind us with our two suitcases in tow.

Close, but too far from home to be safe, my mother told my father, "We can't make it." Bala Miller, a friend and musician and pioneer of Nigerian highlife music who my father sometimes sang with, lived only ten minutes away. As dusk fell, terrified, they pounded their fists on Bala's door. By then, three and tired, I was fully wailing. The house heard my cries. The three of us gained entrance, and there we waited out the night. The next day we made our way to Kaduna and Jamila, my parents relieved to find their firstborn safe. Bobo was Igbo, and the Igbo were often targets of persecution—a fact that made both my parents' fears tremble even louder in the violence of a slow-passing night. It was 1987, and with our move to the U.S., we were exchanging one dangerous country for another.

A QUARTER OF A CENTURY LATER, IN THE MAGICAL NORTH OF Brooklyn, I've conditioned myself to run, cook, make love, eat, sleep, with my body showered by the knives of the inherited and complex traumas white people have forced on Black folks in what is supposed to be a shared country. On the track, white men in professional bicycle gear ride so close they taunt the boundaries of collision. All around me: migration. Dog owners happily let themselves be yanked by their leash. Children learn to ride bikes while other children test their recent mastery of the open road. Solo runners pass solo runner after solo runner, having found the only place in this city other than the train where we can be alone.

In my periphery, I see a cop looking at me as I try to look like someone who has come to the park to do exactly what I am doing and nothing else: run.

We are four generations from slavery. There's a news ticker in my mind: police called on Black people for talking on the phone in our hotel lobbies; for waiting at a Starbucks for a friend; for barbecuing in public parks; trying to use community pools; for napping in the common rooms of our colleges; coming home late from work; not playing golf fast enough; for helping the homeless; shopping while pregnant; birdwatching; on the very first day of our very first job delivering newspapers; trying to cash a $1,000 paycheck at the end of a long week.

White people calling the police on Black people doing everyday things is a reminder to me of all the ways that one single white body can embody a whole country, and employ it in a way no Black or brown person can. I read that another innocent Black man is exonerated after decades in prison. Can I prove where I was on this Wednesday of last year?

The pain in my back screams, knowing it takes only a single white body to transform mine into a national spectacle that will have me dead or alive.

∞

When I moved to Brooklyn, I settled into the unicorn of a Black-owned brownstone in a garden apartment at the edge of Crown Heights and Bed Stuy, where the city seemed to seldom honor any street cleaning schedule. I noticed I was the lightest-skinned person in the neighborhood, a highlighter on the segregation. Was I a warning to my own people of the gentrification to come? My spine swelled and contracted with the pain of that question.

Weekend train service was constantly suspended, marooning us, save the slow drag of the overcrowded shuttle buses that never seemed to come often enough to make up for the inconvenience or how many of us lived there. Staring down Atlantic, we could see the newly erected Barclays Center two miles away, our sparse trees growing more abundant and lusher as they reached out into Fort Greene.

On this edge of Crown Heights, fenced-off concrete fields stood in place of parks. Fresh produce was sparse, police plenty. More often than not, they stood in clumps of two, three—sometimes four—on street corners, in front of the C train turnstiles where those of us who got off the train were careful to swipe in those who waited fareless, at the edges of the entrance. Police lingered, threateningly, outside the doors of fast-food restaurants and liquor stores—the only establishments that outnumbered the bodegas and laundromats.

I'd seen stings. I'd seen setups. I'd seen Black man after Black man stopped. Anything, it seemed, made police numbers swell: holidays, parades, graduation ceremonies, heat, boredom, news stories, quotas. Even Black joy dragged them from their stations. The police stood, hands resting on the butts of their guns, hoping to make a day on their feet worth it.

On my body, the years of pain blended into all the years of pain that had come before. I scrounged together co-pay money for physical therapy and chiropractors and scoured Groupon for massages and acupuncture deals. I wanted to feel better, but no doctor could tell me how.

I was stretched, needled, pulled apart, connected to electrodes. I was hung and I was spun in belted contractions that looked made for a Frankenstein. I was not completely out, but I was no longer completely in. The radius that held my home life and its errands seemed to be devoid of queer people, or at least any I could identify.

I was always in pain. Worry, fear, and anxiety seeped out of my skin so readily a trained nose could have smelled me coming. There were days I hobbled, days I called in sick, days I cried, and days I cried out. Pain shot through my body as I tried to overcome a limping gate, not wanting to draw attention to a body that was supposed to be too young to be so injured.

When I told Dr. Lamb all this over the phone in one of our Saturday morning sessions, she'd *mmhmmm*'d the way Black women do. The cadence of her voice, like warm bread rolls, urged me to continue. I explained to the both of us the work of keeping myself safe on the streets, in grocery stores, and especially at work, where the white violence roamed free and unchecked, pushing me to the brink of a hyper-perceptive exhaustion. I want to close my eyes, but Breonna Taylor couldn't even safely sleep. I felt like I was in the waiting room of emotion.

"I know grief," I told her, embarrassed, forgetting for a moment that speaking to another Black woman released me from having to convince her my pain is real. I often forget that this armor I wear can also be set down. Dr. Lamb listened, doing her best to stop me from weathering away. "But this isn't it, this isn't grief—or if it is, it isn't mine," I told her, thinking that maybe this grief I'd been shouldering belonged to America instead.

"I'm in a nowhere place." I continued trying to describe how so much fear and anxiety has driven me numb, and how it's like the whole world of me seeps out instead, through this physical pain I carry, which sometimes gets so bad it's hard to walk without emergency cortisol. Dr. Lamb knows I've limped all over the world, from London to Gambia to the freest place I could find in America: New York, New York.

IN MY SLOWLY GENTRIFYING NEIGHBORHOOD OF CROWN HEIGHTS, the dollar stores were in disrepair. African and Caribbean men sold perfumes and incense from behind folding tables. They set up shop in front of the dilapidated Shop 'n Save that seemed to be the mecca of wilted produce. Bodega owners hushed their children in Arabic, sparred lightly about politics with the Black locals who'd made themselves known entities, and carefully watched the ones that hadn't. Chinese liquor-store owners tossed change through the small holes in the bulletproof glass and yelled *Next!* The cops that loitered never seemed to smile. Not at children or old ladies. Not at each other. Not at themselves. They were the watchers and we who they had been sent to watch.

Meanwhile, Black folks under fifty lifted their chins in acknowledgment to one another. Older Black men tipped their caps, aunties and grandmas cast out rhetoricals like "How you doing, baby?" We all knew how monstrous the shape of our nation's shadow could be. Strangers or not, we witnessed each other, knowing how quickly the shadow could arrive and one of us would need to warn the others: *Run!*

The large building across the street from my apartment, which took up the whole block, remained boarded up until, when the boards eventually came down, like millions before me, I was priced out. It was a neighborhood where the promise of America was gone, though its intent was ever present.

I was steeped in fear and dread, but still, everywhere I looked reminded me, memory could save your life. Summers, Crown Heights reminded me of summers with Qjuan and Regi, and how their still-boyish smiles could be like a kiss on your heart. I thought of my grandma out on a porch. The way my aunt Liz's laughter was as deep voiced as mine, and all that, as a child, I would have identified as home. America was always burning, but we were making our Black Periods.

I smiled as, up and down my Brooklyn block, Black children ran through open fire hydrants. Grandmas like mine hung out of windows keeping a watchful eye. Fathers, uncles, sons, and brothers stayed up late prepping the meat that, come morning, would become another side hustle as they sold barbecue from their sidewalks and front stoops. We wore curlers and house shoes in the street, played cards, chess, and dominoes in folding chairs, and threw footballs in the empty roads. We helped neighbors get groceries, slung our children's school bags over our shoulders so they, so excited to tell us about their day, could do so with both hands.

2.

My play cousin DeShawn is in prison. My father sighs heavily, like someone who, having taken their eye off the ball for a second, has just heard it drop. In his voice, I can hear him wring his hands. He's got no new details to share, other than a guttural agony buried so deep inside him he can only moan for this dark-skinned boy who, even as a child, always lingering about our house, stood in doorways a rail-thin six-foot-five. This always-blushing boy who still leans heavily on one hip and bites his top lip like he did when we were children, his eyes smiling, shining like rough stone in the sunlight after rain.

Hopefully, DeShawn will be released in time for Christmas. Meanwhile, his sister Shanice has been helping out. My auntie Gina, their grandmother, who was good friends with my mother in Akron, tells this to my father, who tells me that DeShawn was holding for somebody else. That Shanice has been training to be a beautician, and Auntie Gina is real proud at how Shanice has stepped up with De-Shawn's two boys and daughter.

My father's voice trembles with fear. He sucks his teeth in to both the phone line and the situation, unsure who he's supposed to be mad at. "Do you know what they could do to him in there?" he asks. He forgets that he's raised me to be someone who knows the answer.

My father has spent his whole life teaching his daughters to be afraid of prison. He's warned, for Black people, it's never been a matter of guilt or innocence, it's that being Black in America means prison stalks you. Its foundations were laid on our skin. Our safety has always demanded that the specter of prison occupies our imaginative and community spaces.

Though he didn't have the terminology of "school-to-prison pipeline," both he and my mother had strict expectations of our behavior. In stores, we kept our hands at our sides, knowing touch could lead to suspicion, and that in a world that found Black people constantly suspicious, any look of want was all it took.

My parents banned cable TV, live concerts, snack foods, and allowance. They found the idea of children out at night, and thus curfews, ridiculous. They reluctantly gave Jamila a curfew of eleven P.M. her freshman year of college, before she vanished from the U.S. again, this time to study in Thailand. I didn't yet understand my parents' strictness, but the child in me took it to mean we were always in danger. I went to school subconsciously aware of how thin the line was for me between a teacher and a prison guard.

Decades later, in adulthood, I'd realize, though our parents were strict with our bodies, they had that "Black abundance" approach to our minds. As Mariame Kaba writes, "every vision is also a map."

Through stories of the Black Panthers, we learned that *we* were the pioneers of America's national free-lunch program in schools, that we had a right to self-defense, and an obligation to educate each other's minds as much as we did to protect each other's bodies. Through books chronicling resistance and revolutions and Nigerian women in politics, we witnessed the work of freedom, never questioning if women could be in charge. My father's favorite war story from his draft service in Germany during the Việt Nam War involved General William Westmoreland, who, visiting my father's barracks for inspection, walked in and saw a large drawing of Malcolm that my father had been working on, took one look, and then marched back out. My parents were laying a foundation of resistance so that even if it was something I might one day stray from, it would always be there waiting for me to find my way back to.

I'D MOVED TO NEW YORK AFTER FIVE YEARS IN CHICAGO, WHERE, in the overly white North Side neighborhoods, the only white people who ever looked me in the eye were the cops. The clerks in shops on Mag Mile watched me unabashedly, hoping their suspicions would prove right. Cabdrivers sped up after seeing my color. In a land before Lyft, in a city where temperatures drop to thirty below, this was often a deciding factor in the question of going out at night come winter. It was back-splitting to live so fearful, with all my hackles up, and yet to *still* be the one who made white people afraid.

In Chicago, non-Black houseless folks yelled slurs. It was the racist food service, the friend who earnestly asked, "Why are Black people such bad tippers?" It was the way segregation painted my nightlife white, once again, like Clemson, rarely leaving me anyone but slightly racist white guys and white women to fuck. It was in convincing anyone outside of the South Side or Pilsen to rent you an apartment. Watching white people with distasteful looks watch Black kids on the train as they giggled, happy to be done with the school day.

By the time I'd arrived in New York, I was twenty-six and my parents had been mostly right about mostly everything. In this body, I was assumed guilty, and that meant prison came with me everywhere. Like every woman, I already understood restriction. No alleys at night, no bars alone, no drinks I hadn't seen poured. And though womanhood drew borders in this country that I am supposed to feel is mine, whiteness made Blackness the border. Declared my body a moving weapon inside white America's fear of infiltration. I was its starting measure. A lie was revised into an origin story. A road map laid for the oppressions to come.

The generations between my great-grandmothers, my grandmothers, my parents, me, and the next, are a hallway I can peer down. Though, first, I'd have to tell you about the darkness.

3.

How do *I* even begin to tell *you* about the darkness?

> *Do I start with the bodies?*

Skin rich as the land they come from. Eritrea, Ethiopia, Somalia, Congo, Nigeria, Senegal—the whole Sub-Saharan. All of them looking a little bit like my mother.

> *Do I start with the night?*

Moon falling on black waters.

ONE MIGHT SAY *BLUE-BLACK* TO DESCRIBE THE WAY THE AFRICAN body carries land on its skin. One might say *incandescent:* with home, longing, leaving, fear—belief in the journey. The sea too large for them to know that their god won't make it across the border. Upon their arrival, the god they meet has already pledged allegiance to those who wait to call them *enemy, infiltrator, criminal, illegal.*

The waves smash them into one another.

It is the haunt of the transatlantic all over again. Human beings drown, fallen into some forever darkness haunted by the souls of people renamed slaves. Those thrown overboard or who jumped ship. Surely some above in the boats must have crossed over ancestors below. Like then, squeezed into boats by the hundreds, like corks in wine bottles, dozens suffocated from the pressure of one another's bodies.

"Stepping Over the Dead on a Migrant Boat," the revised online article title reads, but when I see it in the October 6, 2016, *New York Times* print edition, it runs with the title "Just Like a Slavery Boat." Neither title able to comprehend or allow the coexistence of "Africans" with human life. For this sparsely worded photo essay, a collaboration between the white American reporter Rick Gladstone and

Greek photographer Aris Messinis, less than six hundred words accompany twelve photos.

In one photo, one of the worst, I stare at a group of African men in life jackets huddled in the back of an inflatable gray boat. Three others in life jackets and tattered clothes edge along the side, holding on, stepping over body piled upon body. So many bodies that the bodies lose their borders, their boundaries, lose all consent, becoming tangled with the bodies of the other dead.

Though America bled into the skin of the daughters she made, my mother had skin like this. A nightshade. Nuh, bearing his Gambian father's even darker coloring, is a black sky around the lit moon.

In the photo that is one of the worst, where the dead pile on the dead and the living cling to the edges of something you wouldn't necessarily call life, it is the skin I don't look away from. So much of it that, were any breath left in their bodies, their positioning would resemble a passion instead of the Fall. A man in bunched-up yellow shorts and nothing else tops the pile of loss, his arms and legs spread out—another Christ on the cross. A baby blue Western T-shirt covers his face and a tight, curly beard, grown in the time it took to flee, peeks out, wrapping his chin and neck. A man pinned underneath, chest also bare, T-shirts piled on his neck, turns his head ever so slightly against the leg of the man in the yellow bunched shorts, as though he is kissing his thigh in reverence. But it is the woman I cannot unsee.

All but her torso is pinned beneath the limbs and parts of other's bodies. Her tank top is stretched tight as a drum while the heel of someone else's foot pushes through, across her hip, as though about to run. But what pulls the eye in the photo is her bare breast. A headless African woman exposed. Our bodies now only parts.

Is it the horror, the lack of dignity, the gaze that seems close enough to reach a hand out, but snaps a photo instead? Or how suddenly I am ten years old, lying on my parents' bed in Akron, Ohio. My mother changes while cradling the phone to her ear. Speaking Hausa through a calling card, her breasts, dark, round, are an almost exact image of this faceless, fallen woman. Is everyone reminded of their mother this way?

Other than "this week," the article offers me no date of when this nightmare was captured for film. Instead, the photo essay turns their images timeless. Erases the border between their African/dark/Black bodies. They exist forward and back. The photos of their death are simultaneously the photos that stared me down the year prior, of two-year-old Alan Kurdi as he lay face first on a Turkish shore, the waves coming in. Their African bodies, even in death, grieve.

WHEN MY FATHER CALLS, HIS VOICE SHAKES SPEAKING ABOUT THE migrant detention centers at the southern border. In the moment, he is an utterly terrified father. He says the detention centers are worse than prisons. Even worse care, and new inventions of abuse. There, children are beaten, molested, attempt suicide. He says some are saying the children are not children anymore. Some say "lock 'em up." Others turn the channel. He tells me our U.S. courts have found no U.S. wrongdoing in the case of fourteen immigrant children stripped naked in a Virginia detention center, strapped to chairs with bags over their head, and beaten in cold cells. He tells me the Smithsonian wants to purchase the drawings of the children who some say are not children anymore. Like Blackness, the Mexico–United States border is one of the most frequently crossed in the world. When he speaks, I can almost hear his paintbrushes weep with rage and a fear he's got nowhere to place but with me.

As a Black person in America, images from the migrant detention centers become palimpsests of horrors. One result of Clinton's disastrous 1994 crime bill, Kaba points out, is the framework it laid for immigrant detention, noting that the people "most incarcerated within immigrant detention are disproportionately Black immigrants."

America's prisons could not exist without my Black body or without my existence in this country, and the humanitarian crisis of the detention centers could not exist without the scale prison has achieved on my body. Not only have U.S. prisons been created on bodies like mine, white Americans, over centuries, have desensitized themselves through our bodies, too. My body has lost the ability of metaphor. I am conduit. I am pain regarding the pain of another. "The convergence of 'tough on crime' and 'tough on immigration,'" writes Harsha Walia, "sustains racialized control, while also ensuring a compliant labor force through the containment of surplus labor that exists alongside the outsourcing of maquiladora labor and the insourcing of migrant labor."

I see pictures of the vice president, cabinet officials, Democratic and Republican senators touring the detention centers. Some leave tears, others *God bless Americas*. All leave the door locked behind them when they go.

There is more here than just the spectator or the coward. There is all of history, and sometimes the pain you are regarding is also your own. The very thing that fuels state horror against other marginalized people is Blackness—me.

We are illegible as belonging *in* this country rather than *to* it, and the police kill us in our homes, on our neighborhood streets, in Walmarts, in our cars. Running from the end of a barrel, I watch America chase brown people, aiming at anything dark it sees coming, after honing its sharpshooting on me.

Thy will be done, says the Havsuw 'Baaja land, stolen and renamed the Grand Canyon. *Thy will be done,* says a lynching. *Thy will be done,* says another immigrant detention center built by the same corporations that build our private prisons. *Thy will be done,* says Darren Wilson. *Thy will be done,* says Dylann Roof's bullets leaping through the air. *Thy will be done,* says another Havasupai Elementary student dragged from school to prison. *Thy will be done,* says a U.S. president renaming Covid-19 the "China virus."

4.

It's November now. Politicians peacock across my TV screen. This is the stage where wanna-be actors come to prove themselves the *most* American. The *best* lover of this country. Where day after day, brown and Black faces say what their white counterparts never have to. *I, too, am America,* someone tweets. All of them trying to prove and position themselves as belonging enough to our country to be elected representatives of it.

Citizenship: *O Captain! My Captain!*

My carrot and stick.

Is there a word for this in any language? Patriotism, I suppose. White America demands of Black and brown people an illogically strange gratitude, where I have only recognitions: of my privileges, of my safeties, of my fears. Of the freedoms, rights, and possibilities that this country did not give me willingly, but that my ancestors demanded and won through a physical pain, a bloodletting. Violences so unfathomable and revealing, the white imagination dismisses—this record of their crimes—as myth.

The news reports there are many dead, most by the hands of white men. Eight in Odessa. Ten in Dayton, Ohio, where Cousin Regi texts, "Hey Fee Fee." He lets me know that everyone is okay, though it was a place he frequented Saturday nights. A woman he knew died. "She just had her second baby . . ." My cousin trails off.

Twenty-two lives are vanished in El Paso in a white man's protest to immigration. Twenty-six in Sutherland by a domestic abuser. Six in Isla Vista by a resentful virgin who leaves behind a rambling manifesto. More are dead today, tonight, this morning. More tomorrow.

There is both the violence to attend to and its veil. The violence veiling the positioning. The positioning being those who are raised to call violence by its first name. Isn't all violence *in defense of*? Of self, others, the roof over your head, sovereignty. Of ego, dominance, money, land. Of a lost America that only white people can make "great" again.

"What we saw today was a facility that is providing care that every

American would be proud of," I watch a U.S. vice president say in 2019 of the migrant detention centers that some of us are calling concentration camps.

I must be more precise: so often violence is not just *in defense of* but, more accurately, more true, violence is often *in defense of a history*. That history can be a narrative, an inheritance, a legacy, or a bloodline. It can be a violence in defense of a history of country, men, though in the U.S., it most often defends white supremacy.

∞

In 1999, the Columbine school shooting tore the maw of my world open. I was fifteen. The summer after Columbine we arrived in South Carolina, and I was still mentally preparing for my transition from St. Maria's single-sex education to public school at Fort Pleasant. Beyond Rodney King's beating and O.J.'s chase and trial—of which, the latter, I remember unfolding live on TV at St. Maria's in a classroom full of my white peers—I had never seen the news report so relentlessly on a single story before. Every newsroom, newspaper, radio station, and magazine covered it for weeks. It was talked about in homes and in classrooms. *What did it mean?* Everyone wanted to know.

They banned trench coats, backpacks, and Marilyn Manson. No one could get the story right. Then, one after the other, white boys and white grown men, who the news said were more sad than bad, bulldozed their homes, middle schools, high schools, colleges, churches, workplaces, local malls, country music and garlic festivals with bullets. That so much violence could go unchecked was as terrifying as it was ridiculous. Their targets were Jews, women, girlfriends, ex/wives, Muslims, children, immigrants, Asians, Black people. They positioned themselves as acting in defense of either the nation or white men, but what was the difference? Politicians were unable to agree if guns killed people, or if people killed people, and guns the unknowing participants in a crime.

We are four generations from slavery. I've inherited a sharecropper's back. Each fear I wear, a gear that's been overly tightened. In America, I'm rarely ever more than a few thousand feet from a white man with a gun who knows his country has his back. Like that one October in Georgia. I snaked the edge of an ocean that had attenuated into marsh. Each curve that hugged the border of the water, each bridge that extended for miles, left you feeling like you were a skim on the surface. Massive oak trees lined the roads. Their branches dripped with heaps of Spanish moss that shimmered silver in the sunlight.

A group of motorcyclists flanked my rental car, passing me like birds in formation. It was fall, the heat suspiciously high. They appeared to be a motorcycle gang, a few wore their leather. The others wore only T-shirts with slogans that flapped in the wind: YOU CAN'T HAVE MY COUNTRY. IF THIS FLAG OFFENDS YOU I'LL HELP YOU PACK. CONFEDERATE LIVES MATTER. IF YOU CAN READ THIS YOU'RE IN RANGE.

I was driving to a writing retreat on a plantation with a suspiciously, vaguely recorded history, two original Andy Warhols of Jimmy Carter, and anthropological drawings of Indigenous people adorning every wall.

I was thirty minutes outside my destination, the roads growing lusher and more isolated. With no barrier between their bodies and the warm wind that blew in off the marsh, the motorcyclists' shirts waved like flags above their waists. I counted four holstered guns among them, had to assume there were more I couldn't see. I was on a road in a state in a country where I knew better than to feel safe. A place where my grandma and her mother had sharecropped cotton. A road populated by what were, for me especially, dangerous men.

I knew Georgia allowed open carry. If they all had permits, am I to be relieved? I think again of the phenomenon of white male mass shooters, America's *hear and see no evil*. However troubling it may be to the U.S. populace, mass shootings could not continue unchecked if they were not, at their core, an authentically patriotic act. A violence *in defense of* an essence, the open secret that a Ku Klux misogyny is at the other end of the umbilical cord in the birth of the nation.

Whiteness is a border that shifts to justify and arbitrate who has a right to use violence and call it defense. A border that rescues victims from those it labels acceptable losses or deserving of their fates. A border that sends DeShawn to prison for what I've watched white people do in bar bathrooms, on boats, in stadiums, drugs snowing from the dressers of their apartments. Whiteness is a border that sets precedent.

In Florida, the border shifts to say you can kill an unarmed seventeen-year-old Black boy if you don't like the looks of him. But will go to jail for at least three years if, in Florida, you are a Black mother like Marissa Alexander, who fired a warning shot in the air to stand her ground in front of her abuser. In "my" country, my fear will seldom, if ever, be acknowledged at all. America will use my skin to try and weaponize me despite my empty hands.

"Life is not a spectacle," wrote Aimé Césaire. "A sea of grief is not a proscenium, a man who wails is not a dancing bear." But in America, Black fear is made the spectacle, the proscenium, the dancing bear.

Is it the bullet of America or the fear of the bullet of America that is killing me?

TO BE BLACK IN AMERICA IS TO, WITH A RATIONAL MIND, LOOK OUT from a position of fear onto a nation full of lies. The haints here being:

- the bullet,
- the weapon,
- the hand that holds it,
- and the nation in which stands the hand that holds the weapon that holds the bullet.

I know America relies on lies to weather my blood. With a subtle word, it's tried to kidnap my mind. The Black Period taught me to see the bones of this country. Now I can see the musculature, the circulatory system. The bruises hidden below the epidermis. I see the scars that don't match the stories.

In New York, I try to keep a side-eye on the angriest white man in the room/on the train/walking toward or behind me on the streets. I read that Arizona has "refurbished" their gas chambers in preparation for executing people using hydrogen cyanide—the same murder weapon of Auschwitz. In a nation of atrocities that has rendered unimaginable, improbable, and impossible both the memories and fears of whom it has violently oppressed, safety is a trick question. Though, a passport and birth certificate certify me a jus sanguinis citizen— a citizen not by birth but by my father's bloodline—I know nothing in this earthly world can make me appear to America citizen-sized. *I come from both captives and the people never captured. My blood is a story that intersects. I am of both/no lands, my bones are of two directions. Today, I promise myself:* I'll walk outside unafraid to rest my hands inside my pockets.

IN 2020, WHEN THE PRESIDENTIAL ELECTION WAS FINALLY CALLED, I was in the park. It was warmer than usual. Like every Saturday, I was walking to the farmers market to buy Stephanie weekend flowers. I knew something had happened by the way Black people were suddenly laughing all around me. And then there was the way the fall sun cast itself off our faces—like a soccer ball bouncing off a chest—while from Black folk to Black folk, we smiled, nodded. It was like the relief of a cop exiting your rearview. The time it took for your worried blood to find your worried body once again, finally over. The valves in our bodies releasing just a little steam.

And then the whole park exploded in cheer. Live music rang from all corners as if joy had been here all along. Joy had only been lying in wait! I wanted to cry, to call everyone I loved and say: *hey, I love you!*—and I did manage to call a few—and then all I wanted was silence. Two things were true: Things were better. Nothing had changed.

In the world my parents dreamed of, the one they worked so hard to get, but which failed to manifest as more than an apparition, we still can't agree on what a nation is for. And yet, I just want to be free on this stolen land where, yes, Black children play with a price on their heads.

"Revolutionary consciousness leads to the struggle for one's own freedom in unity with others who share the burden of oppression," writes Joshua Bloom in *Black against Empire: The History and Politics of the Black Panther Party*. In the wretched year of 2020, even as we debated among ourselves, I watched Black and brown people work, in and across communities, to flip Michigan, Georgia, Pennsylvania, Wisconsin, Arizona. We did so knowing no presidential election will ever save us or change the world. Instead, we chose to build change a home in our daily and collective actions.

In 2000, when Jamila was nineteen and our mother newly a citizen, the two of them excitedly cast the first vote of their American lives together. That year, the country voted for Al Gore by majority, but George W. became president. Then came Obama, with his audacious hope, deporting people by the millions as America refused the same old lesson: don't make gods of men.

Afrofuturists like Sun Ra and Octavia Butler believed that what guards the present is Blackness being an always future tense. I was taught that my vote is never an investment in the government. (That would be suicide.) It's an investment in my community (my hope). Is it a meaningless gesture? An act of solidarity? A small ingredient that might buy the Stacey Abramses and Mariame Kabas of the world more time? Or is it simply a way to say to other Black people: *I love you, have hope.*

As children, though we were only just beginning to understand our country, we knew the sheer miracle of surviving it had turned our elders into living ancestors. Daily, our ancestors demonstrated resilience and stressed perseverance while warning that the world waiting to meet us offered no justice, no peace. Our bodies were trapped inside our nation's limited imagination, but Black hope built to-be-charted territories. Hope is a conversation with that which is im/possible.

5.

In my mind: South Carolina.

The stars above my father's house shine hard and ambivalent. This place I confess to love is also the place that handed me my first lesson in the danger and deceptiveness of beauty. This mecca of the slave trade that destroyed the bodies of my ancestors but could not take their legacy is, to the eye, lovely to its core.

Beauty can get you in trouble.

From its Lowcountry to its islands, from its coasts to its colonial-era cobblestones. In the summer, the moon shines bright like the voice of someone who has loved you for the longest time. The trees stretch their branches out like chandeliers over the smell of growing earth. No matter the season, in the South, the sun comes up from underneath: a flashlight, lifting the grass, the leaves, the branches. But there is a ghost story here. The beauty is made of mostly blood and bones. Rapes and whippings. Of stolen children, and people robbed of their names. Or it is written as a love story, depending on who tells it.

I don't know the day, or where I was when I finally realized the origin story I'd long been carrying wasn't mine. But I was older than you'd think. I was somewhere floating around in my twenties. By then, I was living in Chicago. After moving from the white school I'd known my whole life, whatever a three-year interlude at an integrated public high school had reminded me of, a conservative white college helped me again to forget. The origin stories my parents had given me, I'd long set down by the side of the road. Kwanzaa was something in my rearview. I was driven by shame. Part of the shame came from being a part of a people who had to write their own origin stories in real time, and with the whole world watching if it wanted to. It took years to find my way back to the Black Period. Years to see that my shame could be something temporary, like a nation, like a border. Like anything with walls.

In the America that waited for me every day, I didn't know how to carry an origin story of mixed Black and African blood. Growing up, even my Black American father wore almost exclusively African clothes. Kwanzaa was a pan-African holiday, and I was pan-African, too. I was a melting pot of beginnings, and like Kwanzaa, I never felt like I held any of my origin stories accurately. I had been gone too long to be Nigerian. I was Black, therefore not really seen as American. Foreign born, I couldn't access the American child's daydream of being president. I was too queer to be safely anyone's citizen. My origin stories had no boundary lines I could map. I grew up and out of my parents' home and along the way forgot the world was full of countries where people knew how to pronounce my name.

In America, when strangers and acquaintances asked my mother her name, she responded, *Hauwa,* not Tini. She'd returned to her baptismal name. The one that meant Eve—that name that pulsed through generations of our family like a heart.

In the gaping distance my mother saw between herself and her home country, did she feel like the first woman? How Eve wandered the newly created earth, cast out despite being of the rib. Her daughter, I roamed in search of a clearer origin.

I WATCH ALEPPO EXPLODE. ON MY TV, AN EMERGENCY RED CROSS "shelter" shows a string of faces somehow simultaneously alive and suffocated in soot. They sit, mouths torn open, but silent, war having assailed them with everything it could: the sight of bodies being torn apart by the homes that fell on them, the smell of a whole life burned, and the sound they say you cannot imagine unless you have been under it. Bomb after bomb, there is picture after picture. Women and children, mothers and daughters, young girls and baby boys. It seems as though only the women and children survive—the cursed keepers of memory.

On another channel, protesters in Hong Kong are beaten in the streets marching for their right to speak against their government. On every continent, Muslims are systematically killed and oppressed. Palestinians are still trying to freedom ride out from under their bombed homes and hospitals, out of an Israel-enforced, United States–funded Jim Crow. In Chennai, Cape Town, Mexico City, Cairo, Tokyo, Jakarta, São Paulo, Bangalore, and Jamila's former adopted home of Beijing, they are running out of clean water. In Zimbabwe and Venezuela, the price of bread skyrockets to a month's wages.

Today, I can barely breathe. So consumed I am by a feeling I can't name. The feeling like a desperate thirst quenched by water—I am an American citizen. This passport my bloody talisman. The boot on my chest rocks. Shifts its weight. A moment of reprieve. And though, when I stretch my hands out, sometimes thinking that I can feel America's borders, the pieces of paper that tether me to this land feel thick enough to lean toward prayer.

I've had education, my family has always had healthcare. For a time, my citizenship provided me, a child, more rights than the mother who raised me, and my passport allows me to travel both the world and the country I call home with a freedom—however restricted— that far outpaces that of the Undocumented. Two rooms away my wife—so kind, so patient, so tender with my pain that she gives me a back rub almost every night—sits under a blanket reading in her office, together the two of us sculpting both a life and a home. That Stephanie is white makes an already complicated love more complicated. We who are written by this country as opposite ends of a spectrum. But like most things, through love, tenderness, work, it works.

I know that it is this small haven of a city inside this precarious ship of a country that provides the two of us the space to do the work. Black, queer, a little foreign, this land, more than any other, astronomically increases the chances that I get to live. And though it is not uncomplicated, for better or worse, the people of my country having been able to fight for me *in* our country grants me all this. But what does it mean to need your oppressor?

I know that in my place of birth, girls who are never found go missing every day. Something that is also true, but in a different way, of Black girls in the U.S. My awareness over what living in the United States makes possible leans sharply in my mind against a country of ICE raids, a country that abandons its own in New Orleans and Puerto Rico, that poisons children in Flint.

Someone always gets rich in disaster, my father likes to remind me.

But from Indigenous water protectors and climate justice advocates like Josephine Mandamin, the Water Protector Legal Collective, and the NDN Collective, to the legacies of Marsha P. Johnson and Sylvia Rivera, to the Black Panthers, to the work of the Native American Disability Law Center and the resistance of Havasupai Elementary families, to the Havsuw 'Baaja's insistence on the sacredness of their language, stories, and land, to the abolition work of Angela Davis, Ruth Wilson Gilmore, and Mariame Kaba—I know at the root is more than the wound. I know whiteness isn't the limit. Not when Indigenous and Black folks, by America's design, have always lived on the outskirts. If there is an outskirts, logic says, there is a map leading to a different way. A way beyond the centuries of this racial capitalism that is months away from devastating the nation, the nation who, while scapegoating Asian and Asian American people, will leave the entire country to die at the hands of a virus.

But what is a country? How do you make one? Can a stolen orchard bear anything more than stolen fruit?

Side by side, my mind replays a home video my father took of Yaya in Nigeria, speaking at length to my mother in Hausa, next to another video he took a decade later in South Carolina where my mother speaks back.

Yaya wears a bright wax-print blouse and a matching headwrap—Hausa swirls the red, yellow, and blue cloth that adorns her still stroke-free body. A shy-girl joy kidnaps her face as she says "Tini," my mother's *beloved* name. Something in my chest cracks open to think of my mother being missed, not as *my* mother, but as someone's child.

For a full hour, Yaya speaks. Her shyness to be talking to her daughter via videotape falls off as, inside her Hausa, the language of her body changes. From Yaya's face, I can distinguish when she talks about our family from her exasperation about the country—this Nigeria my mother, still alive in that moment, is missing.

In Akron, my mother, suddenly a daughter, suddenly Yaya's child, holds a mic in her hand. She is a carbon copy of Yaya. My mother's face wears her mother's same shyness from behind oversized nineties-style glasses. Suddenly, from me, to my mother, to Yaya, I feel like the inside of a matryoshka doll. My mother's Hausa flows from the orange velvet chair my paternal grandmother once recorded her own story in, the chair that still sits in me and Stephanie's Brooklyn living room.

In a red-and-black African dress, my mother says her daughters' names, and like always, our names sound different, easier, strung up between her phonemes.

WHEN I CALL MY FATHER TO ASK HIM HOW I CAN GO ON LIVING heartbroken by this place for so long, he recites Muhammad Ali's "Me, We!" He means memory, honor, and obligation. He means this country needs a credible witness, and it's up to us, because accurate witness is something that whiteness will not provide. He says, "After all your grandmother and my grandmother survived, who are any of us to quit?"

We give our children over to a future through the promise of our imagined nation, while the country we inhabit tries to unimagine us: in its movies, literature, politics, its cultural and historical records, despite only being rendered real by our existence and the records *we* hold.

As Sehgal implies, when it comes to rising from the ashes, history begets transformation.

Whether I was Icarus or phoenix, I had to name the fires.

6.

In every name, there is a story. In my sister's, there is a joke. After having Jamila, my parents came to the U.S. from Nigeria to visit my father's family. I had yet to be born. My parents had thought they were giving her a unique name, only to arrive to a country where Jamilas were everywhere. Jamilas had taken Black America by storm.

It is a story my father tells as he laughs, head tipped toward a memory like he's lost inside one of his own drawings. Smiling, he always finishes the story by saying that when I came around, they tried harder. But in my father's story is another: the one that tells me how deeply my parents believed in the power of naming, and how close to history we are that the right to name our children is still brand-new against the scale of time.

My mother died before the explosion of online footprints. I'm traces of her. I'm the manifestation of her imagination—it was she who taught me how to dream. She is a chest of things. Paperwork. Documents. Cloth and clothing in African trunks that my father keeps stashed at the back of his bedroom closet.

The chests hold her Nigerian outfits and fabric that I would, over a decade later, be grateful to have tailored, wearing my mother like a second skin. Jewelry boxes full of gold for me and Jamila to divvy up. Her wedding band. The earrings my auntie Mairo brought her from Saudi Arabia. The five gold bangles that adorned her wrist every day. A necklace with a charm in the shape of a Quran. Inside, it holds a mini version of the Holy Book, inscribed with a single Arabic prayer. It holds my parents' marriage license and a dozen copies of it—a habit of my mother's, who kept copious copies of every official document like someone refusing to fall off-record, her holster always full of papers that could prove or explain our family's presence.

It holds our entire family's immunization records, a paper declaring her graduation from secretarial school in Kaduna, proof of high marks and a reference letter that testified to her strong character and constitution. A copy of my father's divorce papers. Proof of child support payments to my brother, Gerald, the distance between him and my father troubling my father's mind. My father's love letters from his and my mother's first year of marriage living on separate continents. Her old address book, chaotic from revision and trying to keep hold of friends as they migrated through the years. Both of their international drivers' licenses from the seventies, the two of them looking like a Black Bonnie and Clyde, and a blueprint for a house they were going to build on land they'd purchased before the country fell apart.

A fastidious record keeper, my mother kept a manila folder for every year of our lives. She stashed birth certificate copies, our old report cards, picture-day photos, doctors' notes, hearing tests, hand-scrawled Mother's Day cards. Every certificate of her daughters' achievements and every newspaper clipping that bore my father's name and proved him an artist and man of accomplishment.

There's her social security card, every last one of her Nigerian passports, showing her slow transformation from an African, to an African in America, to an African in disguise. Her clothing slowly assimilating over decades before the first U.S. passport appears. It is a trunk of gains and losses. The contents evidence that life splits you like a river.

Like every immigrant I've known, my mother took the process of naturalization seriously. Her nerves excited, jittery as a dice game. After all, a test was a test. At night, in Akron, she studied in the tiny sewing room just off my bedroom, sometimes asking Jamila and me to quiz her on presidents and capital cities.

A woman of two continents, immigration carved my mother into a woman of two contexts. She was African. Dark-skinned. Accented. Once naturalized, she, like my father—like her children—was, the paper said, also an American. The caveat "black" written before "American" in invisible ink. But what I want to know is, how often was she afraid?

Did this country shroud her, and what was that final straw that made her wear, once again, her Islamic name? My mother died too young for me to have known to ask her what it was she wanted from all *this*. Was it freedom, an American Dream, or never having to fear she and her family would be separated?

I do know my parents tried to resist America. They'd been married four years. They packed their bags. My father returned with my mother to live in Nigeria. After years of trying, there, in my mother's home country, the miracle of children came.

My parents, now parents, bought land and drew a blueprint for a house in a buckling country. A country on a continent under the thumb of foreign policy, the World Bank, and the International Monetary Fund—all of which would force the entire continent into collapse. It is the old immigrant tale, and you've seen this one before: *A Love Story*. A chase scene! Bloodcurdling scares. A heist. Death haunts the journey—*The Body Snatchers* find you by way of assimilation.

From what she left behind—from what my mother did and didn't give us—I know she wanted her daughters to have more than our birthland, at the time, could afford. That she and my father brought us to America in search of the opportunities that in her home country, colonization had stolen. And she knew enough about America to grasp the necessity of your own story inside a country where the idea of free Black people was still so brand-new. I often wonder, if she were still alive—like so many immigrants after raising their children stateside—would our mother have wanted to go *home* home? Our father would be smiling, his replaced hips—aged and rickety—remembering when, as four, we'd been fleeing coups.

HERE SHE WAS IN HER AMERICAN LIFE. A WOMAN WHO SELDOM told stories of Nigeria or her childhood, home was not a thing my mother could turn into past tense. In America, Nigeria was in the kitchen, in the privacies she guarded inside language, always on the phone with a relative, where it was Hausa she spoke. More than half of her tongue and more than half of her mind forever a stranger to the family she lived with. Still, the sound of her making my father laugh reverberates through me, like a flower in my chest that's perpetually blooming. They'd laugh so hard they'd have to steady themselves. With one hand on their stomachs, they *tee-hee*'d around one another like wobbly spun tops. They'd throw their free hand out to catch the kitchen island or the back of a chair, though more often than not, they grabbed each other.

There was how, into my middle school years, before bed, in the face of my pleading for more information, hints, breadcrumbs, answers to our mysteries, my mother delivered me Nigerian fables. An approximation of a country and of a history—her Black Period.

Everywhere we called home, my mother tended her garden. She lassoed roses, daffodils, and her favorite, orange marigolds, around every house we lived in, her body steadied by an "Allahu Akbar." Like my paternal great-grandma Lizzie in her own Alabama garden, my mother pulled tomatoes, basil, thyme, and red and hot peppers from her garden to our kitchen plates. In the earth, my mother, legally hyphenated, newly "African-American," sucked her teeth.

Which of our countries left the deepest wounds on her in the end?

Was she thinking about how the ground beneath her had been made rich with her ancestors' graves? Was the wind scrawling?

America—

she loves me

she loves me not

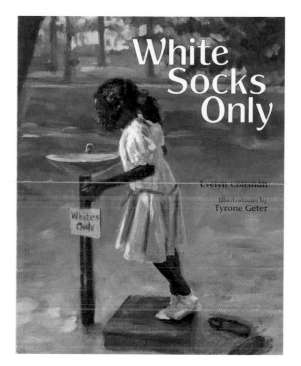

White
Socks
Only

Evelyn Coleman

Illustrations by
Tyrone Geter

2

3

4

5

7

8

THIS CAN
STILL HAPPEN
ANYWHERE

AGE IX

TESTIMONY

Susan has loosed me on the neighbors,
A cold representative,
The scariest face you could think of.

—CORNELIUS EADY, "Composite,"
from *Brutal Imagination*

You know how a storm can make a neighborhood go quiet?

The trees don't say a word.

A hurricane has taken out half the branches.

IN PROSPECT PARK, CAUTION TAPE SURROUNDS DOWNED TREES, which look like swords with their tips broken off. Men have gotten to the work of mulching them. Walkers, runners, and cyclists of all races disappear behind face masks with Black Lives Matter slogans or African print.

I've just come off a badly twisted ankle from running without paying attention to my footfall underneath the overgrowth of the park's back trails. This time I run slow. With my heart matching the pace of a limping deer, my back aching. The sound of ducks in conversation drags across the water.

It is nowhere near cold, but fall is coming, and after our first Covid-19 summer, everyone behaves like they know it. The hurricane originated as a tropical storm off the coast of Africa. It's left several towns in Puerto Rico without electricity or drinking water, and eighteen dead, but the news barely mentions it, focusing instead on mainland lives.

Days later, something called a "derecho"—a devastating line of windstorms—pummels Iowa with hundred-mile per hour wind across an area nearly eight hundred miles wide and damages 43 per cent of the state's crops, and yet it will go barely reported on outside of local news. In Iowa's eastern city of Cedar Rapids, Micronesian and Tanzanian immigrants set up refugee camps from the blueprint of old memory in front of their destroyed homes and, with no surprise in their voices, tell a hometown reporter no help from the government has come.

I read that corporations like Chevron, Shell, Exelon, JPMorgan Chase, Bank of America, Morgan Stanley, Goldman Sachs, and Wells Fargo (who are all responsible for environmental, housing, economic, and health inequities in Indigenous and Black communities) also fund the police through backdoor foundations in Seattle, Chicago, Washington, New Orleans, and Salt Lake City. There's a genocide going on in my country. As of last count, there's more than one.

By August 2020, the year of our Lord the Pandemic, Monika Diamond, Nina Pop, Dominique "Rem'mie" Fells, Riah Milton, Brayla Stone who was just seventeen years old, Merci Mack, Shaki Peters,

Bree Black, Dior H Ova, Queasha D. Hardy, and Aja Raquell Rhone-Spears will all be dead, putting 2020 on track to be the deadliest year for trans people—a record that will be usurped by November 2021. Whatever it looked like to emerge from erasure, it wasn't supposed to look like this.

When the news reports that Isaias was the most impactful wind event in New York City since Hurricane Sandy in 2012, they'll be talking about power outages. I'll be thinking about how any kind of power is just the ability to keep yourself and who you love safe. I'll be thinking of two dead boys named Brandon and Connor Moore, and making a list of how much more can be lost in the worst hurricane season on record. *Do you remember?*

Remember?

Do you?

∞

It was 2012. Wind took out the city, Nasdaq, the New York Stock Exchange, the New York Marathon, and NYU's hospital, like candles extinguished off a birthday cake. The tides rose to reach the new moon. Though not the Goldman Sachs building. It remained illuminated like a lighthouse guiding the Beginning of the End of the World to its port.

Water the shape of God's fist punched its way through skin, ribcage, the heart, leaving parts of Red Hook, DUMBO, Lower Manhattan, Staten Island, and Queens submerged, each a modern-day Atlantis. Across the five boroughs, the young/able/resourced frolicked. Friends called, texted, slid into each other's DMs, and bounced from one blackout party to another. Hurricane Sandy, two-faced with those lost to darkness and the sound of careless revelry.

Running from June 1 to November 30, the storms of the Atlantic hurricane season follow the same paths as the ships of the Atlantic slave trade. Black lore calls it retribution—our stolen—our ghosts turned haints coming through the weather. All of us swept up in history's retribution.

Two hours before the storm, I'd relocated my books, piles of writing papers, and family photos to higher ground, finally deciding to abandon my dimly lit garden apartment and walk the thirty minutes to a friend's. The air, not yet fully wild, had become rebellious enough for both me and my father to question my last-minute decision-making.

As I walked—my father on the other side of my earbuds—the wind pushed large piles of trash down the empty streets. Across what was/ is Lenape land, all of Brooklyn was an abandoned saloon-town. The quiet making room for the *anything* that promised to happen.

At Kyla's, we waited out the storm with snacks, her portable piano keyboard, Stevie Wonder, and gossip. Outside, the city was quiet in a way only made possible by impending disaster. The wind snapping like a whip in the distance.

The next day, I returned to an apartment intact. An aftermath that, in the end, affected me very little. I returned to lights still working despite the millions thrust into darkness for weeks and a governor who was focused on economic consequences.

The air had thickened with humidity. All down the block, bodegas quickly reopened their doors, their owners stunned and wide-eyed as they calculated losses amidst train closures and low foot traffic. At the Port Authority, MTA workers passed buckets of floodwater from the train tunnels up to the light, trying to separate the walkways from the destruction misnomered with the name of a woman.

The MTA is well known for its crumbling infrastructure and long delays that I've seen drive grown people to angry tears. It's the skeleton that runs through the city, and even before Sandy, our skeleton was finicky and brittle.

Someone who can't help but consider *all* the dominoes, even before the first falls—who can't help but consider catastrophe—in the wake of the storm, I imagined various scenes of disaster:

- Being trapped in the silver bullet of a B train, stalled for hours.
- Suffocating underground in the August heat.
- Being trampled on an overcrowded platform by a fool yelling fire.

- A white man with a gun.
- Panicked people turning Lords of the Flies.
- But worse than the unimaginable was what had already been imagined: the sound a grieving mother makes that never ends.

In Sandy's aftermath, it took police three days to find the bodies of Brandon and Connor Moore, Glenda Moore's two- and four-year-old sons. Her husband, Damien, an NYC sanitation worker and Irish immigrant, had been called in to work during the storm. Glenda, and her boys were fleeing Staten Island when their jeep plunged headfirst into a watery ditch. Car trapped, she exited the vehicle, a son clutched tightly in each arm. Beneath torrential rainfall, the three of them clung to tree branches for hours. Eventually, Glenda sought help from neighbors who refused her and her children refuge—refused her even after the storm waters ripped Brandon and Connor from her arms— every one of them turning this Black Madonna away.

All these years later, her grief still has its own sound. Her loss a sideways guillotine, forgoing the head for the knees. And I think, *this* is what Black folks mean by anguish: a grief so angry, it leeches color from the sky.

Lord, this woman, Glenda, holds on. Though no pictures evidence the hours she spent trying to grip her boys and the water between her hands.

Still, she rises —above flood,

- her children's terror,
- transforms from a body,
- completely to sound
- and she can be heard
- above the storm,
- in the aftermath's aftermath.
- Her neighbors deny her ascension.
- Deny she was sound rising above flood, rain, their abandonment.

- Deny that for twelve hours, her voice was an elegy in the streets.

Above the high tide of Sandy, Glenda's begging climbed neighbors' porches, knocked on neighbors' doors, begged neighbors for hours to help her find the Black sons these neighbors had refused to help save.

This is America—one neighbor, Alan Walker, intimated as he reported angrily to a newscaster that in the flood Glenda sounded like a much bigger, much Blacker man—and what was he supposed to do with *that*? As Walker talks, I watch his whiteness shift. He stands not far from the tree Glenda and her boys swung from. The bald fear that made him tremble all night with his back against his door morphs into confusion, a flash of betrayal when the white newscaster tells him, unequivocally, no, it was a mother at your door. But his confusion is a brief outburst, barely a thousandth of a second. Then, like a man who, without reason, convinces himself he's being tricked, I watch his anger take back over. *This is America,* his shoulders seem to say. And *isn't* this America, where Black boys are gone before even being gone—where, whether Walker means it to or not, his whiteness winks, and Glenda's grief stands 5'3", 130 pounds?

Easier for me to describe than what Glenda and Damien Moore have lost are Walker's shoulders. He rounds them like a stock character to show the newscaster how a phantom hulking Black man threw a concrete flowerpot at his door trying to break in. Because, yes, this *is* America, and here, I know, even in a hurricane, whiteness claims the monopoly on fear. Walker, like his neighbors—like their NOLA counterparts—thinks we only weather storms to loot them.

Though in a hurricane Walker would not open his door for a Black man, in the storm's aftermath—like Susan Smith, the white woman who drowned her two young sons in a South Carolina lake, then blamed their murders on a fictional Black man—I see him grip the ghost of a Black man's hand like his life depends on it. He spins himself into righteous denial. *No,* Glenda—this neighbor insists—was never there. I watch his denial flick her boys from the trees, and into the marsh where their bodies are discovered days later, twenty yards apart.

To this news Walker begrudgingly concedes, "It's unfortunate. She shouldn't have been out, though. You know, it's one of those things." His voice, still agitated, begins to bear relief. He settles into his own rediscovered innocence, having found some place out of his purview to set down the blame. But I am wed to Glenda's loss. And if I could untether, still, wed to it is how I'd choose to remain.

On my computer screen, I study Walker for whiteness's body language. Walker gestures low. Shrugs his shoulders. Left palm up. Walker appeals to the newscaster, to viewers like himself. His open palm asks for trust, the benefit of the doubt denied Brandon, Connor, and Glenda. His positioning implores his allies to stand by him on dry land. I know this tether of movements: the begging gesture. The language of bodies I've always been hungry to know: in regret, the mouth purses. In desire, the eyes dilate. In shame, they look down. But first, to read whiteness I had to learn to read whiteness reading me.

I spent my middle-school weekends running my fingers over the spines of psychology, self-help, and sociology books trying to understand the silences both in and outside my house. The library stacks confirmed what I suspected: the world was just data and data could be broken into parts—a string of dates, the names of the dead, and the names of the streets that took you home. Data was a mouth twitch, an averted eye, the involuntary shrug of a shoulder.

In psychology books, I read how motive doesn't promise itself to logic but to our own personal narratives. From self-help books, I learned those narratives were difficult, if not impossible, to change. Sociology revealed: this is *America*. And whiteness employs its own body language to explain why it lets its neighbors' children drown. What do Glenda and Damien call *living* now? What does it mean "to be saved, when what you are delivered into is abandonment," asks writer Tavia Nyong'o.

I close my computer screen. Switch to my phone, where scientists warn—the world now without Brandon and Connor Moore—that in some places, climate change's erratic temperatures will make the time it takes to round a snowman's head, or to turn a shadow into a snow angel, intolerable. Soon heat will lose its joy. With our bodies trapped inside, fireflies stand to lose our adoration.

How does a child learn the way dusk collects above the head like a woman gathering the hem of her dress without being, summer after summer, beneath the sky?

THE BLACK PERIOD · 241

IN AN OLD HOME VIDEO, DAY TAKES ITS TIME TO VANISH. WE SIT ON the back deck of the house we lived in briefly in Kent, Ohio, before moving to Akron. Our voices the same volume as the dusk. The memory no different than the poem:

> Even
> After
> All this time
> The sun never says to the earth,
>
> 'You owe
> Me.'
>
> Look
> What happens
> With a love like that,
> It lights the
> Whole
> Sky.

Even the moon listens to Hafiz's poem, waiting discreetly in the sky for the sun to pass the baton.

My parents, Jamila, even my uncle George—the sole consistent white man of my childhood—is here. Fireflies flicker, offering their torches. My mother brings over jars. My father presses holes in the lids with a scratch awl from his frame shop. Jamila and I giggle, sounding like my nephews. The video confirming that despite the passing decades, in the present, neither Uncle George's nor my father's voices have aged.

We are only catching fireflies. But for some reason, I memorize the moment. This *tonight*, waiting for fireflies to transform, where my parents want for their daughters a lesson in mercy and a magic that requires no sacrifice. This Black Period moment when Jamila and I are, unequivocally, children. Unequivocally, little girls.

For centuries, Black people have been fighting to return childhood back to our children. For centuries Black mothers like Glenda have weathered white blight storms. Have weathered an unnatural violence, only to be delivered by the hands we've survived to storms fabricated off our oppression.

How far back in history whiteness has the courage to look is equal to the credibility it yields to a Black or brown body—is equal not to the question, but the question's premise: was Glenda Moore ever there?

Against the Black-splash of her grief, Walker condemns her presence: "She shouldn't have been out," he says—her guilt presumed and interrogated. Her sentence: two capital punishments.

"We live with the ghosts of slavery," writes Angela Davis in *Freedom Is a Constant Struggle,* speaking of this world where Black and brown people can't safely fruit, and where Glenda's neighbors' necks point only in the direction where history has no future implications. Century after century, what does loss snatch from the mother-blood? If Glenda and Damien's neighbors' necks could turn back, would Brandon and Connor still be alive?

A fact that this grief has its own fingerprint. But, too, there is repetition. An echo falling backward in time where Black mothers count, numerous as sheep, all the ways their children can be copped by the state. The War on Drugs, which seems to mostly frequent the homes of the Black and brown. The foster care system that hangs on its tails, profiting from ~~selling~~ scattering our children into the white world.

There is economic poverty—despite how much we work—which only serves to leave us time-poor for ourselves and our children. There is the festered body of the prison-industrial complex that occupies its own shadow in our houses. The entirety of the fifteenth, sixteenth, seventeenth, eighteenth, nineteenth, twentieth, all we've known thus far of the twenty-first, and life in the aftermath—the Wake—of enslavement and Indigenous genocide. And there is the exhausting lie of our own country.

But still—I remind myself—the longest arc in history is kindness. Like that of a woman knitting baby booties on the train. My grandmother's eyes lit by softness at the simple sight of *only* me. My mother sitting on her heels in an Eastward devotion. Like mean Aunt Sarah in the kitchen setting her meanness down. Grits, ham hocks, collard greens, cornbread—Aunt Sarah's kitchen magic inherited from those who made feasts from scraps before turning them into our family heirlooms. There is the kindness of a parable. Every Station of the Cross. My first-grade teacher, Sister Betty, forever faithful, demonstrating the kindness witness lends sacrifice.

FROM OP-ED WRITERS, NOVELISTS, AND ESSAYISTS, I READ THINK pieces that declare, thanks to white America's dilution of the idea, that empathy is falling out of fashion. Though no one has told this to the poets who keep arriving to sit with us in our grief. In "Poetry Is Not a Luxury: The Poetics of Abolition," Black feminist researcher and curator Nydia A. Swaby calls abolition an art form—"a creative work that blends the historical present, memory, futurity, the embodied, the visual and the poetic, with notions of freedom, care and collectivity"—maybe you know the poem I mean?

It's Mother's Day and a woman's voice wet with the story of methadone wrings its own neck in the street. *"I'm so lonely, I could kill myself."* Home from the airport, the poet Aracelis Girmay leans out her window. She sees her landlord's nephew, his arms extended around this woman he doesn't know. Through the poet, we hear the nephew say, *"It's okay. I love you, it's okay."* His stranger-love "tall in his Carolina-Brooklyn swagger." The nephew, the poet, the page, and us, all in "the common circumstance of being there." The poet's poem, warning us: we are loved. It is Mother's Day.

In this poem she calls "On Kindness," is she also meaning grace and possibility? Does she also mean the Black Period? That "everywhere I go / I hear us singing to each other." And maybe empathy is simply how one love finds another. Even if accidentally, Girmay, an Afrolatinx poet, calls the Palestinian American poet Naomi Shihab Nye's name.

A Palestinian woman, lost in translation, wails in the Albuquerque airport—the poem, Nye's "Gate A-4." The woman, a grandmother on the way to a medical treatment, in search of legibility, of someone who speaks her mother tongue. Nye, who—in times like these—still volunteers her Arabic, calls the woman's sons on the phone. Nye calls her own father, some Palestinian poets she knows. The grandmother, finding her language, her laughter, and a stranger's kindness, offers homemade mamool cookies to the other women in the terminal, where not a single woman declines—all of them, in that moment, realizing they have waiting in common. Girmay's *common circumstance of being there.*

"This," Nye ends the poem, "can still happen anywhere. Not everything is lost."

As sun scorches the land, as heat climbs the trees, as our grief multiplies, and in the swelter, we die by our own hands, suicide rates are expected to rise an estimated 1.4 percent in the United States and 2.3 percent in Mexico by 2050. The calefaction, like any disaster, will hit Indigenous communities the hardest—their sovereignty braided into their ancestral lands. For these communities—already ravaged by colonization and land theft—drilling and climate change will leave them even less of their country, their stories, traditions, histories, and scientific knowledge for future generations to inherit. But still, in these two true moments of witness, Girmay and Nye remind me what it is possible to do for each other, and now, *not everything is lost.*

Friday, November 9, 2012, on Lenape land, Brandon and Connor Moore are laid to rest in a single casket. A photo shows Glenda and Damien holding hands, sobbing, at the threshold of a church—the difference between the beginning of the world and its end, the feet between a neighbor's front door and a hurricane. The unreachable freedom pole: the white imagination. And though I know "this can still happen anywhere"—I do what I can to stay wed to their grief, its specificity. The people gone, not actually forgotten.

Glenda and Damien's sons' names are more than moans tossed at a Monday-evening moon. With their bodies left abandoned to the marsh by a field of white Samaritans, it's their names—Brandon and Connor—we're obliged to rescue. Like Nye, "This / is the world I

want to live in. The shared world." Where a woman walks through
the airport and—in times like these—still volunteers her language.

> Where one stranger says,
> *It's okay. I love you.*
> Another,
> *This can still happen anywhere.*

WHERE THE PEOPLE COULD FLY

AGE X

INHERITANCE

—Kunta Kinteh Island—
Independence Day, 2019

The sea sounded like a thousand secrets,
all whispered at the same time.

—DIONNE BRAND, *A Map to the*
Door of No Return

TRAVELOGUE, JULY 4, 2019, 9:02 A.M.—EARLY MORNING, AND A
packed van drives me, Stephanie, my father, my pregnant sister, her
husband, Alieu, and my two nephews from Senegambia to Banjul. A
drive that takes us through villages where Gambians sit outside on
buckets, texting or talking on mobile phones, the tin roofs of their
mud houses held up by long, thick branches with slingshot tips.
Where the locals who can spend dalasi after dalasi purchasing bottles
of water in between turning empty lots into storefronts and two-story
hand-built homes for the British and Chinese money that floods in
like I imagine water and news cameras must have flooded into the
Ninth Ward through cracks in NOLA's neglected dam.

We pass cabdrivers waiting on line outside Portuguese gas stations
to fill leased German cars. Women walk along the side of the road,
almost exclusively in traditional African clothing. Most of the men
wear American or European jeans and T-shirts. Like in the U.S., here
both white supremacy and patriarchy make a tool of the men, their
clothing replacing one history with another. And though trash litters
almost every road, the filth, undoubtedly, is colonial, the "second
scramble" for the blood and riches of the country and the continent in
full pursuit.

All summer Jamila and her family have been in Alieu's home
country, where five out of seven of his siblings still reside—a country
that the ministry of tourism, with a New York branding company,
has dubbed "the Smiling Coast," after the way French and British

colonization carved Gambia's borders into the face of Senegal like a mouth.

My father, Stephanie, and I have just arrived. Jamila and Alieu have a two-story rented flat, a two-bedroom where our father is staying for his month duration. Directly across the street, and a two-minute walk to the beach where the only thing between America and us is the Atlantic Ocean and the sun, Stephanie and I book a suite for our two-week stint at a resort hotel almost entirely emptied of the British tourists who, come November, erase the country into a pool-party getaway.

At night, rain pours down on our tin roof above us like God themself has come to collect—the hands of the divine, once again a carpenter's, discarding sharp-toothed nails from a high bucket as though looking down on their creation, trying to decide whether to start over or repair.

Mornings, we drink coffee and fresh juice in bathing suits, watch as teal Abyssinian rollers spread their auburn backs obstinately. Speckled kingfishers caw in nearby palm trees, taking their brief rest before the final leg of their journey to feed from the water. As we reach Banjul, the same birds circle. Around us, hooded vultures, jacana, fish eagles, yellow-billed storks, and nightjars pry themselves out of the woodwork that Africa makes of the trees.

In Gambia, 3,356 kilometers from Nigeria, I am a stranger but close enough to my first homeland to be satisfied. It is relief on my body to be out of America. Something new in the world has opened up to be on this trip with both my family and the woman who, in a year, I'll marry. *Possibility, possibility, possibility.*

TRAVELOGUE, JULY 4, 2019, 10:00 A.M.—WE SQUEEZE EVEN MORE tightly onto the deck of a large ferry. We are many: locals off to see relatives, seeking work, showing foreign wives and new in-laws our old homes; we are tourists European, Black American and white, schoolchildren mimicking a journey our relatives and ancestors took thousands of times. We are laymen and professional merchants hawking cashew nuts, fresh and dried mango, water bottles, and cellphone minutes. I watch the sun hover in a distant haze over an early-morning horizon dotted with fishing boats.

I don't want to rouse suspicion by being one of those tourists who, everywhere they go, is overly moved to gasps and tears, but in Gambia the sun has its own sound. It arrives, a conductor bent over in the sky. Below, local boy children's laughter, shy against the happiness of being together, rolls against their bare chests in the fresh light as they convene for surf lessons. Their laughter breaks the air in two.

I've been letting myself think about my mother more and more. If she were still alive, she'd have slapped some sense into Jamila's first husband. She'd have fallen in love with her second and his country. Alieu, who, like my mother, and like me, can be so shy.

In Gambia, I am a safe-enough distance from my mother and my mother country to dip into the waters of wondering how much of my mother country I have left.

In Barra, both my brother-in-law Alieu and Yusef, our driver turned guide, warn the two-hour-long journey that will deposit us at the shore village of Albadarr, where fishing boats await us in a lull of waves, is treacherous.

TRAVELOGUE, JULY 4, 2019, 12:00 P.M.—WE CRAM INTO AN OPEN jeep with no seatbelts that moves us through overcrowded streets full of people hawking goods and mothers begging with children on their backs, through the strong mollusky stench of ocean and the corpses of sardinella, horse mackerel, shads, catfish, and bonga that the fishermen lay out. The women smoke and salt the fish bodies, unbothered by the flies that hover around them by the hundreds.

The city dissipates to rural roads, thins to villages. Our driver maneuvers, one arm hanging out the window, the other moving back and forth like a windshield wiper as he avoids the craters that dot the road like giant mole holes. In Wolof, Alieu and Yusef wrestle for the precise English words that will properly translate to us the nuances of land and history. At the edge of his seat, my father's eyes grow wide with disbelief and with fear for the rocky road.

Jamila and I had returned to our birth continent in 2004, a year after our mother's death, to pay our respects to my maternal grandmother, Yaya. But our father had not been back to Africa since a work sabbatical in the nineties—a fact he now wears across his face and body.

Beneath the thick tires, the road rocks, its knuckles becoming fists. I stare out at six-foot-tall termite mounds and even taller cashew trees. Baobabs stand like thick-necked lightning against the tapestry of white clouds before the roads give way to dust completely. Yellow trumpets swing from their branches. Palm trees dot the skyline like torches, and every mile, the scent of mango trees trails.

It is a rocky road, but one that, over hundreds of trips throughout the years, our driver has mastered. He laughs, good-bellied, at almost every swerve. He knows the road like we like to think we know our lovers' bodies, remembering every place the earth in front of him bellows or craters. He knows when it's better to drive along the steep edge of the road, the low-seated jeep tipping at an almost forty-five-degree angle. We bounce, bounce, bounce. I, Jamila, and my father look out at our former home continent. The root system feels so close to repairing the wound.

TRAVELOGUE, JULY 4, 2019, 12:45 P.M.—AT THE SHORELINE OF Albadarr, a spattering of merchants sell baskets and small tourist carvings. The island of Kunta Kinteh, both a speck of land and our history, sits like a flat disc on the water. The long, slender fishing boats that will take us the final leg are waiting for their patrons at the end of the dock. Young men and boys balance at the very tips of the bows, waiting to take us on a ten-minute ride to a disappearing place.

At seventy-five, my father has never been on a boat before the large ferry we just rode, a fact he does not disclose until we've been pushed off into the water on this second, much smaller boat fit for ten.

My father clasps his hands over his lap like a church boy, tightly smiling as Jamila and I stare at him with a mixture of amusement and concern.

Despite the smell of rotting sweat wafting off the tattered life jackets we wear, my brother-in-law's face maintains a steady, wide grin. He gently tugs his son's ear, trying and failing to get Nuh, three, to sit still in his lap. Zayd stares up at my father, grinning wildly like a boy looking up at the sky. Though there are sixty-six years between them, they look eerily alike, like echoes of each other peering out from two different vantage points of the same timeline.

Looking to the left, Stephanie touches her chin to her shoulder, her mouth soft, her fingers gripping the wooden benches we sit on, and her brown curls unlooping in the wind as she takes in Africa for the first time. A visual artist and photographer, by the time we got together, Stephanie had already spent the last ten years walking around, searching for the relationship between the built environment and history, photographing the wrought iron fences of American cities that still bear the Adinkra symbols of the enslaved peoples that built them.

It was simple, my coming out. My sister owed me one, and I told her to do it. I was nervous, and wanted to be on the other side of the confession without having to hear whatever my father's initial reaction might be. Jamila called our father up and then he called me, told me, "After your mother died, I promised myself I'd never let anything come between us." And that was that. History, grief, and time had cleaved a clearing for the conversations we'd been afraid to have. A new Black Period had begun.

WITH OUR EYES TOWARD THE DOCK, WE WATCH STUDENTS ON school trips waiting for their turn to be taken to the small island that is both a beacon of memory and a shadow of their country. Despite where and what this boat will lead them to, they flirt. Their skin glowing, their smiles buzzing bright—all of them so young that, in their imagination, history only bears the weight of a feather.

In our boat, the grins of Black Americans, white Europeans, and Gambians spitball at one another. Later, at our hotel, I will wonder, on this continent of my birth now so distant to me—this continent that treats even my brother-in-law as *gone* after an eighteen-year absence— how my Americanness stamps me. Wonder, in this moment, in this continent where I have to hide my queerness, which line Gambians might place me in, white supremacy or Africanness.

We float less on the water and more on its sound.

Behind us, a large white pole with nothing strung to it grows smaller and smaller in the distance. It is the Freedom Pole, and we are instructed to watch it disappear. *This,* our guide says, is how enslavers taunted the enslaved with freedom. Bored, this first generation of British enslavers told people beaten, starved—reduced to the nerve ending of fear—that if, from Kunta Kinteh, they could swim back to shore, touch the pole, freedom would be theirs—one of the many ways our bodies were forced to transform, over and over again, not just into commerce, but also into objects of sport. Here, man and God were dangerous bedfellows. Here, men turned themselves into deities.

And like any god, white enslavers performed mind-boggling feats of cruelty. They were Zeus raping the women, Ares who bore the curses. They were Epiales with nightmares draped across their skins; they were Charon, the ferryman of Hades, dragging our souls through the water; Ker, god of disease and violent deaths. The Book of Genesis's vengeful flood.

TRAVELOGUE, JULY 4, 2019, 1:05 P.M.—NOT EVEN HALFWAY TO the island and the distance we've crossed seems impossible even for the well-fed and healthy. The distance between the end of the world and its beginning, just over eight kilometers.

In the beginning God created the heavens and the earth. The cadence of my childhood nuns spills from my mind and floats across the water. *And the earth was without form, and void; and darkness was upon the face of the deep.* Was it a question of why walk the plank when you could run?

And the Spirit of God moved upon the face of the waters. From the boat, the earth is blue and bright. Freedom's hunger fills the river. Fills every gap between lands. *God said, Let there be light: and there was light.* There was hunger making an impossible distance appear plausible. These, the years crocodile populations swelled. The fact of our bodies in the world changing—feeding—even the seas. Was the hunger to be free the spirit of God or was God the deception?

God who had declared the sun, made no direct claims to making the water. God had only *divided the light from the darkness.* Then, the darkness reigned. Was it as dark as that first decade without my mother?

TRAVELOGUE, JULY 4, 2019, 1:20 P.M.—A GIFT OF THE RIVER, Kunta Kinteh Island—the island of Alex Haley's *Roots* fame—has formerly been known as both James and St. Andrew's. We haven't yet learned from the tour guide that the river is taking Kunta Kinteh back. Formerly six times its current size, thanks to man-made climate change, a lasso of eroding shore maintains a slippery grip on its two remaining acres. Today, it's an ever-shrinking dot in the Gambian River.

From the fifteenth to the nineteenth century, Kunta Kinteh Island played a crucial part in the slave trade. Frequented by merchants and explorers, it served as one of the first zones of cultural exchange between Africa and Europe. Once a Portuguese settlement, Spain, France, Germany, and England all fought for control of the island that helped form the very first trade route to inland Africa, becoming a place where hundreds of thousands of enslaved people were shipped off to the New World.

Once we're docked, the island seems even smaller than it did from a distance, as though something beyond the physical world is eroding below our very feet. People wander in and out of earshot of our tour guide.

We are on a crumbling island, but everywhere the shackles of the world remain intact—the remnants of iron chains, still attached to the stone walls in tiny hovels where ancestors were imprisoned by one colonial empire after the other, to await their day on someone's auction block. I stand where people were sorted, separated, branded, in the ghost outlines marking the room where our names were changed.

I know every decay is the mulch for a new beginning. I'm trying to understand what it was that began here on this continent that, on every map of Pangea, looks like the glue. If in America I lived in the Black Period, Africa had to be the supereon. It was the first bucket of time that held all the rest, and the home where Lucy, the first known human ancestor, got her start. And if we go even further back than that, the trees and greenery that now sprout on Kunta Kinteh were yet to be born. The whole world was still without flowers.

A millennium later, vegetation not meant for land creeps the shore like hands pulling the island down. Roots and sapling trunks pry open cracks in what is left of the rubble. Everywhere, I'm surrounded by a fragile ruin. The split-open faces of former forts and their missing walls gape toward the ghosts of the water. Like any death, it is the skeleton—both on land and in life—that's the last to decay.

Here, on this tiny island of Kunta Kinteh, I am both tourist and blood. Both a stranger and a daughter come home. Some come for tours, or pilgrimages, others for the Year of Return, all have come to witness and to be reminded. To see that, *yes*, there is a reason our Black life looks and feels this way.

In spite of it all, the Black Period was what, with all the tribes turned enslaved people coming together, Africa made in the United States. The Black Period was what collective made out of us. In America, *in the beginning,* we were our own big bang.

ON KUNTA KINTEH ISLAND, I STAND ON TOP OF *THE* PROOF THAT, though history and the present are lovers that unleash on each other an intimate terrorism, they nonetheless hold hands. My witness becoming a way to reinforce that it *had* all, in fact, happened. But still, we of the modern era took a somber but inescapably beautiful journey on a warm day of clear and calm skies, a journey that once, for my ancestors, had been full of death, devils, and terror. My ancestors stared into the heart of darkness and it was a white man. But now, with so much buried/forgotten/washed away, what are people, after seeing this, able to believe?

Beneath my feet, the blood of Kunta Kinteh Island speaks. No schoolbook I ever held ever told our story like this. My back hurts a little less here. On one hand, it's the relief of a few weeks off work, absolved from the daily racism that aggressively dots my days.

From the highest point of the island, an American poses for a picture, his Black Power fist thrust defiantly in the air. Next to him, Alieu is a satisfied man with a son in his arms, one at his hip, and another in my sister's belly. He squints into a distance that for so many of our ancestors who trekked to this island offered only death.

My brother-in-law is a man come home. My brother-in-law is showing his family his family. There is more than enslavement here, there is the space between us—how *what* and *who* survives the shell of oppression tells the story of an island, even after that island is no longer there.

—Jambanjāli—
Leo Season, 2020

> I want to say more than this. I want to do more than recount
> the violence that deposited these traces in the archive.
>
> —SAIDIYA HARTMAN, "Venus in Two Acts"

"PEOPLE TELL ME, 'I DON'T HAVE LAND,' I SHOW THEM THEY DON'T
need it," Nfamara says over video chat. A raspy laugh falls through the
slight gap of his two front teeth. His voice is gravelly but smiling as he
points to tin cans, discarded containers of cooking oil, and rubber
tires. Vegetable plants grow from each.

If Gambia is the smiling coast, then all the Badjies wear it. From
eldest to youngest they are Buba, Isatou, Nfamara, my brother-in-law
Alieu, Fatou, Ebou, Hawa, Alhagi Moduo, and Abdou. Where Alieu is
shy and quiet, his older brother Nfamara, like their eldest brother
Buba, has a personality that turns the volume all the way up. With the
exception of Buba and Abdou, the youngest, who live in Sweden, the
remainder of Alieu's siblings still live in Gambia and all contribute in
some way to the family farm.

This three-hectare plot that overwhelms the eye with green is
their ancestral land. Their parents died over two decades ago and a
year apart, but the way Alieu and his siblings speak of them has me
expecting the parents to walk through the door at any moment. Ask
any Badjie sibling and they'll tell you their father was the best farmer
Gambia's ever seen, that their mother was as sweet as the mango trees
Nfamara grows. Looking at the smiles of Alieu and his siblings, it's
easy to see how the ghosts of two people can hover.

Nfamara studied agriculture in high school and at university, and
later worked for the Gambian Ministry of Agriculture before returning full-time to Jambanjāli to work their family land. But still, even
with all his training, he credits his extensive knowledge of agriculture
to their father. With the help of Buba, a well-known veterinarian in

Sweden—and also the first African/Black contestant on the show *Expedition Robinson 2000* in Sweden, known elsewhere as *Survivor*—they've extended to additional plots for a total of ten hectares.

Brightly painted concrete walls surround the main plot of land that Nfamara tends. Each bears a message on behalf of a begging earth: *Cutting A Tree Without Replanting Is A Crime Against Humanity; Your Destiny Is In Your Own Hands; Our Next Generation Should Not Suffer Because Of I And You; Agriculture Is Both Science And Arts; Make Tree Planting A Hobby.* When it comes to the earth, he wants a different world, though he'll settle for a changed country.

Nfamara smiles with his body and talks with his hands. He holds up a thin piece of jagged Styrofoam that looks ripped from a refrigerator box. On one side of the Styrofoam, a plant has begun to flower, on the other side, webs of roots push through in a tangle. He's tied half-full water bottles to trees. Inside, plant clippings have begun to sprout. Other water bottles he's hung upside down, snaking plastic tubing through them for a homemade irrigation system. A composter, an up-cycler, Nfamara's a leave-no-trace kind of guy.

The summer before, when we'd visited Gambia and the farm, we'd all been stunned by this Eden Nfamara had built. From my father to Jamila to Stephanie to me, we all kept telling him that if this were America, he'd be a rich man. He only laughed good humoredly and shrugged. Listening to Nfamara speak, it strikes me only now that money as a goal is the America in me.

Through a screen and spotty Wi-Fi, he tells me that Gambia imports 60 percent of its food, including its staple, rice. In the evening he'll be going on the radio to talk about the impact of Covid-19 on agriculture. "I'm showing people they can feed themselves with the resources they have," Nfamara says. "What do we do when something like Covid happens and impacts trade, so, you see," he says, turning his wrist over in the way my mother used to do whenever she posed a question without a question's lilt.

Development has taken most of the country's farmland. "Gambia should be growing our own food, thank you." At the farm, they grow cassava, mangos, tomatoes, and a slew of plants I've never heard of.

"When I was a boy, this whole area was forest. You'd see wild tigers and lions. All of that is gone. It rains later ever year, thank you." He speaks in this way, saying "thank you" at the end of every sentence that addresses the land. Today is Nfamara's birthday, and he is in many ways, like me, very much a Leo. And like Leos often do, we instantly like each other. The way the bones of the earth reverberate inside him like a hard-struck tuning fork is another thing we have in common.

ON OUR GAMBIA TRIP THE YEAR PRIOR, MY MOTHER REVERBERATED in me everywhere. I hadn't realized how unsteady I'd been to return to my first continent with Stephanie in tow until we'd landed back in the U.S. It's dangerous to be queer everywhere, from Africa to the States. When I finally moved to NYC in 2012, it was clear the queer mecca that *I* sought—like all meccas for me before—would have to live in my imagination.

My queerness walks a line. You can see it, but it's invisible to the catcallers of men who believe all women are available to them. Stephanie and I seldom hold hands on the streets of our neighborhood. The times we have, we've been hollered at by disappointed or angry Black men who find my queerness in particular a personal slight to them.

Years ago, before we were living together, we walked back to my apartment one evening holding hands. "I know you aren't coming to my neighborhood with that shit." In the darkness, a Black man followed hissing behind us, angry for the four blocks it took for us to get back to my place—which was in the adjoining building of the apartment Stephanie and I occupy now as a married couple, after digitally eloping in our living room four months into the pandemic. You can get used to never being safe anywhere.

In Gambia, I'd been relieved and grateful that, like him, Alieu's siblings were welcoming to both me and Stephanie. By then, I'd already known I wanted to marry her, and we'd already begun making future plans and discussing marriage and a life with kids. Meanwhile, at the restaurant attached to the apartment Alieu and Jamila rented for the summer, Stephanie and I every morning bought fresh juice and—like everywhere outside of our hotel suite—we pretended to be just friends.

In Gambia, Stephanie and I were illegal, just as we were in my birth country, just like we were in so much of America. On that trip, we sat on the back balcony of our hotel suite in bathing suits and straw hats sipping ice coffee, flirting with each other as we pretended not to think of the dual lives we'd always have to live or the pocket-sized closet we'd need to travel with for whenever the world demanded we stuff our queerness back in. But from the hotel suite's tin roof, birds cawed. The children of the Blues—Otis Redding, Sam Cooke, Nina Simone—hung their voices out of our travel speaker—their voices spilling into the bright Gambian mornings, full with memory and the echoes of the queer Blues women who were our ancestors.

I'd been in love with Nina Simone ever since I'd heard her sing "Don't Let Me Be Misunderstood" as a kid. Her voice was like the inside of an heirloom piano that had survived the beautiful impossibility of every Black generation. Even as a child, I immediately recognized her voice as important. There was something in the way she made sound that was directly related to the way, as Black people, we waded these waters we'd been given.

Nina was jazz. She was classical. She was Blues. She was a tuning fork at my ribs and stomach. She was reverberation, reverberation. Her voice knew what it was like to have a body that needed its ache shook out. But above all, her voice, no matter what she sang, made you feel good as brand-new love.

One of our last days in Gambia, the day we visited the farm, we went to a nearby beach where heat, wind, and salt water carried the smell of fishermen and their work. There are so many smells to a country, and I tried my best to capture every one. Rubber burned in the distance. Mangos ripened on their branches, competing with the ocean salt in our noses. I focused hard on breathing in and out. It'd been sixteen years since I'd been in Africa. The distance I felt crashed against the intimacy. It collided with the shore.

.   .   .

ON THAT 2004 TRIP TO NIGERIA THAT JAMILA AND I TOOK TO VISIT
Yaya, I'd stayed for a month and a half, after changing my ticket so I
could remain for an extra two weeks, even after Jamila returned to the
States. With my mother gone, inside Nigeria was the closest to her I
could ever be again, and I wasn't ready to give her up. With my older
cousins, who were the children of my auntie Mairo (who loved me as
much as my aunt Liz did and seemed to find a joy from my presence
that Aunt Sarah should have), Jamila and I were taken from home to
house, where we met my mother's childhood friends and those who'd
known her before she'd emigrated to the U.S. at the age of thirty-five.
The age I am now, which feels so frightening, but such a curious age
to be starting over, and in your spouse's country.

In Nigeria, men I'd never met who were friends of our family
showed up at random intervals to scope Jamila and me out as prospec-
tive wives. But the day I remember more than all the rest was the
day at the hairdresser with my distant cousin, whom we all called
Patience a nickname from a too-long birth that had stuck. Between
cousins, me, and Jamila, we visited the beauty salon a few times over
the course of our trip. With the salon's fans whirring against the rainy
season's mugginess, I sat in a chair that faced a mirror on the opposite
side of the room while my hair was attended to. Nollywood movies
blared from a TV that had been hung from the ceiling corner.

For most of my life, I'd been told and have accepted that I looked
mainly like my father's side of the family. My American grandmother
had strong genes, and from my father to Jamila to me to my nephew,
Zayd, my American grandmother's face is the face that hovers. But in
Nigeria, when we visited my mother's friends and our family, they all
said ah-ah! kai!, smiling whenever I walked in a room. They couldn't
believe how much I looked like my mother. It was new knowledge to
me, and I treasured it.

All over Nigeria, I walked around inside that moment when a single piece of knowledge suddenly makes your whole life different. In
America, it had been obvious to me, by common sense alone, my
mother was unusually beautiful. But in the white worlds I inhabited,
no one ever seemed to respond to her that way.

I'd caught my own reflection in the beauty salon's mirror and was taken aback. A ghost stared out. For the first time in my life, I saw my mother all over my face. We had the same nose. We had the same way of burying our chins in our chests to guard our laughs. Our dimples were twins. Was this genes or apparition?

In that beautician's chair I couldn't stop turning my chin to look at my reflection, but also, there was a woman, a beautician's assistant, who couldn't stop looking at me. *Was this flirting?* It was flirting. Looking like my mother, I was feeling, for the first time, truly beautiful instead of simply being a girl with "nice features," which always seemed to connect to my paper-bag lightness.

Feeling swollen with courage and confidence, I stared back. The woman was cute. But I had to be careful, with my cousin Patience there. As clear as any memory, I can see that woman sweeping the floor, sweeping her way toward me and leaning into my ear to whisper, *You're very beautiful.* Thank you, I whispered shyly, awkwardly back.

Even to this day, I've never quite mastered the art of the flirt. Always feeling a little too awkward, too shy, too obvious, too much like a simulacrum of an ideal, and never wanting to risk the embarrassment of thinking I'm wanted by someone who's not wanting me. Compounded by my uncomfortableness at being on the receiving end of a compliment, if I happen to realize someone is flirting with me, it always takes me by surprise, and I fumble the ball. But after the woman had leaned in and whispered into my ear, whenever someone was going to the beauty salon, I volunteered to tag along.

The woman oscillated between long looks in my direction and assisting the other beauticians, as they all spoke in their language and laughed. Did they *know*, I wanted to know? Their laughter toward the woman who flirted with me seemed like friendly teasing. Was she *out*? Was there a world in my origin land where a queer woman could have freedom, safety, *and* friends? And how could I arrange for us to have a moment alone? I could tag along to the store when she went out to buy drinks. I could stand outside the shop hoping she'd take a break.

The last time we visited the beauty shop, I remember how deeply Patience sucked her teeth as we drove away. Her whole body making a *smch* sound—a reminder that the sacred sound could turn on you. "*Ah-ah,* there was something wrong with that girl. The way she kept staring at you," Patience said, disgusted, as she went on to tap her temple and wonder out loud if the woman was "slow" or "sick in the head." I didn't know if Patience was just talking out loud or if she was sending a message. Either way, I heard her loud and clear. It was like the walls of the car were collapsing in. The heat of the whole country concentrated inside of me. I was humiliated, horrified, scared to death, blacking out into the want of my whole erasure.

A year or so later, Patience would come to South Carolina to visit my mother's grave. I remember watching Patience zigzag around one grave, then another, not wanting to disrespect other people's ancestors. When it came to queerness, it turned those you loved and those who loved you into two different people. On one hand so careful with the dead, and on the other hand, the living queer so disposable. If, in the U.S., I was God's abomination, in Nigeria, I felt like Allah's, too.

As we drove away from the beauty salon, I sat in the backseat of the car next to Patience, and without ever discussing it, we both decided I'd never go back. Driving away from the flirting woman for the very last time, I stared out the window. I inhaled my birth country looking like the woman Patience and I desperately missed.

∞

Back in Gambia, on a farm in Jambanjãli, Nfamara holds me in the palm of his hand. He walks me around the farm by spotty cellphone and shows me the saplings of trees he knows won't reach maturity till long after his lifetime. "The bark of this tree will cure constipation. All these ones are good for asthma." He's traveled up to four hundred kilometers to fetch a single clipping from an endangered tree. More than farming, he's trying to bring Gambia's extinct species back.

Like the way development ruins the land and everything natural to it, everywhere in the world, the world is trying to make queerness extinct. And yet, everywhere I am illegal, my existence is ancient. The fact of my queerness is as old as these trees in Gambia that are running out. All along the transatlantic slave trade, Europeans imported homophobia in at the same time they were exporting African bodies out, all to further justify the continent's need to be colonized. But what does an origin story like *that* mean for queerness now? My own queerness wants to know.

I thought back to being in Gambia the summer prior. However we all were navigating it—me, Stephanie, my father, my nephews, Jamila, Alieu, the Badjies—all of us were creating a world, even if small, where queerness could breathe. Maybe together, we were another version of that moment in Nigeria at the hairdresser's—a queer woman flirting across a room, her courage encouraged by her friends. Maybe, not everything is lost. Or, to conjure Sehgal again, "What would it look like to emerge from erasure?"

Could it look like *this*? Could it look like *us*?

Nfamara and I hang up. I think of him bringing back to life what capitalism and settler colonialism have culled via development, oppression, and extraction. Nfamara cares about the land in a way I've never seen. As though to sleep, he digs a hole in the earth, roots, and gives himself back to the night.

∞

EARTH, WIND & FIRE

AGE XI

REVELATIONS

Y FATHER ONCE TOLD ME, "IN NATURE, THERE'S no such thing as a straight line." He was talking about art and observation, but he could have easily been talking about history. How it is only the hand of man that draws a straight line, whether it be on the page or in a textbook, where straight lines are drawn to erase a crime or someone else's story. It was a Nigerian woman—my mother—who showed me that we only need to look at a map of Africa or America to see how the ruler of settler colonialism vivisected land, tribe, and home into straight lines, intentionally leading directly to structural collapse, disease, poverty, community discord. That it leads right to all this wind and fire that we've turned into climate disaster.

At the tippy-top of Runyon Canyon, I shove down my distaste for needless danger and heights, hoping my back will hold. Daniel leans in with his six-foot-five frame, peeks over the edge. The bump in his nose and his muscles make him a well-read Greek statue with softly styled brown hair. Around us, California is lost to routine. Dogs scamper recklessly off their leashes. At 2.7 miles, Runyon Canyon reaches an elevation of 1,320 feet, all hikeable. And it is hiked by the most beautiful people of all colors, shapes, creeds, sexualities, and genders, bearing the whitest smiles I have ever seen.

Eyes shining like a childhood photograph, Daniel laughs my favorite laugh at how the canyon guards itself with so little: no ropes, no guardrails. Around us, the sky is clear like a tricky, beautiful Medusa. The ground beneath us so rocky, the paths so narrow, amongst a violently daring lack of safety precautions. Pinching his muscle tank between two of my fingers, I yank Daniel back from the edge. Beyond our view, large patches of Los Angeles stand completely blackened.

Behind a mountain range sits a formerly green state park torn apart by fire. All around us, all these Edens, burning, dying, gone.

FOR THESE RECENT ROUNDS OF CALIFORNIA WILDFIRES, THE WIND has blown in Daniel and his partner Steven's favor, sending both the smoke and flames west. On one side of the mountain, an illusion of a clear day. On the other: a mother can't see her child's hand in front of her face. Between New York and California, Daniel and I are like windup walkie-talkies. One of us in the city whose trash never sleeps but instead piles up higher and higher, and for longer periods of time, as the neighborhoods move from white to brown, Asian, and Black. The other, now in a city of celestial and cement stars, burning brush, drought. The both of us inhabit the safest cities possible for our queerness, cities that, come any disaster or emergency, will be too congested to flee.

Meanwhile, 2,419 miles away in Columbia, South Carolina, hurricane season is underway. Not having lived in the same state as my father for over a decade, he resides in both South Carolina and my imagination. From the top of a California canyon, I see my father inspecting the yard around his house. He gathers scrap wood, loose nails, the power tools he uses for framing, random pieces of rope, metal and iron, a bowl of bottle caps, and the empty shells of found bullets—all of which he's sure he can find a place for in his next drawing or painting. He jostles loose two outdoor sculptures that have reclaimed their deep depression in the ground, once again, like the previous year, gingerly laying them sideways in the grass. He lets out a soft, low groan that reveals he's taking his time to bend his replaced hips carefully.

My father knows better than to stray outside the earshot of a warning. Columbia, South Carolina's capital, is two hours from the coast, where the smell of pluff mud and Confederate jasmine overtake the senses. From Charleston—a beach city most famously known as the setting of Pat Conroy novels and for the slave-trade hub at James Island—Columbia inherits a hand-me-down weather. And the news has already warned my father, Hurricane Charley/Joaquin/Matthew/Irma/Florence/Dorian is on the way.

In the Lowcountry, those who can afford to evacuate on the interstates from Charleston or Hilton Head, where all roads lead inland to Columbia, the state having reversed all lanes into a one-way arrow. Those who can't afford to leave, who get the orders last, or who cite *evacuation fatigue* after years of locking their homes up to uncertainty, are left behind—receivers to a storm.

A reminder that not all choices are willingly made, they hunker down, hope, stay. And though a hurricane means death is on its way, the winds have yet to pick up.

The dead-not-yet-dead bear no familiar or familial names.

Like my father, Daniel's parents want to know what their children are prepared for. Where, in a hypothetical world turned real, our generation will flee. Some say Canada, others Europe. I do the math. Climbing the canyon, the sun smiling, I ask Daniel, Y'all got a go-bag? Ask if they've taught their cats, Wolfgang Fireball and Purrtricia Ourcat, their safe words. Together, me and Daniel's preparedness boils down to a few cases of bottled water and two overindulgent senses of humor. Still, even though we are both queer, in the apocalypse, our difference will split us.

A white man in America, history has given Daniel a safety net. His father, a retired Virginia Tech professor—and physicist at VT during the shooting that claimed the lives of thirty-two—inherited a farm in North Carolina that he's been retrofitting with solar panels for the end of the world. If it comes to it, Daniel thinks that's where he and Steven will go. But, like most Black families in America, the Geters—despite all the land we've worked—have no land to inherit or pass down. No southern nooks that in dire times can realistically be beacons of safety. Not a single gun.

Around Daniel and me, people sprint the narrow paths as though, beyond lacking a fear of death, they want to test it. Already Black in America, the additional risk of this steep-edged canyon sends the tension in my body and my chronic pain into overdrive. My country is always trying to extinguish me. Still, I can't afford to die.

As an artist, my father's life's work has been in witness. As a layman, he tracks the uptick of deadly disaster and its finger-like tentacles we can both see spreading across the globe. Regardless of the hundreds of miles between us, I know my father is thinking of a coming danger that is not only his. He's thinking something bigger is coming.

Even from this Runyon Canyon vantage point, my mind hears him pointing his voice skyward, still unable to find more than a hairsbreadth of difference between himself, his children, and those whom FEMA comes last to rescue. My father, the widower, is thinking of Katrina or Maria now, his face a grimace, his eyes the wet before tears. He is thinking of his mother and grandmother, who worked hard to give him and my aunts access to the kind of life that would allow them something that was theirs to protect. Thinking of how the extractive conditions of white America birth the storms that, so quickly, wash life away, and what comes next for Black and brown people after devastation. He is thinking of how my grandmother, having already fled once, would be surprised to find her only son back here, on the southern side of freedom. Every coming disaster kicking loose the sediment of my father's old but never outdated fears.

I know how a coming storm injects an extra shot of weariness into his joints. I see him there: right hand on his hip, elbow cocked out, left hand resting on his left knee like a kickstand to steady himself against arthritis and the foreshadow of winds.

African/American, queer, intellectually and spiritually militant for Blackness—and one day, I hope, with a family in tow—in Armageddon, I will be conspicuous. It's like a movie about the apocalypse, except movies don't cast me in the aftermath—despite Black folks having passed through the end of the world more than once. Amid all this climate disaster, even if the world stands in the end, I worry if our bodies will.

AS DANIEL AND I HIKE TO THE TOP OF THE CANYON, FOR A BEAT, the drought surrounding me slips away. We move from topic to topic, laughing easily in and out of conversations we immediately forget. Together, Daniel and I enjoy the Indigenous Peoples of Los Angeles's land, though, if there is a plaque that marks the fact, it is nondescript enough that I don't see it.

The Gabrielino-Tongva/Kizh—also known as the San Gabriel Mission Indians, the Gabrieleño Band of Mission Indians, Gabrieleño, Gabrielino, Tongva, and Kizh—once relied on this canyon for their seasonal campsite, where they hunted in an area they called the Nopalera. Before the Gabrielino-Tongva/Kizh's displacement by the United States government, they built their villages in the Los Angeles Basin and their homes along rivers. Tongva refers to "people of the earth" and "Kizh" is derived from the willow houses they lived in. Both namings encapsulate the idea of home, and signal toward how they inhabit their own lands. The original 405 freeway, one of the three main portals that connects the San Fernando Valley and the Los Angeles Basin, was built on top of the Gabrielino-Tongva/Kizh Nation's ancestral footpath through Sepulveda Canyon.

A tourist, I've read that what can daisy-chain two canyons is the Colorado River, from which LA gets most of its drinking water. This single force of a river makes Runyon and the Grand Canyon touch. Through a series of pipes, before LA's water reaches the Colorado, it runs into Lake Havasu, which derives its name with the Havsuw 'Baaja tribe, who call the base of the Grand Canyon home, and who share the other end of the Colorado River. Between the Gabrielino-Tongva/Kizh and the Havsuw 'Baaja, the river sits—it's the living embodiment of two cans and a string.

But *how* do you *own* a canyon?

Where does naming come from?

The Gabrielino-Tongva/Kizh—this seven-thousand-year-old tribe—were dubbed Tongva by ethnographer C. Hart Merriam in the middle of the last century. Interviewing one of the tribe members, Mrs. James Rosemyre (née Narcisa Higuera), at Fort Tejon, Merriam asked her the name of her tribe. Back then, the Indigenous Peoples of Los Angeles referred to themselves by proximity, by the villages they inhabited. And so, when Merriam asked Rosemyre the name of her people, she said the name of her home village (and the original name for the Mission San Gabriel): Toviscangna. What the white man could not fully comprehend became *Tongva*.

California recognizes the Gabrielino-Tongva/Kizh as the Gabrieleño Band of Mission Indians, after the Spanish missions planted like weeds along the Gabrielino-Tongva/Kizh's territory—missions they were enslaved to build.

IF THE BODY BOTH HAS AND INHERITS MEMORY, WHAT IS IT OUR bodies remember?

From the top of a canyon in California, I can still see my father standing in his backyard in South Carolina, bending like his grandmother picking another man's cotton in a Georgia field; like his mother cleaning another woman's house in Alabama, then Ohio. My father, bending into the possibility he could be out there all day.

As the winds pick up, I know, too, so does a familiar worry that a force beyond his control will wrap its hands around his life. It is a ghost worry, a worry that holds the strife he's lived, the strife he's witnessed, the strife that lives in the memory of Black blood and bone, and the strife that he, a father, grandfather, and griot, tries to suss out of our futures.

It's always one more thing, my father surely thinks, with no time to consider that the mixture of exhaustion, fear, and worry is punctuated by a body memory from a history we live in the perpetual present—a history that belongs to not just him. How else to explain that my father, a painter and teacher, bends like the child of sharecroppers whose body has inherited the physical memory of being someone's slave?

Everywhere Daniel and I look, there is so much land I barely understand it. Can barely fathom the valleys of blood that run beneath. By white hands, Runyon Canyon has been sold at least seven times, never once to any benefit to the Gabrielino-Tongva/Kizh. Disinherited—renamed—the Gabrielino-Tongva/Kizh were homeless on their homeland. Arrested for their dispossession, they were turned into prisoners and forced to work off their bail. Today, there are around five hundred Gabrielino-Tongva/Kizh Nation members, though it is believed that the official population is closer to three thousand people.

What would it look like to emerge from erasure?

Inside me echo Sehgal's words. But how does anyone emerge from an erasure like *this*? Having been robbed of their language, in modern times, many of the Original Peoples of Los Angeles use Kizh, or Tongva—a reclamation of their identity, their heritage, and their right to name themselves: Tongva, Kizh, Gabrielino-Tongva/Kizh. Perhaps this is one answer.

I IMAGINE THE AIR AROUND MY FATHER. HE IS ALREADY IN THE embrace of an ominous stillness that guarantees something stronger is coming. Far enough inland that he won't need wood boards or nails, instead, from the outside, he secures the windows of the front room where he keeps his largest pieces of artwork with thick sheets of corrugated cardboard and good tape. He is distant enough from imminent danger, but close enough to know that he could lose a tree. Other neighbors have. Some cut them down or back in anticipation. Storm after storm thins shade from the streets, turning the neighborhood bald.

His modest and racially mixed community circles a man-made lake that interrupts Sandy Branch, a natural stream running for 1.4 miles as it quietly spills a little bit of itself into one passing stream after another. Water you cannot swim in in the increasingly hot summers, there have been times I've visited when the lake stunk as though an invisible factory was sitting on its chest. In the last century, South Carolina has warmed, by some estimates, almost a full degree. Every decade the sea creeps up in inches, eroding the beaches—which, every year, another hurricane attempts to destroy.

In South Carolina, the ground is sinking. Wetlands can't keep pace. Fleeing starvation, one day the egrets will migrate themselves into endangerment. Sooner than I like to think, as salt marshes disappear, shrimp, oysters, and catfish will become delicacies even in shore towns. And despite all this water, from the skies and the seas, drought will come for the crops. Livestock will be harder to breed and milk. Which is all to say, shit rolls down hill—jobs will go: from the farms, fisheries, distributors, restaurants, and retailers.

At the very top of Runyon, referred to as "Indian Rock"—a name that signifies the wrong gaze—Daniel and I laugh into one another as foliage crawls across the canyon. All of Los Angeles—the Hollywood sign, the skyscrapers, the burnt tips of trees made invisible in the distance—licked by a breathtaking, blue morning haze.

The beauty is a mirage over the newscasters who, rehearsed but solemn, report on the millions of acres of California already lost to wildfire the prior year. A mirage over the prison labor that once again saves the day, as inmates hustle up in chain-gang formation, their matching orange uniforms striped with neon to keep them surveilable at night. Having demonstrated a history of nonviolence, the inmates are paid two dollars a day to run toward fire.

Though they are there saving the homes of those whose histories and freedoms keep them in prison, when released, their criminal records will prohibit them from becoming firefighters—much like they are banned from participating in the lucrative, now legal, majority-white economy of recreational marijuana dispensaries. Instead, once released, they will be cast back into an invisible land—one that, even for the non-Black, will resemble Black space—and this soft morning haze that takes my breath away is mostly smog. But for now, across this beautiful, stolen landscape that is almost guaranteed to burn, these human beings—who will be labeled "criminals" even when free—when called, will rush into someone else's fires. So many fires the local news can barely keep track.

Less than thirty miles south of where Daniel and I stand, even though my eyes can't see it, I feel the city of Compton. That *we-ness* of Blackness calling me out.

Before N.W.A.'s legendary 1988 rap album, *Straight Outta Compton*, and its infamous track, "Fuck tha Police," the community-run Communicative Arts Academy "held Compton as canvas and muse, renovated buildings across the city, and transformed vernacular, underutilized structures into venues for and objects of art," writes Jenise Miller, a Compton-based Black Panamanian writer and urban planner. From the 1960s into the 1970s, the CAA was a hub of Black power and Black pride. Funded by the Office of Economic Opportunity (OEO), the CAA set up in a vacant skating rink they called the Arena and transformed it into multiuse studios and a community center. At its height, the organization had a two-hundred-seat playhouse, a sculpture workshop, a darkroom, a dance-and-recording studio, and an orchestra. It held over seventy different classes and attracted celebrities like Muhammad Ali. Today, the Arena is the site of a shopping mall.

At the end of 1972, the Nixon administration and the OEO discontinued its funding. After three years of trying to fund themselves, the CAA was forced to close permanently. But it was because of the CAA's work with the Black artist Elliott Pinkney that the walls and buildings of Compton became Pinkney's canvas. Most of Pinkney's eight murals have been lost to time, but thanks to restoration, a few can still be seen, including *Beacon of Hope* at West Fifty-second and Main.

Today, Compton lives in the popular culture as a scene from movies like John Singleton's *Boyz n the Hood*, or Ice Cube's iconic "Bye, Felicia" *Friday*—due, in part, to an influx of drugs that the Reagan administration allowed to flood into Black neighborhoods, and the militarized policing tactics that followed. It's a city where most Black children will experience an array of complex traumas inflicted by way of poverty, racism, LGBTQ discrimination, environmental racism, ableism, gun, and domestic, sexual, and/or police violence. A city where many young people have already experienced more violences than many soldiers, all of which reshapes the architecture of developing brains, creating devastating obstacles to learning.

But Compton is also the same city where students in the Compton Unified School District (CUSD) filed their 2015 federal class action suit to have their complex traumas acknowledged under federal disability protections. It's the city where Black and brown students and teachers, not knowing what the future held, provided students at Havasupai Elementary—who also have disabilities caused by complex traumas—exactly what, in a few years, they'd need to win their own suit: legal precedent.

In the corner of my eye, I catch a glint of something that wobbles my knees. I follow the dominoes like my parents taught me, thinking of Black people, the *we* of us that, like my father, makes me sing. In the sky, an invisible god sucks their teeth at me, asking, by now, don't I know, loving and being obliged to only *my* own ancestors won't do. It's not enough. I owe something to the students of Havasupai Elementary. I owe a debt to the Gabrielino-Tongva/Kizh.

Standing on stolen ground, next to a white man who, despite all the American history between us, I have allowed myself to deeply love, I think of the different and many kinds of courage that both

Daniel and I will need. My body swirls inside the climate of the sky and the climate of a country, unable to tell the difference. My mind runs to a future, to 2050, where the number of heat-wave days is set to quadruple from fifteen to almost sixty, and where I am sixty-six and it is already five years after the greatest fear of white America has come to fruition, turning them into the majority-minority. By then, perhaps all these stolen canyons will be unhikeable.

The dirt trails of Runyon stretch out like a carnival-game tongue. Its hills rise and fall.

What, exactly, is in a name?

Like this canyon, in this country, my mother was seldom called by her native name. Hauwa was a broken origin story on an American tongue. Her original meaning left behind in the lacuna. Not until I was a graduate student in poetry would I realize my parents had unknowingly named me after Hafiz, the fourteenth-century Persian and Sufi Muslim poet. Until then, I had only met one person in the world with my name, Jamila's best friend's mother. In our childhoods, Iram was a girl with a wide laugh and a serious undercurrent that revealed she was the child of the fleeing kind of immigrants. Her father and her mother, Hafiz, were the Muslim children of Partition.

Growing up, whenever Iram's mother came to fetch her, though we came from different lands, bloods, histories, and violences, I watched her secretly and greedily. My name, in her presence, suddenly a plural possibility. There were *two* of us. And we were the memorizers, the protectors—the poets—of the unsaid and silences. And, too, there was the thrill of the quiet being broken: the hot-blooded excitement of hearing my name for the first time said in another's direction, knowing our names signified, somewhere behind us, we had far more in common. Now, the students in Compton and the students at Havasupai Elementary, and the fight that lives in all of them, reminds me of this all over again.

At the top of Runyon, despite fire, despite storm, I can hear my father singing in South Carolina. Singing from our Black Period. This habit of his that, come hell or high water, his whole life he's never been able to break. I've been taught to live, love, and thrive where colored folks do, in the contradictions. My father's hope, despite all this weather, is a truth I am rooted from. All this burning, and still, I believe, unshakably, we can win—that we already are. That if we keep drawing our maps toward each other, we can never be erased.

In the Compton suit, students and teachers argued that the complex trauma that their communities face is so pervasive that more individual trauma counselors were both needed and not enough. *All* faculty and support staff, they insisted, had to be trained. They legally declared what, inside Black and Indigenous Black Periods, has long been established: to raise a child a village is not only *required,* a village is what a child is owed.

Still, it surprises me to read that, after the courts denied the CUSD's motion to dismiss the case, rather than litigate against the community it's obliged to, the CUSD chose to collaborate, launching its Wellness Initiative. The information sprung from me a happy laugh. I'd almost forgotten that we can work together, it doesn't always have to be a fight. I have spent too much time missing only my own ancestors.

I think of one day living in LA, in this state plagued by earthquakes, wildfires, mudslides, drought, and flooding, full of polluted cities. A place where Stephanie and I, in our queerness, might more easily hold hands, but where the federal government still refuses to provide the Gabrielino-Tongva/Kizh—this seven-thousand-year-old tribe with federal recognition, and thus federal aid. America's attempt to finish the work of erasure that settler colonialism began through genocide.

Still, in what the Gabrielino-Tongva/Kizh name themselves, I find a history, a truth, a story not just resurfaced but claimed, a story that, after an erasure, the Gabrielino-Tongva/Kizh have written back in— *home—their* bespoke Black Period.

AS PART OF THE CUSD'S WELLNESS INITIATIVE, TEACHERS, ADMINistrators, and support staff receive training to help them understand the effects that trauma has on students' ability to learn, with the goal of creating trauma-sensitive classrooms and environments safe for

learning. They are taught repair over punishment, a move that re-
duces the school-to-prison pipeline by cutting off the source that fuels
it—our children—and by inextricably tying educational justice to the
work of prison abolitionists and those working to defund the police.
"Hope," Kaba says, "is a discipline," and "abolition is the praxis that
gives us room for new visions and allows us to write new stories."

This new model of education, fought for by Compton students
who, like Havasupai Elementary students, refuse to be thrown away,
has improved academic achievement. Between 2015 and 2019, stan-
dardized testing showed that literacy and math proficiency both in-
creased 15 percent. Graduation rates rose a significant 7.7 percent and,
in 2017, the school district transitioned from an "orange-level" suspen-
sion rate to zero expulsions in a school district with over twenty-three
thousand students.

I think of the CAA and how, even though state divestment forced
them to close, half a century later, it still serves as a model for
community-based arts all over Compton.

"You have to act as if it were possible to radically transform the
world. And you have to do it all the time," says Angela Davis, attesting
to the power of the "not yet." Like the end of North American slavery
and the work of abolition, the hope of the "not yet" is rooted in that
which is im/possible, and in the understanding that the present lacks
the imagination necessary to fully conceive the potential of the future.

And though the progress is incremental, and though, in the face of
all our varied historical traumas, the victories can feel so small, I can't
help but think that this is the genius of community. Compton, this city
that lives in the popular imagination as exclusively poor, Black, Latinx,
gang-riddled, and swollen with bullets, is also the same city filled with
the same people that provided the students in the Havasupai Elementary case precedent—instantly making the *we* of all of our communities bigger. How can I look away from that?

TA-NEHISI COATES WRITES IN *BETWEEN THE WORLD AND ME,* SPEAK-ing of white supremacy, "They made us a race. We made ourselves into a people." It's a people, not a race, that makes hope a social space. Hope *is* dangerous because, like Blackness, in its social function, hope changes communities and thus economies. Black hope is deadly to the racial capitalism that built and buttresses America precisely because it's the lie of America that our hope calls into question.

Maybe being raised by an artist has made me susceptible to hope. Cornel West says that America produces consumers, and a democracy of consumers is but a simulacrum of itself, but art produces citizens. Hope, then, is both an art and an antidote to capitalism, and thus against destruction.

What if *this* is how we emerge from erasure?

By insisting that the state prioritize their mental health and help them to develop coping mechanisms around their complex traumas, the students in CUSD revealed the miracles we can make for each other. Robin Wall Kimmerer's reminder, "If one tree fruits, they all fruit." We are a *we*—"there are no soloists."

Grabbing Daniel's bicep, my back begins to spasm. If we don't leave soon, he will be carrying me down. Stray goats stand absurdly on inch-wide ledges, my reminder: we are the ones pushing in. The returning greenery of the hills buries and grows up from all the blood that's been spilled.

Somewhere, smoldering embers are still catching California dry brush. Some spread, some turn to ash, float along the highways. Somewhere, flames, like lava, blur hell and heaven into a single horizon. Somewhere, what burns eventually drowns—into lakes, streams, reservoirs, and drinking water. And though it's a reality that if I open or close my eyes, California will be on fire, I could move to LA just for what's left of the trees. I think of my father in his art studio. He grips a piece of charcoal, draws a version of a dark woman with a tree growing out of her every seam. She is Black. She is African. She is both my auntie and a stranger. We are people of the natural world.

In one oil painting, the legs of an African woman in a yellow dress give way to roots as she stands in a desert. In another charcoal drawing, an African woman stares out, a grimace of resolve and determination on her face that the viewer would do best to take as a challenge. Her hair, kinky, grows out from her head, turns to branches, then to another bird in flight. My father, skeptical to the notion of God, is still always trying to get us to heaven.

BEFORE OUR DESCENT, DANIEL AND I GAPE OUT INTO THIS LAND WE don't call Gabrielino-Tongva/Kizh Canyon. I do my best to look in all directions and see that rendering our Black Periods amidst the violence of a stolen country, and our insistence on our right to name ourselves, is something that Black and African people hold in common with the Gabrielino-Tongva/Kizh.

I see my American great-grandmother, the land beneath her stolen, her knuckles gnarled from one of its many poisonous fruits: cotton

I see my grandmother, Yaya, her Nigerian life marked by British colonization. Time: the string between us. The people forgotten—not actually gone.

I see my father drawing us growing from the earth.

WEIGHING OF THE HEARTS

AGE XII

JOY

when the smell of midnight thickens on the carpet
coalesce the words. Chase them. Until they scatter
out of your mouth.

—SHELELL FREEMAN, aka Ai Elo,
"A Lesson on Scatting Under the Influence"

Yaya, I watched you outlive a daughter. Watched you survive stroke after stroke. The first grandmother, in the first country, I ever knew, illness, my mother, and Nigeria are the languages we had in common. Though this is me forgetting that, like my mother, like my uncle Muhammad, Uncle Garba, like Auntie Mairo, and Auntie Asabe, I, too, carry your cheekbones. That I walk around looking like both my grandmothers. Looking like the gap between Nigeria and Georgia.

What I don't know about you I remember clear as day. What you don't know of me is the story you authored. In the living world we briefly inhabited together, we had no words for me to translate myself to you, not Hausa, not English—we barely even had *this*: our shared birth country. But we did have the blood.

In this place your feet never touched, I've feared I would live myself out of country, house, home. There were times there was no one to call when I needed to say: *body*.

With you now in some Jannah, finally returned to Hauwa—*Eve*— perhaps it will be easier to speak.

Yaya, some think this new world a hoax. In America, doctors cry and beg for ventilators. Like always, Black and brown folks die first—most. With the streets around the park closed to cars, parents shout out behind homemade medical masks, "You've got it!" "Hold straight!"—their children trying for the first time to ride with training wheels off. Covid-19 weaves its way through our hair, their wheels, the wind. It's a pandemic world, a community project. For any of us to live, a stranger's got to love you. When it comes to Africa and the Western-dominated vaccines, you know our shared birth continent is in trouble. Meanwhile, my current one swells with lethal anti-Asian sentiment.

I've been trying to either outrun or emerge from so many erasures. Written history leaves me straddled across the unknown, the deletions, all that's left to tell. Yaya, who I always remember laughing, did I learn my sadness from you?

Meaning "black bile," melancholia gets its name from the Greek. It's a feeling that has no top, heart, or base notes—has no scent at all. An absence that seeps out from the body, it's loss defined by an "excess of."

For Freud, melancholia was disease. It was like holding loss up to a mirror and having the only thing reflected back at you be *you*. In *Mourning and Melancholia*, Freud distinguishes mourning to be "the reaction to the loss of a loved person or to the loss of some abstraction which has taken the place of one, such as fatherland, liberty, an ideal, and so on." These losses are also at the root of melancholia, but with melancholia the gap made never closes, the absence becomes indistinguishable from the self. It's duende meets saudade. For these purposes, let's call all of the above—the beloved, the land, the freedom, and the archetype—*Hauwa*.

Below you: stars.
Canis Minor—
"little dog"

Yaya, Ancient Egyptians named this constellation Anubis, after
their jackal-headed god and guardian of the dead.

In Gambia, where three of your great-grandsons live, the Serer
people believe the jackal the first animal on earth. The jackal knows
who will die, who will soon be attending a funeral. Soothsayers, every
one.

Having outlived the death of a child, you were a new kind of mother. We, the grandchildren you hadn't seen in over a decade, had come to witness and be witnessed. With the money our parents saved for their first empty-nest vacation, our father sent us to you, hoping our presence might salve the freshly broken link between generations. We, who buried your daughter in the place she lived but that I'd never once heard her call home. Guilt makes me want to dig the woman between us up. My love won't leave anyone alone. With me, not even the dead rest. Mistake me for the jackal.

Ah-ah, Jamila, Hafizah—
Hafizah, Jamila. Ah-ah.

That last time we saw you, you couldn't stop saying our names, couldn't stop yourself from laughing as tears cascaded down your face.

I sat there watching my mother's phonemes sing out of your mouth. Your body heavy with its loss of control, your face still beautiful despite the teeth that had abandoned it, the second stroke that tugged one half down—despite the jackal leaning his breath against our windows.

In Hausa, you smiled. You begged Mimi, your eldest daughter's youngest child, to translate your grief over not having a shared tongue. Our laughs finding each other despite language's generational divide.

You raised a daughter who could not speak of the past, which meant she could not speak of you. With her dead all these years, I understand the impulse to hoard the memory of someone because you fear losing their reality. You could not read or write, but the ghost of you in America made legible a life where books could be my freedom song. With your name never on her lips but still swimming inside of her, your daughter, book by book, built a bridge back home for her children—from *Anansi the Spider* to *The People Could Fly*. In America, these were the stories my mother knew how to give.

Melancholy, Greek gods named Oizys. Of course, a woman. She is daughter of Nyx, goddess of night, and twin to Momus, god of mockery. In Greek mythology, melancholy is made of immaculate conception, not from the violence that swims through every one of their mythological worlds. Vengeance paints their gods, who are always depicted white. Prometheus loses his liver every night. Dionysus is cut from his mother's womb by Zeus. Zeus, who condemns Atlas to hold up the whole sky. I am like Atlas in this way, my body holding up the burden of a country made of myth and lies.

A myth can form mountains.

In another Atlas myth, Perseus, half-god/half-man, wielding the face of the beheaded Medusa, turns Atlas to stone.

In North Africa, Atlas names the folded mountains that stretch out, held together like a string of pearls, from Morocco to Tunisia. The Atlas Mountains stare out into the Atlantic Ocean, whose name is derived from the same. Atlas—this Titan, this pre-Olympian god who bears the weight of the heavens—is both stone and water. Simultaneously witness, bystander, vehicle, and grave to the transatlantic slave trade. It is Atlas who sees all—the stars in the skies, the hells made of the waters—but whose truths remain unable to rectify the lies of history.

I know I'm American because I accept my pleasures at every cost. I have become wholly a citizen of a country that convinces itself there's no line it can't come back from. But history is as much a weapon as it is a shield, and U.S. empire is the silencer on the gun.

I am afraid to imagine you, who represents all we've gained and lost. They say the jackal is a lonely thing. In the Bible it is the animal shape taken on by abandonment and desolation. It makes homes out of the former cities and towns left by humans, scavenges the flesh of whatever is left. Monogamous, territorial, some lore calls it opportunism—cunning—this will the jackal has to live. It is both in my mind and in the ruins that the jackal takes up residence.

Beyond trying to fill the gap of the daughter who died, I only have four kinds of memories of you:

- 1991, when our mother brought me and Jamila back to you and our country three years after we'd emigrated. Six years old, I hadn't remembered another woman could look so much like my mother.
- The black gourd you pounded yams in that sits on a high shelf in my office.
- The likeness of you in the portraits that my father drew and painted.
- And the charcoal fabrication he made of you crouching before a large basin in the Zaria dirt that I wear tattooed on my right forearm. It stares into the eyes of your American twin—an oil painting of his mother tattooed on my left.

We are either the jackal or the jackal's scraps. We are the empty-bellied in a country that criminalizes hunger. Rising temperatures hunt us while epidemiologists pray heat will quell disease. What a country does to you when it believes you too animal to feel pain—but *painpainpain* in the root system anyway.

Snake oil from the president. Puerto Rico—Maria—forgotten. Earthquakes, hurricanes. Floods wider than the name Noah. The patience of a country willing to kill you slow as a chokehold. Slow as a knee pressed against your neck. Who can hold us now, our bodies deadly with virus. Call it Covid-19. Call it *Yes, sir, officer.* Call it any name you like, as long as you call it America.

In America, nothing can fully protect someone who looks like us. Not the King's English, a high-cotton attitude, or a Black or African name. Still, as though trying to outrun the mouths of our colonizers, Black folks give their children names that dance like lavender on the nose. Lavante (Biggs), Dajuan (Graham), Kyam (Livingston).

We are the remixers of everything in this country, even sound itself.

Some give their children names that mark the next generation with a freedom no living Black person in this nation has yet to taste, though, Allah, we try. Tamir (Rice), Ashaams (Manley), Ahmaud (Arbery). *Jamila, Hafizah.*

In this country, the same name that beckons a cop we gift our children as armor. Though it can take a while to put that armor on. In the beginning, I was as afraid of my Arabic name as I was of my deep voice, inherited from my aunt Liz, my father's eldest sister.

Do you see how the continents tug at me?

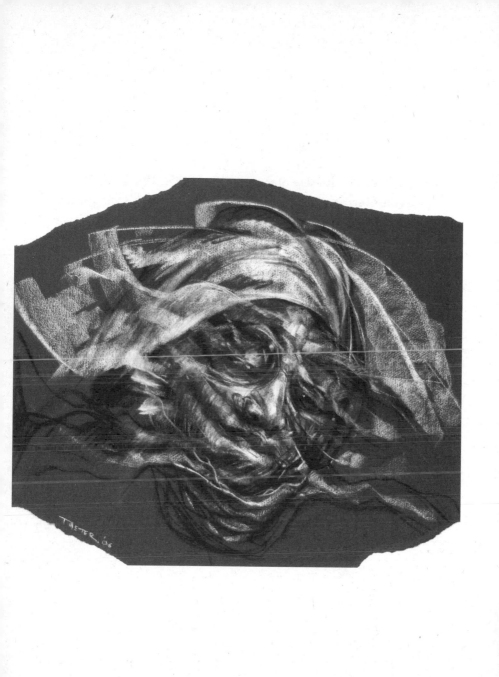

In Egypt, Anubis is usher of souls to the afterlife. This jackal-headed god is the overseer at the Weighing of the Hearts. Yaya, their ancients believed that to prove worthy of Jannah, one's heart had to balance the scales. It couldn't weigh more than truth and justice's feather. Which, my father would say, means the afterlife holds very few white people.

So many of the ones who love us have no clue how much they hate us. From them, I have learned how dangerous intimacy can be. White people don't believe we hear the dog whistle that blows through this country. This sound they mistake for silence, we hear in the signal their bodies transmit. They don't *really* believe being Black in America means that when America breaks you, it's always trying to give the bullet your last name. Even the ones who love us seldom recognize themselves as the gun's chamber. It's taken till now to get quick at cleaving the toxic ones away. To reserve the best of me, like frothy bone stock.

In Judaism, they say a whole heart is one that is broken. The cracks, where Adonai gets in. If the broken heart is the "master key that opens all doors," will holding the Black heart up to light get you to Elohim?

Hold the white heart up to light and it'll lose you a white friend. Every microaggression cheaply costumed in the mise-en-scène. Our reflections, doing the unforgivable, unveil them to be the offspring of this American country. *All* this freedom, *all* this North. *Can't you just shut up and be grateful?* We, who recognize them everywhere, they'll accuse of manifesting ghosts. They'll say Black is in our imagination. We, who hear the thinking behind their thought, say: Black *is* the imagination, the image, the imago.

Yaya, like the sun—like Blackness—the stars have been every metaphor. A star can be a guiding light. The lullaby that puts your great-grandson, Ibraheema Alyaan, to sleep. For some, what's written in the stars is destiny. For lovers, to be "star-crossed" is to be maligned by fate. A star can be what shimmers enough you don't recognize it as dead.

Can you imagine a greater cruelty than the sky being made your burden?

A Titan, Atlas was, according to Greek myth, of a class considered former gods. The Titans were a group of demoted deities whose mythology was appropriated from the Hurrians, an ancient people who inhabited what is now northeastern Syria, and whose ethnicity archaeologists still find it difficult to determine.

When a new ruling order was put in place, these former sovereigns were ejected from their home in the heavens. "This was their 'nature,' and nothing is served by enquiring any further; they have no stories or functions as a collective body in conventional myth, and they had no place in Greek cult." That's how Robin Hard's *The Routledge Handbook of Greek Mythology* describe ancient Greek mythology's Hurrian origins. The text observes that though the origin of their name, *Titans,* is unclear, ancient evidence points to one possible meaning: princes.

Yaya—*are the Titans Black?*

If not, can you imagine a Blacker story?

If Black is also a structural position. The Hurrians ripped from country and throne. Banished to the underworld. Stories erased and stolen. Bodies renamed. This casual and ancient tale of colonization.

Yaya, in Pakistan—the home country of Iram, Jamila's childhood best friend, who has always been my favorite, and where they name their daughters Hafizah, too—the jackal is an animal stronger than the lion. Hunger being one way to partition a homeland in two. Imagine waking up in another country without ever having left. Or is this what the British did to you, too?

Yaya, if the wound is in the root system, doesn't it make sense that the wound obsesses the body?

Like Catherine dying, barely sixteen.

Our childhood was a landscape where we wrote each other letters and watched them grow. We spent hours in AOL chatrooms flirting with boys who were more likely dangerous men. We studied CD booklets until we'd memorized the lyrics of whatever narrated our angst: Cake, Bush, Weird Al, Meredith Brooks. Her parents had left apartheid behind for Bath, Ohio. Her flu turning into pulmonary hypertension.

When I hear *wound,* I think of Catherine. I think of my mother picking me up from my new school in South Carolina and driving straight to Sears. Her mouth sewn shut as she bought me a pair of Adidas sandals without warning, the hairs on the back of my neck standing up. My mother, quiet on the plane as we flew to Ohio for my best friend's funeral—a child's eulogy, the first I ever gave. Their house of grief pulsed with life. Her mother's South African accent sung its hellos to guests like a woman trying her best not to die with a full house. Her father, the biggest man I've ever held, wept. His wound was both a Band-Aid and a matryoshka over mine. Catherine and her younger sister, Lizzie, were Irish twins—Lizzie now a twin in half. A middle turned eldest.

Wound, someone says, and I remember how with Catherine gone, I convinced myself that I—your Americanized granddaughter—was immunized against further loss.

Wound, and five years later, Yaya, your daughter is dead. Now, I'm crawling into Catherine's bed, still clutching the plane ticket her mother bought me. My body not blood, not musculature, not bone. My body now water, alone—a dam cutting itself open.

Wound, the way I dream of Catherine's younger siblings just to know their hair is still red.

Wound, and I want to ask the jackal, *Who suffers more?*

The dead?

The living?

Maybe melancholy is my father singing in the kitchen.

Our childhood turned into a musical just by the sound of his voice.

My father hums his never-forgotten gospels, croons Nancy Wilson, Otis Redding, Bob Marley, Fela Kuti, and lobs foolish southern ditties into the air to remind us, *yes, Lord,* he's still that same Black boy who'd fled Alabama.

Mama, I'm depending on you to tell me the truth, my father sings like a man on a leash, a man willing to start a song anywhere. He tugs a bassline out of his throat. The gesture invisible. But essentially, someone, hand over hand, pulling a bucket of water up a well by rope.

He shimmies his shoulders all around our Akron kitchen island. Rocks his knees in the street like a seesaw. He sings when he shaves, when he pours cereal, when he paints, sang at his own mother's funeral. Where his "Papa Was a Rolling Stone," mine is a music man. Whenever my father sings "Papa Was a Rolling Stone," a song he will make last my entire childhood, it pours from his mouth like baptismal water. His eyes like someone wandering the jackal-filled land between remembering and forgetting. This song, which I do not yet recognize as my father's lament, for my entire childhood, delights me.

Sadness is the boy left by the father, but melancholy is the boy turned man, and Black is that man turning his dirge into a harmony his children can dance to. This, what love can do: turn the kind of life that makes you cry into song. *Da-dum, da-dum.*

The last time I heard your voice, it was a raspy, sweet mango, my mother pulling the draw of okra and tuwo into my mouth, the bitter kuka you taught her to cook that I can never get enough of, and the sour Malta I still can't drink. Your voice inside me, expanding and contracting like a country.

In this way desire, too, can be the wound.

From your mountain-high cheekbones, from your skin the color of fertile ground, joy sprung like fruit from a wind-planted seed. You looked to me like a woman who laughed often. I remember the tender-sweet flesh of delight sending love fleeing your mouth like steam. You and my mother had this in common.

On a walk the other day, the lights of an ambulance flashed. I heard the cries before I saw the woman they came from. "I don't understand. Please help me. Anyone, help me."

A Black woman, skin that hummed like yours and my mother's, stood on the street begging paramedics in face masks for . . . what, I don't know. Answers? A ride-along? She had no safe way to follow them to the hospital. What do you beg for when everything is at stake?

"But that's my mother," she said to the paramedic, really pleading now as people scooted by her, as though her grief was as contagious as Covid 19 —their bodies harkening back to an eighties epidemic. The woman's lips came down hard around the word "mother," as if she was trying to build a shield with sound.

A Black man in his forties and a fade shouted from behind the gate of a front yard that someone needed to help her, that they were doing her wrong. I could see they were strangers. Still, his voice strained toward tears.

"That's my *mother*," the woman said, holding her stomach. From a distance no one could see, sirens kept rolling into the air

Too lonely for his own loneliness, the jackal offers me his neck. Now we're in this together. He says heartbreak, like hunger, is a political condition.

Atlas means "to bear," and some credit him as the inventor of astronomy. A nod to those who bear and who, by bearing, know that levity requires becoming intimate with weight. I still dream of my mother in a language I don't understand. Yaya, Jamila and I are one way to say your story in English.

I am the lacuna—the gap. Or, as *Merriam-Webster* defines me, I am the "discontinuity in an anatomical structure." A lacuna is the name not of the missing but of the space left by what is gone.

It can be in a work of art, "a cavity or depression, especially in bone." Music's intentional silences. The deliberate omissions of an archive. In science, a lacuna is what has not been studied but has the potential to be. In linguistics, it's a word that doesn't exist, but that, grammatically, could—which means it is what goes unnamed.

In a pre-op room in Lexington, South Carolina, my father paints the ceiling with his eyes. The two of us waiting for nurses to wheel him to a lobectomy.

"Can you believe I've had these things since I was fifteen?" And, Yaya, now your son-in-law removes his teeth in front of me for only the third time in my life. His lips collapse into his mouth as he plops his dentures in the container labeled with our last name and a barcode.

The second time I saw my father with no teeth was in a hospital room just like this, his eyes groggy from a triple bypass. The first time I saw him with no teeth, I was sixteen. I was afraid. Only a year older than him by the time he'd had his first full set of dentures. Through my parents' cracked bathroom door, I'd eavesdropped a glimpse of his empty mouth in their mirror's reflection. It was information I hadn't expected to be there, in this new house in South Carolina. That my father was not who he seemed, was a man of foreign parts.

Yaya, think of what your own daughter knew of you. Subtract thirty-two years. Now take what's left and split it in half to account for Hausa's divide. This is what I have of the woman you made who made me. Time makes the jackal hungrier in every way.

Forty when I was born, my father was always a little older than my friends' fathers. The lacuna of his mouth, until that moment, had been filled with my own patchworked version of his story. He was the boy who got oranges as Christmas gifts, a single pair of khakis to last the whole school year. The hospital room was windowless, but outside the sun had long come up since our predawn arrival. Like his refusal to wear slacks, I'd understood even at sixteen that the emptiness in his mouth had something to do with us being Black. With him being a poor colored boy in Jim Crow Alabama.

It was February. My father, two days into seventy-five, had—between my sister and brother—just become a grandfather for the sixth time. We still had a month before "pandemic" became the word of every day. A bag full of clothes he'd worn to the hospital sat crumpled between my feet as, tongue-tied, I stumbled through questions. I wanted to cry.

Why?

"Some kind of infection that could probably be easily fixed today. Anyway, we didn't have money for second opinions," he says, his face soured like wet laundry that's been left too long.

Were you upset?

I continued asking all the wrong questions. My father has two new hips, a triple bypass, stents—was soon to be the survivor of lung cancer and a lobectomy—but he's still got no name, no diagnosis, for this loss, this medical lacuna.

"Of course I was upset," he says, shivering beneath his heated blanket, cold in his hospital gown, his body no longer able to disguise the ghosts in his root system. No teeth in his mouth left to suck.

In dentures, my father learns to drive a car. In dentures, he kisses his first girl. In dentures, he graduates from high school. And having made it to college, having finally learned to love his smile again, in dentures, he's drafted to Germany. Four thousand miles away from home, in a foreign country that calls him "nigger," too, he sketches Malcolm X and, day after day, assembles weapons to kill brown strangers in a white man's war.

Lacuna, lacuna, lacuna

Yaya, I married a white woman. Do you understand the sentence? Both the grammar and the living of it.

No—it is not just time, language, and distance that estranges me from family, blood, story, home, you—it is queerness, too.

Yaya, could you love me alive as much as I know you do now that you're dead?

Before you died, stroke after stroke, you lived. Your body, a premonition fading away. That last time we saw you, your house spilled with generations. All of us looking a little like you and a dead woman.

The stroke that eventually killed you first killed your American counterpart. I was fifteen. Though, with my father's mother, as cruel things sometimes like to do, it took its time. Gussie Mae's mind still strong, still there, but her body locked. For a year, she couldn't move, couldn't talk, couldn't lift more than an inch of her mouth. It's blood that calls the jackal. It's blood that haunts me from every side.

Is it truer to tell a story forward or backward? From left to right, or Arabic's right to left? It happened this way. The sun rising as it set. The five-hour time difference between our countries multiplied over days, then decades.

The jackal: my fear, my grief, my America.

Yaya, if America wanted us at all, I swear it wanted us empty—your language squeezed out of me and Jamila like the last bit of toothpaste. Our names, the words we can still say in every direction.

▶

Trying to keep the camera steady, my father pans up as you stand. I think this is the year Jamila and I couldn't stop listening to Karyn White's "Superwoman."

You blush as you twirl in your green and white wrap, and Yaya, somehow, you are still laughing. Still saying Hafizah, Jamila. *I'd almost forgotten what a name could feel like pronounced so correctly. In your mouth, I am remembered.*

You look so tall, forgive me for taking so long to remember where Auntie Mairo also gets it from. You look so much like my mother, so much like yourself, so much like me, I recognize the children I will one day have and the woman I will one day become. Behind you on the wall, a brown-patterned sheet masquerades as a curtain. Cassette tape after cassette tape flanks your right. Your face holds the look of someone who's made joy their bedfellow—I mean to say, Yaya, I know there were difficult days.

For almost two hours, you speak. In your mouth our names are full of Hausa and history. The daughter you speak to is still living, though she is 5,891 miles away. Teeth have fled your mouth, but barely a wrinkle has found you. Here, even the jackal would find relief.

My father zooms in so close, you take up the whole screen. Behind the camera, Auntie Mairo translates at a volume that can't be heard. Here, we could all live forever. Here, you laugh so hard, I mistake it for a scream.

II

Eventually, your daughter took her life into her own two hands. She gave up red meat, took long walks, praised Allah, and searched books for homeopathic cures to the haints history had poured into her blood. She was an African woman in the United States, attempting to save what her adopted country did not want: Dark skin. A woman of Allah. *Her.*

The cops, forgetting Anubis, the jackal-headed weigher of the hearts, have killed another one of us.

After, dressed up in riot gear, they mace Black protesters, who, even on their knees, manage to maintain social distance. On another screen, white men and white women decorated in American flags and assault rifles rush to the Capitol building to protest the election and the Covid-19 virus. Spit flying, they scream at the police who, in medical masks—their bodies wearing no shields, no armor—stand stiff as the guards of Buckingham Palace. Their faces are so close to one another's, one false move and it's a kiss.

They could kill us all, and Yaya, they are trying. They say, "Reopen the economy!" They put on grave faces when they tell us that for Money to thrive some will just have to die. Die we do. This, how, despite white protestations, you know Jesus is Black, with his impossible burden. His white fandom turning a crown of thorns and a crucifixion into their ecstasy.

When you died, I didn't know what to do. It was my last semester of college. My mother's absence, a lacuna. My grief paving the gap permanently with cement. Like my mother's, your death started with a phone call. And like my mother's, it found me in the same position: cramming for a test.

My father's voice quivered through the phone line.

I returned to my table of classmates, cracked my books, didn't say a word. It was like after Catherine's funeral, flying back to our new home in South Carolina where no one knew someone I loved had died, which is to say, you died twice. It was like the borders of a country closing. The stilled panic of that first time I rode my bike too far from home.

At Christopher Street Pier, the queerest in the city, all the genders congregate. We cruise on foot. Have come to hold hands where the constellations surround us in abundance.

In the not-so-distant past, when love like ours was more illegal, the pier was policed by cops on foot, scooters, and horseback. But in modern days, lovers, and the amateur astronomers club, are what Stephanie and I see.

Through a telescope, we watch Pluto—stripped of its planet status—punctuate the sky brightly, like a period at the end of a sentence hoping to be mistaken for a star.

Yaya, sticks and stones may break my bones but the truth could bring down a whole nation.

A nation being no more than what it remembers.

A nation, a lacuna, too.

Where I am, the bees are black. I've seen a green dress go blue from wading, have watched the jackal's howl grind against the wind. I've kept you in the pocket like a list, unable to check anything off. There are poplar trees. Fall sunlight falling in mortars. The way, despite a pandemic, children's laughter refuses to leave any of us alone. Their joy is a guillotine at the neck of my melancholy.

Not yet a widower, your son-in-law's reflection stares back from our French windows. He moonwalks across the living room, past his pink meditation chair, and on into our Akron solarium. He drops his voice into baritone. *It was the third of September, that day I'll always remember.* And your granddaughters are laughing, and your son-in-law is smiling. Smiling, laughing, and singing, having forgotten this melody is his saddest song. Melancholy, more than grief's shovel, the jackal's hunger, not just a gap.

Yaya, we are close enough to be maimed, humiliated, killed, but still we scream, "Fuck the police!" Pardon our language. We are trying to bring a whole system down: the banks, the prisons, the police and their politicians. All down the streets, cops brandish batons. We chant, dance, organize in response.

I came to history because I was hurting. I came desperate, wanting to comprehend.

And then, one day—one history after another—

the jackal that had been starving inside me realized: scarcity was someone else's myth

—I said my own name, and Yaya, there was joy! I was the descendant of Eves! I took up my mission: *protector, watcher, guardian, memory.*

Finally, in my own mouth, I felt like an easy word

Black is the night, the second sight, the white fright, the satellite, the light, the jackal head of Anubis. Yaya, Anubis, the god drawn in black. We, the color that means:

- life,
- regeneration,
- the Nile's fertile soil

The history between us promising I'll see you again.

ME, WE!
MUHAMMAD ALI!

AGE XIII

LOVE

I am America. I am the part you won't recognize.

—MUHAMMAD ALI

W E'RE HEADED TO THE PROTEST," I TEXT my father, already on the way. He rings me on FaceTime immediately. To my surprise and slight disappointment, he's not one bit mad to know I'm going into a crowd during a contagious pandemic. A part of me winces to see my father's urgency, how much he suddenly needs to know I can face this world alone.

My father won't live forever. Finally, I see it. Part of my father needs to know I can enter hell's mouth and walk back out. He needs to know, even though I can't swim, I can wade into America's waters and see choices beyond drowning or baptism.

My father says, "You do what you have to do." And I know he means Black folks.

He says, "Be careful." And the two of us, in lockstep, hope words can be enough.

I hold my father in the palm of my hand in the middle of a cordoned off street in Brooklyn, and Stephanie standing next to me, waiting for me and him to finish assuring each other we're safe. The bright lights of my father's upstairs art studio reflect off his face, which confirms we are resistant to looking our age. His beard's only recently taken sides with his seventy-plus years. Bald-headed, in a single winter his face completely abandoned black for gray. His newly silver eyebrows arch with a worry meant only slightly more for the police than for Covid. But he knows my worry will keep me alert.

Behind my father, on six-foot-tall sheets of paper, Zayd and Nuh stand life-size, rendered in charcoal, two models in apocalyptic skies. My father's drawn Zayd practically blowing away into a background littered with factory pollution. In another, Nuh pouts in front of a dying field and a black tornado. My father's calling the series "Pandemic," but I remember *Scary Stories to Tell in the Dark*.

He draws one ghost story after another. A master of technique, picture after picture, he creates images of what is gone. In all his endings Black folks make it. But, in the world off my father's canvases, a cop has turned his knee into a rope and let it do the work of America on a Black man's neck. Another officer has kicked down a door, and behind it was an American crime: a Black woman dreaming.

"Oh, please, you know I've seen too much *Law & Order* to get got," I tell the man who taught me how humor can do the same work as love if you let it—and we let it. By now, I know better than anything how to watch. I always remember my parents' naming lessons. I know "natural causes" is what they say when Black people die of America. It's a no-brainer that courage is a useless virtue compared to what happens in my gut when white people feel off. "We'll leave if anything happens," I promise my father before hanging up.

I peek at Twitter, and the human world presents itself cracked in two. Across the country, hospitals overflow like shook pop. The newsrooms of America swap Black Lives Matter protests and unemployment numbers for stories of disappointed Trump supporters and Dow points. They barely mention the concentration camps still open at the border. Violence against Asians and Asian Americans skyrockets. Man-made natural disaster after man-made natural disaster claims the same storm-battered towns of prior years. The cops have killed us again with their knees/bare hands/whole bodies. I wonder, have they grown bored by bullets?

From half a football field away, protesters gather at the tip of Prospect Park in front of the dingy McDonald's that, despite the unstoppable gentrification that's overtaken it, reminds the whites this is a Black neighborhood. Magnolias spill over the park's concrete walls. Volunteers in face masks pass out gloves and hand sanitizer. They bring offerings of free and cool water on a hot June day. It is a sea of Senegalese twists, box braids, shaved heads, and styled afros. Black folks look so good it feels more like a Tuesday version of Afropunk, except we're all so mad. We're sad. We're delirious to be alive and exhausted with the way America makes breathing while Black so deadly, so complicated. I grew up looking at photographs like the scene ahead of us, where Black bodies occupy whole afternoons.

IN MY FATHER'S HOUSE, THERE'S AN OLD FAMILY PHOTO ALBUM. Army-green canvas wraps the cover. It's a rare survivor from his draft days and his reluctant service in Germany during the Việt Nam War. Of all our albums, as a child, I was most enamored with this one, and how it blurred history with memory. The photo album opens with newspaper clippings of the assassinations of Martin Luther King, Jr., JFK, and Malcolm X. There's a brochure from my father's trip to the concentration camps at Dachau, and a copy of MLK's "I Have a Dream" speech, typewritten on his army letterhead.

In the album, my father eventually appears wearing army greens, followed, years later, by my mother laughing into his chest, her afro both halo and full moon. That our histories never begin with us was another one of my parents' naming lessons.

As a child, the photo album told me everything I needed to know about how I was supposed to feel about war. Like why leave home for a fight when you could just the same get got both in and by your own country. We were told stories of Muhammad Ali's draft objections. We were shown the Black art of refusal. Ali had refused both the government and his government name, and instead, had chosen that Blackest "I," the one pronounced "we."

His slave name gone, he said, "Now I can go all over the world!" He had declared himself free. In the photo books and stacks of magazines that my father kept for painting research, I watched Muhammad Ali in Nigeria, Ghana, Egypt, the Congo, while Africans cheered his name and Ali hollered love back.

He had my mother's religion. The man formerly known as Cassius Clay mesmerized me. In part, because he had my grandmother's face. As a child I stared at photograph after handsome photograph, sure he was a relation, and I loved him that way—like he was mine. Which was the way he loved us. My father likes to say Ali made you feel so good, you couldn't watch him alone, had to have a room of shouting Black folks to understand how fast his feet could be.

SOME OF THE DEAD MEN THAT OPENED OUR PHOTO ALBUMS ALSO lived in my father's art studio. They populated the piles of the Civil Rights and *Life* photography books he used for models in paintings and for the children's books he illustrated. Weekends and after school, I spent hours poring through the pages. The photographs showed our men dressed in suits, our women in dresses and heels. We arrived to meet the state the way my grandma and aunts in Dayton did the Lord: in our Sunday best. I pored over black-and-white photos, their margins printed at full bleed. I saw Ali in the ring, Malcolm at the pulpit, MLK in the streets.

I memorized photographs where all shades of Black folks locked arms and marched. Where we covered our faces as we were beaten by cops with batons, eaten by police dogs. We resurrected, bloody as Jesus on the cross his fellow countrymen crucified him on, and I wondered if this was what grandma's pastor meant when he said "baptism by fire." But even in the sweat of trying to survive catastrophic violence, I noticed, in every photo, our skin still glowed. No matter what happened to us, we were beautiful. And what was I to make of that in a world that never treated us as such?

OF THE THREE BLACK WOMEN—PATRISSE CULLORS, ALICIA GARZA, and Opal Tometi—who founded the Black Lives Matter movement, Cullors and Garza identify as queer, and when they said Black lives matter, maybe, for the first time, I knew that meant the *whole* of mine.

At every BLM protest I've been to, you can see the gay. It shows up a little rachet, a *wink wink,* and with the knowledge that respectability politics have never been attainable to bodies at once as Black and queer as ours.

Around me, in the crowd of marchers, our chanting livens the day.

Black folks drip with grief, laughter, and sweat, remembering the days when "I can't breathe" was only the way fall air scratched our red rover lungs and a fading season heaved, just heaved, out of our laughing bodies. We reach back to the recesses of memory where instead of "Hands up, don't shoot," we see our summer-sweaty palms jiving with "Down by the banks of the Hanky Panky, a bullfrog jumped from bank to banky."

I think of my grandmother's fourth-grade education. Of her as a child with her own mother sharecropping American fields, and the lifetime my grandmother would spend cleaning white women's homes to get my father to college. My father believes in a world just out of sight, one that each generation of Blackness pulls more into focus.

There were years my father kept drawing variously radicalized versions of Malcolm X. There was the year of *White Socks Only*, the children's book he illustrated. In *White Socks Only*, he drew water fountains that were segregated and a southern summer hot enough to fry eggs on the pavement or for a firecracker to light itself off.

My father is always reminding me that America tries to erase our histories because our past is our strength. An adult now, I comprehend this in a way I never could as a child. That when it comes to Blackness and the U.S., there is far more to reconcile than any single lifetime can work out. But knowing we live on many timelines, we have to love each other and ourselves enough to try.

IN OUR FAMILY PHOTO ALBUM, AFTER MY PARENTS' SCRAPBOOK histories, photos of the friends and family I don't or barely recognize follow. I do my best to get a sense of these people who are also us. My parents look strangely hip, loose, young as I am now.

In one photo, my mother, predictably, is so beautiful. Her huge sixties afro and bell-bottoms have vanished into one new decade after another. She wears her hair up in an African wrap. My father wears a thick moustache and that smile of his that's like a weight shrugged off, revealing he's just made someone laugh.

In this version of the world, people are still calling my father by the ridiculously hip name he's using to sign his canvases, "Getero." Their friends are calling my mother by her middle name instead of her first.

When we'd first arrived in America, we'd lived in Lynn, Massachusetts, for two brief years before moving to Ohio. Too young to remember much about Lynn, it was less a place to me than it was the setting of one of my father's many prefatherhood lores. "I was fresh out of college, hooked in with the Young Workers Liberation League, but I didn't know I was radical."

In some photos that scatter our family albums, Jamila and I sit plopped on African poofs surrounded by knees and the lanky legs of our parents' friends—artists, Africans, and Black radicals. They've come to our rented Massachusetts brownstone to pour libations, party, and strategize about fighting a power invisible to everyone but all of us.

My father always begins, "They were just walking down the street." He never veers from this origin point. It was the late seventies, and he was working at the Community Minority Cultural Center, where his job was to help bridge the gap between Black and Latinx communities, and to help a community drowning in police violence.

"A *looong* history of police abusing that community," he says, dragging out the bitter poison that constructs the words. "Cases where Black people supposedly hung themselves in jail." Here, his voice will scrunch with the pain of kin. "They claimed that one guy hung himself with a leather jacket," my father says, and one day, I will think of Sandra Bland.

"The woman was pregnant," and he returns to the lesson at hand, his face drained by the futility of innocence on a Black body as he describes how this young Black couple was jumped by a group of young white kids.

"They beat the boy so badly, he was never the same," my father says, never having learned if the baby lived. The police not doing much and my father needing to do something, anything, he wrote an outraged article for the local newspaper and then a letter to Angela Davis, pleading with her to come.

"When she did, she brought Fleeta Drumgo, one of the Soledad Brothers, with her." He'd just gotten out of jail. This story, which he gave Jamila and me again and again, I took it to mean: of course, we owe something to one another. Honoring our collective anger is one way Black folks can love one another even after death.

"John Conyers and Margaret Burnham were there, but the main component was Angela Davis." Despite the pain the memory leaves in his belly, my father always tells the story proudly, his chest filling like the sky when he says Angela Davis's name.

IN THE CROWD OF PROTESTERS, WE HOLLER, WE DANCE. WE HAVE our rage in common, and it makes me whole. "Fuck the police!" and it's like we're singing Stevie's rendition of "Happy Birthday." It feels so good. *Hell,* this tune could be gospel.

In a sea of genders, Black folks wear nail polish, nose rings, high heeled sneakers, tie-dyed hair, loud jewelry, African print, bodies full of tattoos, and midriff tanks with soft bellies and six-packs spilling out. Some of us arrive in T-shirts, some like we've just rolled off the set of *B.A.P.S* or from lunch with Nicki Minaj. Others have reached back to Prince and Dennis Rodman for outfit inspiration. We've come from day jobs, night work, unemployment lines. From childhoods watching the grainy video of Soon Ja Du shooting fifteen-year-old Latasha Harlins in the back of the head over a two-dollar orange juice.

I think of my nephews, three Black boys inside the gun scope of a country. Still, there is comfort knowing all the ways Black folks stay steady trying to stop America from turning our children into ancestors.

We inherited/were born into/grew up in/came of age in/started our lives in a country fueling itself on our deaths. We watched George Zimmerman be acquitted in the name of American "self-defense" for the murder of a seventeen-year-old Black boy holding a can of Sprite and a bag of Skittles. After Trayvon Martin, we watched videos of Eric Garner choked to death by a group of cops for selling loosies. We watched officer Michael Slager shoot Walter Scott in the back. We watched officer Jeronimo Yanez kill Philando Castile live on Facebook. We watched officer Derek Chauvin kneel on George Floyd's neck for nine minutes, suffocating him to death, and the seventeen-year-old Black girl who filmed it win a Pulitzer. We'd seen Tamir Rice, just twelve years old, murdered in front of his sister by police officer Timothy Loehmann for playing with a toy gun. Our bodies are denied. We say, "Say her name," and mean our trans sisters and brothers, too—Roxanne Moore, Tony McDade, Mya Hall.

A statue of Floyd by a white artist was unveiled in Brooklyn on America's first official Juneteenth national holiday, and within days, a hate group defaced the cream-colored statue, literally Blackfacing it with black spray paint. Inches of progress hadn't slowed the miles of bleeding. I thought of Marsha P. Johnson's warning about monuments: "Now they got two little nice statues in Chariot Park to remember the gay movement. How many people have died for these two little statues to be put in the park for them to recognize gay people?" We're angry and our anger runs the streets like hot blood, hot water, hot wine. Our anger runs, with love, in all directions. It dances up hills.

We're furious for Tamir, Trayvon, Michael. For Kalief Browder and Amadou Diallo. We chant George Floyd's name, never forgetting how much we're owed: Emmett, Malcolm, Sandra, Breonna, Felycya. We make protest our repass. We have the memory of griots. Ancestors we have in spades.

We march on the wind of Ida, Marsha, Assata, Angela, Malcolm, Martin, Audre, Ruth, Mariame, the Combahee River Collective. We all carry more than one name, remembering the Black Period's oldest lesson: a good debt, like our shared anger, makes us stronger. We've risen from ashes, and having studied the flames; now, I'm so strong I can hold more names: Brandon and Connor Moore, Havsuw 'Baaja, Havasupai Elementary, Compton, the Gabrielino-Tongva/Kizh.

"THE FIRST DREAM OF THIS COUNTRY DIDN'T SEE ME FREE WITHIN it," Camille once wrote.

It took years to recognize I could dream differently. But Nova, now born into our world—now more than a thought in Camille's belly—is a new dream.

We march the way our parents and grandparents testified. In our Black Periods, and collectively, we harness our anger like love, like we're Muhammad Ali.

EVEN FROM THE GROUND, I CAN SEE THE AERIAL VIEW OF THE crowd. We swell. We are individual fingers transformed into the strength of a fist. Our bodies testify to what we aren't allowed: *life, liberty, the pursuit of happiness.* In unison, we queer what should be our low survival chances. Our anger Black and as graceful as a flock of birds. We be that: *Me, we! Muhammad Ali!*

Ali confirmed that living in our Blackness was like living in a poem. In two words, he made community out of language. Zora Neale Hurston called this "the Characteristics of Negro Expression." No moment in our language is left unadorned or symmetrical. We think not just in words but in hieroglyphics, like my grandma in her front-room "sitting chair." No matter what's going on, inside the Black Period, it can always be said: *She stay steady. He be working. She my sister. I got five on it. Don't nobody know my troubles but God.*

Ali spoke as though he were Blackness's original hype man. Kentucky born, he had the fists of the South. He wasn't afraid to announce to the world that Black folks were unbeatable. He said,

I've wrestled with alligators,
I've tussled with a whale.
I done handcuffed lightning
And throw thunder in jail.

"Fuck the police!" the crowd around me chants. We know that America is the alligator, whale, lightning, and jail. We know Ali's "I" means Black folks. His "I" means us.

A boxer, a poet, a comedian, a humanitarian, a revolutionary, I loved how the cadence of Ali's voice held the determination of Angela Davis. That sour pitch that fell out of her throat when a Black person was asked something ridiculous—"You ask me whether I approve of violence," Davis scoffs in 1972 from a California prison. In an orange turtleneck and afro that shadows her eyes, she tells a white reporter she was overpoliced in LA long before the Watts Riots, that she grew up in Birmingham, remembers limbs, remembers her whole neighborhood shaking from bombs.

"When someone asks me about violence, I just find it incredible," she says to the question's absurdity. "What it means is that the person who's asking that question has absolutely no idea what Black people have gone through, what Black people have experienced in this country since the time the first Black person was kidnapped from the shores of Africa."

Davis who is always speaking of prisons and Palestine, and how, like Indigenous peoples in America, Palestinians—as Davis writes in *Freedom Is a Constant Struggle*—have been transformed into "immigrants on their own ancestral lands." Davis who reminds me, we can only get free *together*, and that the work of liberation—like our obligation—is global and collective, though America positions me to forget.

Ali, the dissenter, had refused the white man's war. He said, "We've been in jail for four hundred years . . . I will not go ten thousand miles to help murder and kill other poor people. If I'm gonna die, I'll die here now, right here, fightin' you."

In his army greens, my father and his Black platoon-mates watched Ali from their draft service in Germany, where they were still being called niggers. In a world where Black people were (and still are) punished for self-pride, Ali fought in the ring and in the streets of America as though one glove said "Black," the other, "beautiful." Meanwhile, the war was maiming, breaking, and disabling both Vietnamese and American minds and bodies.

WITH MY FATHER, I WATCHED RERUNS OF ALI VS. A BLACK BOXER named Ernie Terrell, who insisted on calling Ali "Cassius" instead of his free, chosen name. We watched Ali beat the living daylights out of Ernie. It took my breath away, but my father had been born three years after Ali. Both entered their teenage years with people who'd been born into slavery still breathing, talking, alive on this earth. Watching Ali whup Terrell, I eventually understood that for Ali, for my father, for all of us, the price on our heads was too high, too collectively bound, to suffer any Uncle Tomming.

"You my opposer when I want freedom," Ali said to America. "You my opposer when I want justice. You my opposer when I want equality." He was taking up the mantle for us, and shouting what we also wanted to shout. The poetry of his boasting, his trash talk, his whole being, proved my father's early drawing lessons: Black held the light.

"Want me to go somewhere and fight for you? You won't even stand up for me right here in America." Ali demanded freedom so blatantly, so proudly, white America called it—his Black love—un-American, a disease. But Ali was ashamed of America for being ashamed of *us*. Ali was Blackness turning the light absorbed into our collective energy.

When we finally met Muhammad Ali, it was the early nineties. Looking at the picture of me and Jamila sitting on Ali's lap, our mother leaning over behind him in an African dress, I couldn't have been more than seven. No matter the state we lived in, whenever someone Black and famous came to town, we went to see them—and they looked back at us that way, both proud and knowing why we'd been brought there. Along with Ali, she'd later take us to see Maya Angelou and Wynton Marsalis.

Parkinson's had begun to make Ali's body quiver. My mother pushed me toward him. He spoke in a whisper that shook. He asked, *What's your name*. And I whispered back to the champion of the world, *Hafizah*.

I'd seen him rope-a-dope, his one-two punch. Despite age and illness, he looked even stronger. It wasn't just that he could float like a butterfly or sting like a bee. In the world of Kwanzaa, Africans, and artists, we already knew Jesus was Black. Ali was simply proof we could walk on water.

IN THE WORLD BEFORE COVID-19, STEPHANIE AND I SAT IN A PACKED Joe's Pub, a theatre in Manhattan, where we watched Daniel Alexander Jones's one-woman show *Black Light*, with Jones playing Jomama Jones. Through storytelling, mythologies, Prince, and Sade, Jomama traverses personal, political, and historical upheavals. Speaking directly to the audience, she tells us about visiting her aunt Cleotha as a child.

Aunt Cleotha had an arm that didn't work, and she sat out on her porch late every night with a shotgun. When a young Jomama asks Aunt Cleotha why she's up at three in the morning, her aunt responds, "I'm a witness."

"This is my church," Aunt Cleotha says, and the entire audience leans in, all of us together, imagining her gesturing at the dark.

"But why do you have a shotgun?" Jomama asks, and Aunt Cleotha realizes it's time to give her grandniece "the talk." She tells Jomama that as a girl, her older brother Reggie had come home from the war. Together they'd gone down to Mr. Harrison's store for penny lemon sticks, Reggie strutting proud in his uniform. Later that night, Mr. Harrison, who was white, surrounded their house with a lynch mob, the mob arriving to put Reggie back in a Black boy's place. Aunt Cleotha's injured arm was the result of Mr. Harrison unleashing his dog.

"But why do you have the shotgun *now*?" Jomama asks, with a child's insistence on an answer that satisfies. "They're still out there moving, baby. I stay vigilant so y'all can sleep," says Aunt Cleotha. Jomama marvels that even though it's three A.M., it's not *really* dark. She can see.

"I call this Black Light," says Aunt Cleotha. "If you look into the dark long enough, all sorts of things will reveal themselves to you." The two of them sit together, "waiting for the dawn, learning how to see in the dark."

Inside a sea of protesters, sweet birch, magnolia star, elm, oak, and cherry trees stand, leaf-drenched, praising the sky. A Black child jumps up and down gleefully in response to our self-made spectacle. Like Aunt Cleotha, I want to be a witness, too.

Around me, Black folks dance like it's Kwanzaa, others like its Freaknik. All use their booties. The cops don't know what to do. Having to delay their usual violence, they line the corners of our perimeter with their hands on their tactical belts. Willing to kill us any way they can, they wear no Covid protective gear. They scowl with naked faces, unsure what to make of a people like us who can simultaneously hold fury and joy on our faces—a fury and joy visible even behind face masks—and who dance when in grief.

A Black woman in a halter, setting her sights on a child, hollers, "Come through, baby girrrl, come through!" Black butches dance the electric slide with aging Black queens, while the woman in the halter top shouts, "I see you, T*iimbaa*lands!" "Okayyy, box braids!"

I've been to protests where you could mistake the crowd for a Black marching band's color guard. Even when there isn't music, our bodies know just what to do. We cha-cha, we electric slide, all of us on the same side of God's walkie-talkie. *We,* the remixers of the ancient Stoics.

The original Stoics believed that to experience true joy you had to lean into death. It's in the way we prepare Black children for the cops. How we, being forced to carry one humiliation after another, have yet to burn down this country (though, maybe that is coming). And the way Black folks, despite a pandemic, will rise to protest in order to demand justice for both our living and our dead. Inside the Black Light of our *"Me, we!"* the future is hope-shaped.

IV

THE
BLACK
PERIOD

REMEMORY

What else can we do but grasp at the time we have and can perceive, how beautifully ordinary is this desire . . .

—PARUL SEHGAL, "In Search of Time Lost and Newly Found"

Every time I thought I'd found a beginning, I ended up having to take another step further back.

T

HE EARTH WAS WITHOUT FORM, VOID—THERE WAS
darkness upon the face of the deep. Geologists call these
opening verses of time in the book of Genesis the Precambrian supereon. The first and only, it accounts for seven-eighths
of the earth's four-billion-year history. It was a world that, like an elementary school science project, bubbled with sulfur. No flowers to
be found anywhere on earth. The only building blocks for a brand-
new god were the dust and gas orbiting the sun. No Adam's rib yet to
sculpt from. Just oceans of liquid rock and volcanoes erupting beneath
asteroid skies.

It was a Hades-like world. It was a world the spitting image of a
warning, like the priests of my school days sermoning on about how
easily hell found the faithless. In the Precambrian, geologists suspect,
the moon was born. It took another billion years for the world to cool,
for the volcanoes' eruptions to make the islands that eventually collided into the continents we know.

Epochs passed.

The world of then, still unrecognizable. A foreigner painted in
black basalt, yellow dust, sea. Then, one day, in the days before the
idea of days was formed, webs of green pulled themselves up from the
light-drenched waters. The grass between our toes was still millions
of years away. The inland of our future world still bare and rocky, but
ferns and mosses had begun to curtain the shores. Still, no flowers.
Only the gods of nature slowly architecting palaces of green.

Then, the 180-million-year Mesozoic era arrived. It held inside its
mouth like a pearl the Jurassic period of Steven Spielberg movies, the
first fishes, turtles, and flying dinosaurs, but was still barren of the hot
orange marigolds my mother grew every summer. This was a Pangea
world, and it was waiting for the seventy-nine-million-year Creta-

ceous period, which, aided by the birth of bees, bore the Age of Flowers. In an instant the whole world changed. Was it *exactly* like this? When Jamila fielded what, from our mother, was a simultaneously surprising and unsurprising request—"Drive me to New Jersey?"— how did we not know *this* was our big bang?

Did our mother whisper the question, or did she declare? In her secrecy, our mother was a woman who kept us guessing. She never missed an episode of *Oprah,* loved herself some McDonald's apple pie, and laughed out loud when she read my school copy of *Candide.* There are so many things about her I still can't tell if I've forgotten or if I've simply never known.

In a March 1993 article in the *Akron Beacon Journal,* a reporter once wrote, "Geter is active in teaching African culture and helping native Africans adjust to the Akron area. 'This is my Grammy,' Geter said smiling." She'd been asked about the President's Award she'd received from the Ohio Black Women's Leadership Caucus for her "above-and-beyond" distinguished service to the Black community. I was nine, and she'd been an African in America for six years. She kept the bronze-plated award in her bedroom closet with her green card and everything else she held precious, and where, now, my father keeps her organ-donor medal. But who were these Africans she helped ease into America, and why don't I remember them? Do they know she's gone?

Drive me to New Jersey? our mother asks her oldest child.

When Jamila departs South Carolina for New Jersey with our mother, it's still early enough in fall to accidentally call it summer. Whenever I picture the two of them, it always feels like a chase. Over and over, I've imagined them speeding down the highway with the windows of my sister's silver sedan rolled down, the breeze flowing through our mother's close-cropped afro, flowers sprinting with them up the highway, and our mother racing south to north not for freedom, but for goodbye. This time she's both Bonnie *and* Clyde. She's trying to filch more time from an almost-emptied hourglass. Had she, like her own father, had a premonition of her own death? Did she feel Alhamis, her father's warning of her final Thursday, coming?

My cousin Mimi, Auntie Mairo's youngest child, lived in New Jersey with her husband Hassan and their three daughters. Like she had with me and Jamila, our mother had carried Mimi, and every one of Mimi's daughters, cloth-wrapped on her back. Was it that our mother wanted to speak her native language one last time to someone she loved and in person? With Nigeria so far away, with our mother trying to outrun her own fading light, was Mimi as close to home as she could get? Or was Mimi the only home she could stomach the heart to see?

If our mother knew she was going to die, I wonder, why didn't she race toward me?

∞

When flowers first appeared, like you and me—like everything else on this earth—they came by stardust. The same stars that today still repair our bodies' daily decays. Flowers and us, both celestial remnants, our bodies as old as the universe. The stars, like rocks, like history, laugh at the idea of a single "year." Which is to say we are *intended* to be made of memory.

In the beginning of the world, you should know, flowers pollinated themselves. Through geological time and evolutionary study, like enslaved Africans transforming into Black people, flowers taught themselves to codeswitch into never-traversed territories, into the language of bees and birds.

Strangers in a strange land, for survival, they integrated, assimilated, until the beauty of the foreign world they found themselves in resembled their own image. As anthropologist Loren Eiseley says, flowers "got into strange environments." Eiseley describes the Age of Flowers as a soundless explosion. Like what, as a child, I'd imagined Beethoven felt when he made music—a beauty without definition.

To make this explosion palatable for human consumption, geologic clock analogies can compress the world down to a year, a day. A single hour. In the sixty-minute version of the earth, the explosion of flowers—which, in reality, lasted millions of years—exists for only the last ninety seconds. Humans appear with just a single second left. The birth of a nation doesn't even make the clock.

∞

When my sister's second son, Nuh, was born, save his father's eyes, he looked like no one else, like he had arrived on earth from an un-placeable moment in history. A Black boy living in a pre-Covid Bei-jing, he was a night-skinned anomaly to the people who lived there and who were constantly—and without permission—trying to take his picture, until by three years old, he'd developed a temper.

From English, to Mandarin, to his father's Wolof, to his Arabic les-sons, there was so much language, language came slow to him. Now, trapped in my father's house in South Carolina—the six of them out-waiting a pandemic—surrounded by Black faces, Nuh, five years old, has found his way to more and more speech, and every day becomes a little more legible. Here, in this legibility, his temper has transformed, and he's a child who makes jokes and laughs all the time. In his joy, this little Muslim-Gambian-Nigerian-American child, who has al-ways had a face that's seemed all his own, suddenly began looking exactly like my mother.

How startling, and too, *hallelujah,* to see a ghost. It took me months to tell either Jamila or our father that the woman we wanted back had appeared. Was I sure? There was something to Nuh's smile, the way my mother's dimples raced up his cheekbones as he, still stubborn, tried to hold his ground and disguise his happiness.

The progeny of her progeny, Nuh wore her shy eyes and button chin, her dark skin, so smooth it always read to me like celebration. When I finally told my father and Jamila over video chat, I watched them call Nuh over. Their eyes grew big with the woman we loved arriving so suddenly on Nuh's face, and for them to see. Between us there was this new sound, this new laughter. Our history had found us. And what a relief.

What would it look like to emerge from erasure?
Would it look like this? Does it look like *her*?

∞

Flowers appeared, and they grew a seed at their heart. The seed they held there was fully embryonic and nutrient packed. Like Black people, flowers were revolutionaries. They left a mark on and changed whatever and whoever crossed their paths. Their nectar and pollen beckoned insects. Flowers lassoed themselves around hummingbirds. Like lovers, flowers and hummingbirds evolved together and with no one able to say who fell first. As flowers spread, they became the building blocks for what powered evolution: insects, lizards, mammals. Flowers arrived and—like Black people—immediately they sustained a whole world.

In the Age of Flowers even grass was rare, and then slowly grasses began spreading and establishing themselves as groundcover. For survival, flowers, like Black folks, developed their own double consciousness—that *two-ness*—two thoughts, two souls—that "sense," as W.E.B. Du Bois writes, "of always looking at one's self through the eyes of others."

Flowers lived as prey while also being universal building blocks for everything we know. In their double consciousness, seeds were known to hide in an animal's fur, ride bees' bellies. They buried themselves whole in the intestines of birds and waited to be passed, undigested, miles away.

∞

Can you keep track of them now? My sister and our mother snaking I-95. The radio is on. What are they listening to? What is our mother thinking? I want to know what it must have been like for our mother to know this was her final goodbye. But no matter how many questions I fling at my sister like needles looking for a little blood, Jamila can tell me almost nothing of this lottery-like moment she spent with our origin story as our origin was coming to an end.

The asphalt road ahead of them is smooth, and my fearless sister loves to talk and loves to drive almost as much as she loves a last-minute reason to leave town. Leaf-peeping season has just begun. Did the trees stand like soldiers who, with our mother's blessing, had put their armor down?

The chlorophyll cells that saturate leaves with green had just started the work of draining toward fall's yellows, oranges, reds. Our mother, the sequoia of our universe, was on her last bloom. My father would be there to catch the last leaf of her as it fell. But in the slow trod she recognized as her own dying, all the other leaves fell from her privately and alone.

Our mother could keep any and every kind of secret, even the companion she'd been making of her own death. She stares out the windshield to where the trees lining their journey come together at the horizon like a kiss.

∞

What would our mother think of my queerness now? We were both products of our colonizers, and there's a chance I'd have had to lead her back to the Black Period where she could love me again. There were years I went back and forth between scenes of love and rejection. Until, like with Kwanzaa, I had to write a story that would let me be whole. A wound in the root system, I'd eventually learn, though it might scar, could be healed. I could leave the jackal in my rearview.

As a child, the adults that raised me modeled a world where justice was, so obviously, the work. It was when the Black and African adults around me were scheming, planning, shit-talking, and preparing for the daily revolutions they waged that they seemed to laugh and sing the most. There was the sweat of the fight that dripped from them, but, too, there was that from-the-feet exhale, that deep breath finally come, from doing the work together. There were times it was hard to tell the difference in their voices between strategizing and having a good time.

I can't name the day, the year, the tipping point. But one day, I woke up inside myself with the Black Period feeling almost completely gone. I wanted to emerge from erasure, but only between God and Allah could the amount of shame I'd been carrying be named or understood.

When I was small, the seed of white America planted itself inside the fertile soil of me, and everywhere, its poison ivy grew. I hadn't known to keep a measure of forgiveness for myself. I hadn't known it was possible to shake the fear of one's own reflection, or what to do with the anxieties that made me feel like immovable stone. And what would happen to me if I held my shames up to the light?

∞

I don't need to know what happened when Jamila and our mother got to New Jersey. Even if I did, my sister can't remember enough to tell me. Instead, I want to remember Jamila in the driver's seat of our mother's life as she unknowingly helps the woman who made us chase the last bit of her own daylight.

Not wanting to imagine our mother scared, I think of Jamila's smiling chatter riding next to all that joyous quiet they also must have sat in. I hold on to other things: our mother's scarves, her green card, an empty bottle of her J'adore perfume that moves with me to every home where I've tried to make sense of what she would have considered an extravagant buy. Where and who was she when she made the purchase?

Christian Dior's J'adore is bookended with amaranth, musk, and blackberry base notes, and a top note of fresh mandarin. At its heart are jasmine, plum, orchid, and rose. Depending on the time of day or the day itself, jasmine flowers can have a nutty or banana-like scent. There are hours, or days, it can smell like mango or peach. A full day's harvest yields six million jasmine flowers, but just one bottle of J'adore perfume. Climate change is making flowers less fragrant as, all over the world, temperatures rise. It's incredible to think of how something so new (us) could bring an end to something as old and necessary as flowers. Seventeen years later, and our mother's empty bottle sits on my bookshelf, still holding her special-occasion scent.

∞

When book critic Parul Sehgal asks, "What would it look like to emerge from erasure?" what is the verb the answer demands?

Is it Toni Morrison's work of rememory, which Morrison describes as the sweat of "reconstituting and recollecting a usable past"?

Where had the version of the world where I could love myself or be loved in begun?

Where had it ended?

Where had it turned to convince Black people to leave behind Black people like me?

To emerge from erasure, I had to write myself back in.

Why rise from the ashes without asking why I had to burn?

"In the beginning"—

IN ONE VERSION, IN A LONG-AGO TIME STILL MILLIONS OF YEARS younger than the Grand Canyon, Aristotle, from his pulpit, built a philosophy on top of a foundation where slavery was written as both a destiny and a right, and Africans, the "burnt faced" peoples of the world.

Once upon a history, white people palimpsested their bodies onto gods. They built a Hades on top of an already-made world. Built ships. Turned into hostages we whose souls refused notions of property. Or once upon a history, Columbus sailed the ocean blue. He sailed and sailed and sailed and sailed, sailed the waters red. Indigenous blood flowed from land to river. African and Black blood flowed from ocean to land. So much blood it made a shadow so big that only if you were searching for it could you see the Black Period inside all that "America."

So often, history, like heartbreak, has felt like a rope tethering the ends of a timeline. I think of the last time I held my youngest nephew, Ibraheema Alyaan. Only three months old and he felt so familiar in my arms. I see Zayd, Nuh, and my brother-in-law preparing for salat in the bedroom once reserved for my visits. Nuh, still strong-willed and led easily to distraction, oscillates between play and litany.

When Zayd was smaller, five or six, he drew his prayer over Jamila's like a boy practicing his letters on tracing paper, his prayer more a practice of reverence than reverence itself. Now, almost ten, he wears the face of someone who's achieved it. My nephew, a believer. Though they'll never meet, Zayd recites the Takbir with his grandmother's focus. *How beautiful it will be*, it is impossible not to think when Nuh and Ibraheema's faces also come to this.

∞

In the beginning of myth, our mother gave us a book. There, we learned we came from ascension. We came from Black folks who, remembering Africa and freedom, sung themselves into flight. In Virginia Hamilton's *The People Could Fly*, it was memory and rememory that melodied you free. This was before, for Black folks, there was any such thing as North. Ascension not leading to Dayton, New York, or Chicago, not leading to heaven, but leading to Africa, leading home.

Everywhere our mother looked, including inside her children, was an adopted country. Assimilation spreading its tentacles until, with our ancestral language no longer in common, the best she could do was remind us that whatever we were—American/(Nigerian)/Halfrican—no origin story had ever been written by a plantation.

To my father, an origin story always began with women. With my great-grandma Lizzie nourishing thirteen children and then her children's children from her Georgia garden, as if she were some kind of Jesus with his two fish and five loaves of bread feeding the five thousand. She, the only kind of Jesus my father could believe in. Our origin story was my grandma Gussie Mae, raising a whole family under the weight of a fourth-grade education and the economic inadequacies of domestic work. An origin story began with the first step leaping into a run from Alabama to Ohio, and that southern leap back. Were always more about what we do for each other—the care—than they were about place. They were Black origin stories washed by the sun: about who stayed, who came with, and who sent money home. Origin stories where, at every turn, someone was singing.

∞

Why do we remember some things? And why do we work to forget others?

Calendula, the other name for marigolds, is derived from the Latin word "kalendae," meaning "small clock" or "small calendar." The flower our mother loved to tend the best was *time*. In India, marigolds are an offering hung everywhere: temples, weddings, funerals, festivals, hotels, restaurants, in windshields. The bright-orange marigolds that our mother loved represent courage and sacrifice. Marigolds also serve as a way to remember the 1.3 million Indian soldiers that fought in World War I in service to the British, and the more than seventy-four thousand who lost their lives.

All that death in service to an empire that had left sixty million of their Indian subjects to die over the course of the eighteenth, nineteenth, and twentieth centuries. The weapon was genocide by famine. Empire being empire, marigolds being marigolds, I think of India and our mother's Nigeria and all the violent ways they must have had British rule in common. Our mother's marigolds, my instant, insistent reminder that there is this kind of kin all over the world.

On the occasions my dreams are feeling kind, I dream of our mother planting orange marigolds in our garden—her body tending these small clocks. No matter the neighborhood we live in, our mother conjures flowers. Like her grandson Nuh, she wears the frown that I know, underneath, is actually a smile. She wears a big hat beneath the sun and wipes sweat from her forehead with the wrist of her garden glove. She sits on an upside-down plastic bucket and leans into her work. I know that leaning over like this will lay her up in bed with back hurt, but for now, she is happy to have her hands in the earth.

Black folks, we *be.*

We be the whole verb of the wor(l)d.

∞

On my Brooklyn runs from one park to another, through my headphones, Public Enemy asks, "How You Sell Soul to a Soulless People Who Sold Their Soul?" *Banned from our damn so-called country,* the song begins. By the second verse, Chuck D is *spitting in the wind 'til it knocks a tree down in the woods*—which has always been the work. Then a chorus of voices declare, *Allahu Akbar,* behind D's translation: *God is good.*

Is "Allahu Akbar" what our mother was thinking as she and Jamila drove away, their hands tossing a goodbye out the car windows while Mimi and her family looked happily on?

So many years have passed now, Jamila can't even remember how long they stayed. How quick a trip could a last goodbye be? As they left, hugging my cousin, our mother did something I'd never in our briefly shared lifetime get to see: she cried.

The first time Jamila told me this, it was immediately after the funeral. I was just settling into a decade of being scared all the time. She'd started to say the words as though an afterthought, in that way she still loves to drop heart-sized bombs. It was only as the words came out that my sister, in her grieving dress, recognized that the tears of our never-cry Fulani woman were a warning flare.

> *Question: What was the light like as they drove back to South Carolina?*
> —Our mother knew, like it or not, she was soon to be buried there.

> *Question: What of the flowers that lined the highway as the car pulled back across that southern border?*
> —Behind them, the sun not yet set, but wanting to.

∞

Despite all the white spaces I've populated and the ghosts of the ones still populating me, I'm always shocked to be reminded Black folks are barely 13 percent of the U.S. population. *How can this be?* I see us everywhere. Our minds, our bodies, our science and invention, our literature, and our love songs preserve the stories (white) America is constantly trying to erase. Time seems to get shorter and shorter in white America. In this modern world, they won't even save their children. Not from gun violence, not from floods, virus, nor a president.

Before the first colonizer, before the first kidnapped person that looked like me, when this land known as the United States was referred to by many of its Indigenous inhabitants as "Turtle Island," capitalism was nowhere in sight, and still *a whole world.* There were the Havsuw 'Baaja peoples being birthed from the floor of the Grand Canyon. They lived, they fought, they loved, they sowed. It was the world before it was ravaged, like people, by our shared colonizers, the world before cash crops turned the land gray. The earth, free and belonging wholly to itself. Sunlight rushing in. Nothing had yet been extracted. Here the soil was so rich, so clean, it was black. It was the Black Period.

∞

Look, there!

My sister is pulling into our parents' drive. Done playing chicken with fate, her body is stiff from a goodbye made on the run. Our mother is *all* the way back now, in this temporary home death will make permanent.

If my mother knew I'd be all right, did she know how long it would take for me to get here?

∞

This is what it looked like to emerge from erasure:

At Kwanzaa, during those years the world seemed too white and me too queer for me to love myself, there was always a light snatching me toward an opening that existed on the other side of America's tunnel. It was a reminder that, in the rooms we shared as Black people, there was always an ancestor who would double back for us.

Sing a song full of faith that the dark past has taught us
Sing a song full of the hope that the present has brought us
facing the rising sun of our new day begun
let us march on till victory is won.

At the end of every Kwanzaa celebration, from child to adult, we clasped hands and together sang the Black National Anthem, "Lift Every Voice." From elementary to high school, every day, as students, we rose to recite the pledge of allegiance in unison. It was a pledge of fealty to a nation that does very little to take care of those who live in its country. But in those Kwanzaa rooms, what was national could also be Black.

In "Lift Every Voice," we sang a melody of repair, reclamation, and revision. It was a song I loved so much that, shy, scared and embarrassed as I was, I sang it despite having no sense of tune. It was a song that, even if you weren't ready for it, tugged you toward your own liberation. It was a song of want, the work of rememory. A song where suddenly, history was the most manageable thing we'd ever carried. History was the harmony that made our hips swing in the same direction.

And *that* is it. That's the feeling I've been trying to get back to my whole adult life. The way the first note of "Lift Every Voice" quivers inside me like a memory I didn't realize was lost. The memory arriving wet with the sweat of trying to find me. That place where I could live inside what was true—that Blackest form of attention.

We have come over a way that with tears has been watered, we sang at Kwanzaa from child to ancestors, both the dead and living, that populated those rooms. Our tears carried pain and joys unspeakable. They watered the nation that our bodies and wombs had tilled for centuries. And like Loren Eiseley says, the flowers bloomed and bloomed and bloomed.

Do you understand what I mean when I say I've sat on the laps of my ancestors? I was brought up in a nation that left me knocking on the outside of its door. My ancestors are the people who raised me and the people who raised them. Their bodies came in all shapes, sizes, and makings.

With their tired, or ailing, or disabled, and loved bodies, aunties and uncles, mothers and fathers and man-friends sang the Black national anthem with swagger, their lips pursed, dimples showing a knowing look. Even our mother, who, like me, couldn't really dance, moved her hips. Adults shimmied their shoulders and leaned into the unbreakable circle, which only together, our bodies could make. They leaned in until they were almost halfway bent over. They leaned in like gospel singers who had crossed over to R & B. Their whole bodies let us know: *yes, Lord,* the lift was coming, but, *oooo, baby,* the Black Period was already here.

∞

EPILOGUE

BLACK LIGHT

IT'S THE SEASON OF THE COLD MOON IN THE AFTERNOON.
Half past four. Darkness rises from the East.

From all pockets: a funk band, a solo R & B singer, kids who take their violin lessons outside on dollar-store folding chairs.

What's left of the leaves cascades from blood reds to marmalades, then light-soaked honeys. The pine trees veer toward the spectacular. They retain their needles, their summer color. Black and brown folks go around inside bespoke Black Periods.

Even if, like the sun disappearing ahead of me, I can't change my position, I've learned how to look this sundown-town country in the eye. The world smells fresh, and despite the police dotting the park's loop's perimeter, something in me sings.

Needing to know what November does to the trees, I spill onto back paths. Today, one of my shy days. I can wake up so shy it feels like punishment, but if I'm patient, the wind-scent of the trees will release my anxieties skyward. I've memorized Prospect Park's hidden waterfalls. I know the trees with so much shade that even after a rain-storm, their trunks remain dry—but still, this knowing isn't enough to shake the pain in my body loose.

All around me, stolen Lenape land. Here and now, it's only me and America's ghosts. Finally, even if only momentarily, I'm free of our ghostmakers. Along Prospect Park's quietest paths, in-sects and chipmunks turn fall's leaves and the carcasses of trees to mulch.

I've lived in New York for almost a decade but still get a thrill from the rare moments where it's possible to be outside and alone. *Finally*, it's only me and the trees. My mask comes down. My vision wobbles against Prospect Park's dusk. Around me, the natural world is starting over.

With a wanderlust rooting, the ache in my spine—this cruelty so physical, yet so invisible only Stephanie and I see it—tracks the blade of an approaching winter. I've worn my good hiking boots. I take my time. I take satisfaction walking through the park trails' muddiest sec-tions. In warmer months, this park fills with blue jays and red-breasted robins. Now, what's left of the birds sing, like me, from some invisible place.

The world feels fragile as the ghosts beneath my feet. It's that time of year when early evening and night mean the same thing. After so much time spent inside quarantining, I remember I'm supposed to vary my vision.

Emerging from the park's invisible trails, I practice looking farther, then farther away. A kid's birthday party is packing up. A jazz band makes its debut. Black folks congregate at the drum circle. *This* is night's church. It's unabashedly evening. *Gone* gone is the sun. The unknowing is coming. A full moon erases—chases the stars.

∞

Stephanie's smile is night-lit, deep, clever against our bedroom windows. Post–back rub, I am touch drunk. Endorphins cascade across the weathered landscape that is my body like flowers silently erupting across the terrain of time. Through our home planetarium—a gift I asked for—we project an exact image of the northern hemisphere onto the ceiling. We play Max Richter's eight-hour concept album, *Sleep,* but we keep sleep on the run.

From our bed, we are drowning and drowning and drowning in stars, and Stephanie laughs when I tell her I miss being in the world with all our crushes, miss staring into a face over and over until I can name why and to where it moves me. This world full of people we still want to kiss, and Stephanie laughs again as I pull up a photo of one of her friends, this other woman who, when she laughs, thrusts her open mouth at you like all that guilts you can be forgiven. I am relieved to be reminded there are so many ways to be married. Maybe, we will inhabit every one.

The night is bright, vast as all that is between us. Above, the same shooting star shoots again and again across the same spot in the sky's projection, cutting through sixty thousand night-lit moments and our ceiling fan. The best thing about the planetarium is that it also turns.

We spin—
 —or the world spins.

Night, so often a metaphor
 for Blackness—is everywhere.

IN MEMORIAM

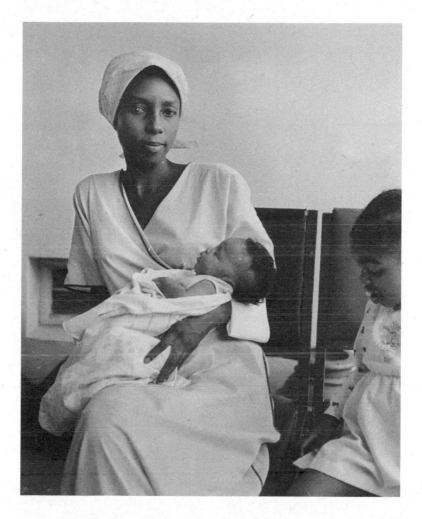

HAUWA TINI ADAMU GETER

December 13, 1952–October 2, 2003

ACKNOWLEDGMENTS

Many of the institutions I've participated in, as well as the stolen lands I've called home, and the cities that this book traverses exist due to the violent removal of Indigenous people from their homelands, including the following nations: Bodwewadmi (Potawatomi), Canarsee, Chumash, Congaree, Diné, the Gabrielino-Tongva/Kizh, Hualapai, Havsuw 'Baaja, Hopi, Kaskaskia, Kiikaapoi, Munsee Lenape, Myaamia, Paiute, Peoria, Tsalaguwetiyi (Cherokee East), the Spiritually Unconquered Indigenous "Uchean" Free People of Color Matriarchal Society, Yavapai-Apache, Yį Įsuwą (Catawba), and Zuni. Colonization means that this account can never be whole, but I have done my best to acknowledge their erasures, stand witness to their histories, and center their sovereignty. For more information, please contact the nations directly.

With love and debt to my father, Tyrone Geter, for painting me a world I could dream into and beyond.

To my mother, Hauwa Tini Adamu Geter, who taught me how to live up to my name.

To both my parents for the many, many Black Periods that they built for their children, where we witnessed how an attention to history and an obligation to community were our greatest gifts, and experienced the strategizing power of hope.

Thanks to my sister, Jamila, who was one of my first examples of braving the world.

To my brother-in-law, Ali, and all the Badjies.

To Karen, Bill and Chris Land for their love and unwavering support.

To all my nieces and nephews, and my family across both continents.

To my aunt Liz who showed me one of the most delightful sights in the world: a Black woman reading.

To Bobo, who in her stories gave me more of my mother to dream into.

Thank you to the dead who are never dead: my grandmothers, Gussie Mae Simon and "Yaya" Hannatu Saleh Adamu; my great-grandma Lizzie, Aunt Sarah, Auntie Mairo, Catherine Simpson.

∞

With gratitude to my agent, Ayesha Pande, for having faith in my roving mind, and for being not just my agent, but also a vital editor and collaborator across these pages.

To my editor, Jamia Wilson, for her insight and her shared belief that the complexity of our stories deserve a stage, as well as the entire Random House team, including Robin Desser, Darryl Oliver, and Craig Adams, Rachel Ake, Maria Braeckel, Ayelet Durantt, Toby Ernst, Barbara Fillon, Marni Folkman, Emani Glee, Abdi Omer, Carrie Neill, Tangela Mitchell, Thomas Perry, Robbin Schiff, Andy Ward, and our authenticity readers.

To Alexis DeLaCruz and the Native American Disability Law Center for taking the time to speak with me.

To Sarah Dohrmann and the women at Diving into the Wreck, where I first waded into the world of nonfiction and found the encouragement to write what became "Theater of Forgiveness," which first appeared in *Longreads*.

To Aracelis Girmay and Naomi Shihab Nye for their words and for trusting me with their sentences.

To the organizations, writers, communities, and friends who have supported the writing of this book: 92Y Women in Power, Bread Loaf Environmental Conference, NYU Creative Writing Nonfiction Program and the Axinn Foundation, VONA/Voices, my friends at Auburn Chautauqua; to *The Paris Review, Bomb* magazine, and *The Believer,* where some of the sentences of this book first appeared; Aba Belgrave, Sari Botton, zakia henderson-brown for helping me to reconsider Kwanzaa; Roxane Gay, Uzodinma Iweala, Tayari Jones, John Murillo, Kiese Laymon, Meghan O'Rourke, Emily Rabateau, Joshua Sharpe, Marina Weiss, Phillip B. Williams, and Keith Wilson.

∞

This book is a result of many conversations and support from: Stephanie Baptist; Ryann Wahl Brewer; William Brewer; my friend and publicist Kelly Forsythe; Brett Funderburk; Dekera Greene; Darrel Alejandro Holnes, PJ Mark; Ricardo Maldonado; my funniest muse Daniel Morgan; Andrey Radovski; one of the world's sweetest miracles, Nova Rankine-Radovski; and Dr. Alice Shepard.

∞

There is a special kindness to those who help us tell our own stories. This book could not have existed in any shape or form without Camille Rankine and Parul Sehgal.

I am forever grateful to Camille for her high tolerance for my "talk to think" ways, for wading through my arguments and comma addiction with a fierce-tooth comb, and for having a mind that has never, not once, let me get away with anything.

Thanks to Parul Sehgal for always knowing what I mean, who allowed me to barricade in her brain for two and a half years, who was so patient, so funny, so kind, among some of the hardest stories I'd set out to tell, and who asks the best questions, and for the conversations and arguments that made the work feel like collaboration.

∞

Thank you, always, to Stephanie, who, along with protecting my time and my energy, protects me from me, who read too many iterations of this book to count, who demanded I rest, doled out back rubs, and cooked dinner for almost two years so I could write—my first, last, and favorite reader, for helping me see who I could become.

With gratitude to the following minds for illuminating the way:

Hanif Abdurraqib, *A Little Devil in America: Notes in Praise of Black Performance* (Random House, 2021).

Africa Is a Country, africasacountry.com.

Sara Ahmed, *The Cultural Politics of Emotion* (Routledge, 2004).

Michelle Alexander, *The New Jim Crow: Mass Incarceration in the Age of Colorblindness* (The New Press, 2012).

Jane Alison, *Meander, Spiral, Explode: Design and Pattern in Narrative* (Catapult, 2019).

Ayşe Gül Altýnay, María José Contreras, Marianne Hirsch, Jean Howard, Banu Karaca, and Alisa Solomon, eds., *Women Mobilizing Memory* (Columbia University Press, 2019).

Benedict Anderson, *Imagined Communities. Reflections on the Origin and Spread of Nationalism* (Verso, 2016).

Roland Anglin, Jeffrey Dowd, Karen M. O'Neil, and Keith Wailoo, eds., *Katrina's Imprint: Race and Vulnerability in America* (Rutgers University Press, 2010).

Natalie Avalos, "What Does It Mean to Heal from Historical Trauma?," *AMA Journal of Ethics*.

Anne C. Bailey, *The Weeping Time: Memory and the Largest Slave Auction in American History* (Cambridge University Press, 2017).

James Baldwin, *The Fire Next Time* (Dial Press, 1963).

Ruha Benjamin, *Race after Technology: Abolitionist Tools for the New Jim Code* (Polity, 2019).

Liat Ben-Moshe, *Decarcerating Disability: Deinstitutionalization and Prison Abolition* (University of Minnesota Press, 2020).

Khaled A. Beydoun, *American Islamophobia: Understanding the Roots and Rise of Fear* (University of California Press, 2018).

Eula Biss, *On Immunity: An Inoculation* (Graywolf, 2015).

Joshua Bloom, *Black against Empire: The History and Politics of the Black Panther Party* (University of California Press, 2016).

Anne Boyer, *The Undying: Pain, Vulnerability, Mortality, Medicine, Art, Dreams, Data, Exhaustion, Cancer, and Care* (Farrar, Straus & Giroux, 2019).

Douglas Bradburn, *The Citizenship Revolution: Politics and the Creation of the American Union* (University of Virginia Press, 2014).

Dionne Brand, *A Map to the Door of No Return: Notes to Belonging* (Vintage Canada, 2002).

Daphne A. Brooks, *Bodies in Dissent: Spectacular Performances of Race and Freedom, 1850–1910* (Duke University Press, 2006).

Sarah M. Broom, *The Yellow House* (Grove Press, 2019).

Austin Channing Brown, executive producer, and Chi Chi Okwu and Jenny Booth Potter, hosts, *The Next Question* (web series).

Michelle Brown, *The Culture of Punishment: Prison, Society, and Spectacle* (NYU Press, 2009).

La Marr Jurelle Bruce, *How to Go Mad without Losing Your Mind: Madness and Black Radical Creativity* (Duke University Press, 2021).

Johanna Burton, Reina Gossett, and Eric A. Stanley, eds., *Trap Door: Trans Cultural Production and the Politics of Visibility* (The MIT Press, 2017).

Judith Butler, *Frames of War: When Is Life Grievable?* (Seagull, 2009).

———, *Precarious Life: The Powers of Mourning and Violence* (Verso, 2004).

Victoria E. Bynum, *Unruly Women: The Politics of Social and Sexual Control in the Old South* (University of North Carolina Press, 1992).

Stephanie M. H. Camp, *Closer to Freedom: Enslaved Women and Everyday Resistance in the Plantation South* (University of North Carolina Press, 2004).

Jeff Chang, *Can't Stop Won't Stop: A History of the Hip-Hop Generation* (Picador, 2005).

Anne Anlin Cheng, *The Melancholy of Race: Psychoanalysis, Assimilation, and Hidden Grief* (Oxford University Press, 2001).

Tracy Clayton and Heben Nigatu, hosts, *Another Round*, podcast.

Ta-Nehisi Coates, *Between the World and Me* (Spiegel & Grau, 2015).

Haile Eshe Cole, "The Repast: Self and Collective Love in the Face of Black Death," *Women, Gender, and Families of Color*.

Tressie M. Cottom, *Thick* (The New Press, 2019).

Anne-Marie Cusac, *Cruel and Unusual: The Culture of Punishment in America* (Yale University Press, 2010).

Yael Danieli, ed., *International Handbook of Multigenerational Legacies of Trauma* (Springer, 1998).

Angela Y. Davis, *Are Prisons Obsolete?* (Seven Stories Press, 2003).

———, *Blues Legacies and Black Feminism: Gertrude "Ma" Rainey, Bessie Smith, and Billie Holiday* (Pantheon, 1998).

———, *Freedom Is a Constant Struggle: Ferguson, Palestine, and the Foundations of a Movement* (Haymarket Books, 2016).

———, *The Meaning of Freedom: And Other Difficult Dialogues* (City Lights, 2012).

Tyree Daye, *River Hymns: Poems* (Copper Canyon Press, 2017).

Barbara Demick, *Nothing to Envy: Ordinary Lives in North Korea* (Spiegel & Grau, 2009).

Kelly Denton-Borhaug, *U.S. War-Culture, Sacrifice and Salvation* (Routledge, 2014).

Mary L. Dudziak, *War Time: An Idea, Its History, Its Consequences* (Oxford University Press, 2012).

Eduardo Duran and Bonnie Duran, *Native American Postcolonial Psychology* (SUNY Press, 1995).

Loren Eiseley, "How Flowers Changed the World," *The Immense Journey* (Random House, 1957).

Caroline Elkins, *Imperial Reckoning: The Untold Story of Britain's Gulag in Kenya* (Henry Holt, 2005).

Roberto Esposito, *Terms of the Political: Community, Immunity, Biopolitics* (Fordham University Press, 2012).

Carolyn Forché, *What You Have Heard Is True: A Memoir of Witness and Resistance* (Penguin Press, 2019).

Murray Forman, *That's the Joint!* (Routledge, 2011).

James Forman, Jr., *Locking Up Our Own: Crime and Punishment in Black America* (Farrar, Straus & Giroux, 2017).

Sondra Fraleigh, *Dancing Identity: Metaphysics in Motion* (University of Pittsburgh Press, 2004).

Lawrence M. Friedman, *Impact: How Law Affects Behavior* (Harvard University Press, 2016).

Hannah Gadsby, *Nanette* (Netflix, 2018).

Amitav Ghosh, *The Great Derangement: Climate Change and the Unthinkable* (University of Chicago Press, 2016).

Dina Gilio-Whitaker, *As Long as Grass Grows: The Indigenous Fight for Environmental Justice, from Colonization to Standing Rock* (Beacon Press, 2019).

Dominique DuBois Gilliard, *Rethinking Incarceration: Advocating for Justice That Restores* (IVP Books, 2018).

Ruth Wilson Gilmore, *Golden Gulag: Prisons, Surplus, Crisis, and Opposition in Globalizing California* (University of California Press, 2007).

Aracelis Girmay, *Kingdom Animalia: Poems* (BOA Editions, 2011).

Phoebe C. Godfrey, "Race, Gender & Class and Climate Change," *Race, Gender & Class.*

Byron J. Good and Devon E. Hinton, *Culture and PTSD: Trauma in Global and Historical Perspective* (University of Pennsylvania Press, 2015).

Avery F. Gordon, *Ghostly Matters: Haunting and the Sociological Imagination* (University of Minnesota Press, 2008).

——, *Keeping Good Time: Reflections on Knowledge, Power, and People* (Routledge, 2004).

Namita Goswami, "The (M)other of All Posts: Postcolonial Melancholia in the Age of Global Warming," *Critical Philosophy of Race.*

Stuart Hall, *Essential Essays,* Volume 1: *Foundations of Cultural Studies* (Duke University Press, 2019).

——, *Essential Essays,* Volume 2: *Identity and Diaspora* (Duke University Press, 2019).

Virginia Hamilton, *The People Could Fly: American Black Folktales* (Knopf, 1985).

Nikole Hannah-Jones, "1619 Project," *The New York Times.*

Saidiya V. Hartman, *Lose Your Mother: A Journey along the Atlantic Slave Route* (Farrar, Straus & Giroux, 2006).

——, "Venus in Two Acts," *Small Axe,* 2008.

——, *Wayward Lives, Beautiful Experiments: Intimate Histories of Riotous Black Girls, Troublesome Women, and Queer Radicals* (W. W. Norton & Company, 2019).

Saidiya Hartman, Canisia Lubrin, Nat Raha, Christina Sharpe, and Nydia A.

Swaby, "Poetry Is Not a Luxury: The Poetics of Abolition," panel transcript, silverpress.org, 2020.

Kelly Hayes, *Movement Memos*, podcast.

Haymarket Books, haymarketbooks.org.

Chris Hedges, *Wages of Rebellion* (Nation Books, 2015).

———, *War Is a Force That Gives Us Meaning* (Anchor Books, 2003).

Rabbi Shai Held, *The Heart of Torah*, Volume 2 (Jewish Publication Society, 2017).

laura hélène, "Shame Within/Without Disabled Peoples: Re-Imagining Representations," *Knots: An Undergraduate Journal of Disability Studies*.

Judith Herman, *Trauma and Recovery: From Domestic Abuse to Political Terror* (Basic Books, 1997).

Marc Lamont Hill, *Nobody: Casualties of America's War on the Vulnerable, from Ferguson to Flint and Beyond* (Atria Books, 2017).

Elizabeth Hinton, *From the War on Poverty to the War on Crime: The Making of Mass Incarceration in America* (Harvard University Press, 2016).

Stephen Hirst, *Hausuw 'Baaja: People of the Blue Green Water* (Havasupai Tribal Council, 1985).

———, *I Am the Grand Canyon: The Story of the Havasupai People* (Grand Canyon Association, 2007).

Sharon Patricia Holland, *The Erotic Life of Racism* (Duke University Press, 2012).

Barbara A. Holmes, *Crisis Contemplation: Healing the Wounded Village* (CAC Press, 2021).

———, *Joy Unspeakable: Contemplative Practices of the Black Church* (Fortress Press, 2017).

Grace Kyungwon Hong, *Death beyond Disavowal: The Impossible Politics of Difference* (University of Minnesota Press, 2015).

bell hooks, *Teaching to Transgress: Education as the Practice of Freedom* (Routledge, 1994).

Richard T. Hughes, *Myths America Lives By: White Supremacy and the Stories That Give Us Meaning* (University of Illinois Press, 2018).

Lewis Hyde, *A Primer for Forgetting: Getting Past the Past* (Farrar, Straus & Giroux, 2019).

Daniel Immerwahr, *How to Hide an Empire: A History of the Greater United States* (Farrar, Straus & Giroux, 2019).

Walter Isaacson, *Leonardo da Vinci* (Simon & Schuster, 2017).

Ha Jin, *The Writer as Migrant* (University of Chicago Press, 2008).

Javon Johnson, "Black Joy in the Time of Ferguson," *QED: A Journal in GLBTQ Worldmaking.*

Taylor Johnson, *Inheritance: Poems* (Alice James Books, 2020).

Daniel Alexander Jones, *Black Light,* play.

Stephanie E. Jones-Rogers, *They Were Her Property: White Women as Slave Owners in the American South* (Yale University Press, 2019).

Tom Junod, "The Falling Man," *Esquire.*

Mariame Kaba, *We Do This 'til We Free Us: Abolitionist Organizing and Transforming Justice* (Haymarket Books, 2021).

Ibram X. Kendi, *Stamped from the Beginning: The Definitive History of Racist Ideas in America* (PublicAffairs, 2016).

Robin Wall Kimmerer, *Braiding Sweetgrass: Indigenous Wisdom, Scientific Knowledge, and the Teachings of Plants* (Milkweed Editions, 2015).

B. B. King, *Guess Who* (ABC Records, 1972).

———, *Live in Cook County Jail* (ABC Records, 1971).

Ezra Klein, *The Ezra Klein Show,* podcast

Thomas Lake, "The Boy They Couldn't Kill," *Sports Illustrated.*

George Lakoff and Mark Johnson, *Metaphors We Live By* (University of Chicago Press, 1980).

Kiese Laymon, *Heavy* (Scribner, 2018).

Jonathan Lear, *Radical Hope: Ethics in the Face of Cultural Devastation* (Harvard University Press, 2006).

Al Letson, host, *Reveal,* podcast

Primo Levi, *Survival in Auschwitz* (Simon & Schuster, 1995—first published in 1947).

Josh Levin, *The Queen: The Forgotten Life behind an American Myth* (Little, Brown and Company, 2019).

Bettina L. Love, *We Want to Do More than Survive: Abolitionist Teaching and the Pursuit of Educational Freedom* (Beacon Press, 2019).

Helen Macdonald, *H Is for Hawk* (Grove Press, 2016).

Carmen Maria Machado, *In the Dream House* (Graywolf, 2019).

Geo Maher, *A World without Police: How Strong Communities Make Cops Obsolete* (Verso, 2021).

Terese Marie Mailhot, *Heart Berries: A Memoir* (Counterpoint, 2018).

Alex Marzano-Lesnevich, *The Fact of a Body: A Murder and a Memoir* (Flatiron, 2017).

Dani McClain, *We Live for the We: The Political Power of Black Motherhood* (Bold Type Books, 2019).

Rose McDermott, *Political Psychology in International Relations* (University of Michigan Press, 2004).

Suketu Mehta, *This Land Is Our Land: An Immigrant's Manifesto* (Farrar, Straus & Giroux, 2019).

Michael Vincent Miller, *Intimate Terrorism: The Crisis of Love in an Age of Disillusion* (W. W. Norton & Company, 1996).

Joey L. Mogul, Andrea J. Ritchie, and Kay Whitlock, *Queer (In)Justice: The Criminalization of LGBT People in the United States* (Beacon Press, 2012).

Stephanie Morrice, "Heartache and Hurricane Katrina: Recognising the Influence of Emotion in Post-disaster Return Decisions," *Area*.

Wesley Morris and Jenna Wortham, hosts, *Still Processing*, podcast.

Toni Morrison, *Playing in the Dark: Whiteness and the Literary Imagination* (Harvard University Press, 1992).

———, *The Source of Self-Regard: Selected Essays, Speeches, and Meditations* (Knopf, 2019).

Khalil Gibran Muhammad, *The Condemnation of Blackness: Race, Crime, and the Making of Modern Urban America* (Harvard University Press, 2010).

José Esteban Muñoz, *Disidentifications: Queers of Color and the Performance of Politics* (University of Minnesota Press, 1999).

Native American Disability Law Center, nativedisabilitylaw.org.

Pamela Newkirk, *Spectacle: The Astonishing Life of Ota Benga* (Harper/Amistad, 2015).

Kim E. Nielson, *A Disability History of the United States* (Beacon Press, 2013).

Rob Nixon, *Slow Violence and the Environmentalism of the Poor* (Harvard University Press, 2011).

Nel Noddings, *Caring: A Relational Approach to Ethics and Moral Education* (University of California Press, 2013).

Noname Book Club, nonamebooks.com.

Naomi Shihab Nye, *Honeybee: Poems* (Greenwillow Books, 2008).

Charles J. Ogletree, Jr., and Austin Sarat, eds., *Punishment in Popular Culture* (NYU Press, 2015).

Kelly Oliver, *The Colonization of Psychic Space: A Psychoanalytic Social Theory of Oppression* (University of Minnesota Press, 2004).

Parker J. Palmer, "The Politics of the Brokenhearted" (Fetzer Institute, 2005).

Carl Phillips, *Quiver of Arrows: Poems* (Farrar, Straus & Giroux, 2007).

———, *Reconnaissance: Poems* (Farrar, Straus & Giroux, 2015).

———, *Riding Westward: Poems* (Farrar, Straus & Giroux, 2007).

———, *Silverchest: Poems* (Farrar, Straus & Giroux, 2013).

Deesha Philyaw, *The Secret Lives of Church Ladies* (West Virginia University Press, 2020).

Leah Lakshmi Piepzna-Samarasinha, *Care Work: Dreaming Disability Justice* (Arsenal Pulp Press, 2018).

Chanda Prescod-Weinstein, *The Disordered Cosmos: A Journey into Dark Matter, Spacetime, and Dreams Deferred* (Bold Type Books, 2021).

Derecka Purnell, *Becoming Abolitionists: Police, Protests, and the Pursuit of Freedom* (Astra House, 2021).

Kevin Quashie, *The Sovereignty of Quiet: Beyond Resistance in Black Culture* (Rutgers University Press, 2012).

Hugh Raffles, *The Book of Unconformities: Speculations on Lost Time* (Pantheon, 2020).

Camille Rankine, "On 'Let America Be America Again' by Langston Hughes," Poets.org.

Claudia Rankine, *Don't Let Me Be Lonely: An American Lyric* (Graywolf, 2004).

Dorothy Roberts, *Killing the Black Body: Race, Reproduction, and the Meaning of Liberty* (Vintage, 1998).

Dylan Rodríguez, "Abolition as Praxis of Human Being: A Foreword," *Harvard Law Review*.

Caitlin Rosenthal, *Accounting for Slavery: Masters and Management* (Harvard University Press, 2018).

Jess Row, *White Flights: Race, Fiction, and the American Imagination* (Graywolf, 2019).

Elizabeth Rush, *Rising: Dispatches from the New American Shore* (Milkweed Editions, 2018).

Edward W. Said, *Beginnings: Intention and Method* (Columbia University Press, 1985).

———, *Orientalism* (Pantheon, 1978).

Lauret Savoy, *Trace: Memory, History, Race, and the American Landscape* (Counterpoint, 2016).

Maya Schenwar, *Locked Down, Locked Out: Why Prison Doesn't Work and How We Can Do Better* (Berrett-Koehler Publishers, 2014).

Karel Schrijver and Iris Schrijver, *Living with the Stars: How the Human Body Is Connected to the Life Cycles of the Earth, the Planets, and the Stars* (Oxford University Press, 2015).

Parul Sehgal, "Fighting 'Erasure'," *The New York Times*.

———, "In Search of Time Lost and Newly Found," *The New York Times*.

———, "The Profound Emptiness of 'Resilience,'" *The New York Times*.

Danielle Sered, *Until We Reckon: Violence, Mass Incarceration, and a Road to Repair* (The New Press, 2019).

Christina Sharpe, *In the Wake: On Blackness and Being* (Duke University Press, 2016).

Leanne Betasamosake Simpson, *As We Have Always Done: Indigenous Freedom through Radical Resistance* (University of Minnesota Press, 2021).

Jermaine Singleton, *Cultural Melancholy: Readings of Race, Impossible Mourning, and African American Ritual* (University of Illinois Press, 2015).

C. Riley Snorton, *Black on Both Sides: A Racial History of Trans Identity* (University of Minnesota Press, 2017).

Susan Sontag, *Regarding the Pain of Others* (Farrar, Straus & Giroux, 2003).

Dean Spade, *Mutual Aid: Building Solidarity during This Crisis (and the Next)* (Verso, 2020).

Hortense J. Spillers, "Mama's Baby, Papa's Maybe: An American Grammar Book," *Diacritics*.

Doreen St. Félix, newyorker.com/contributors/doreen-st-felix.

Eric A. Stanley, *Captive Genders: Trans Embodiment and the Prison Industrial Complex*, 2nd ed. (AK Press, 2011).

Jill Stauffer, *Ethical Loneliness: The Injustice of Not Being Heard* (Columbia University Press, 2015).

Bryan Stevenson, *Just Mercy: A Story of Justice and Redemption* (Spiegel & Grau, 2014).

Keeanga-Yamahtta Taylor, *From #BlackLivesMatter to Black Liberation* (Haymarket Books, 2016).

Lewis Thomas, *The Lives of a Cell* (Viking Press, 1974).

David Treuer, *The Heartbeat of Wounded Knee: Native America from 1890 to the Present* (Riverhead, 2019).

Truthout, truthout.org.

Bessel van der Kolk, *The Body Keeps the Score: Brain, Mind, and Body in the Healing of Trauma* (Viking Press, 2014).

Alex S. Vitale, *The End of Policing* (Verso, 2017).

Miroslav Volf, *Joy and Human Flourishing: Essays on Theology, Culture, and the Good Life* (Fortress Press, 2015).

Harsha Walia, *Border and Rule: Global Migration, Capitalism, and the Rise of Racist Nationalism* (Haymarket Books, 2021).

———, *Undoing Border Imperialism* (AK Press, 2013).

Wendy S. Walters, *Multiply/Divide: On the American Real and Surreal* (Sarabande, 2015).

Jesmyn Ward, *Men We Reaped: A Memoir* (Bloomsbury, 2013).

Harriet A. Washington, *Medical Apartheid: The Dark History of Medical Experimentation on Black Americans from Colonial Times to the Present* (Anchor, 2008).

April Watson, ed., *Gordon Parks: Muhammad Ali* (Steidl, 2020).

Charles White, *Mississippi*, painting.

Sam White, *A Cold Welcome: The Little Ice Age and Europe's Encounter with North America* (Harvard University Press, 2017).

Frank B. Wilderson III, *Afropessimism* (W. W. Norton & Company, 2020).

Isabel Wilkerson, *Caste: The Origins of Our Discontents* (Random House, 2020).

———, *The Warmth of Other Suns: The Epic Story of America's Great Migration* (Vintage, 2011).

Cynthia Willett and Julie Willett, *Uproarious: How Feminists and Other Subversive Comics Speak Truth* (University of Minnesota Press, 2019).

Christopher P. Wilson, *Cop Knowledge: Police Power and Cultural Narrative in Twentieth-Century America* (University of Chicago Press, 2000).

Joseph R. Winters, *Hope Draped in Black: Race, Melancholy, and the Agony of Progress* (Duke University Press, 2016).

Alice Wong, ed., *Disability Visibility: First-Person Stories from the Twenty-First Century* (Vintage, 2020).

James Wood, *How Fiction Works* (Picador, 2009).

Clyde Woods, "Do You Know What It Means to Miss New Orleans?: Katrina, Trap Economics, and the Rebirth of the Blues," *American Quarterly*.

Michelle M. Wright, *Physics of Blackness: Beyond the Middle Passage Epistemology* (University of Minnesota Press, 2015).

Maria Yellow Horse Brave Heart and Lemyra M. DeBruyn, "The American Indian Holocaust: Healing Historical Unresolved Grief," *American Indian and Alaska Native Mental Health Research: The Journal of the National Center*.

Gregory Younging, *Elements of Indigenous Style: A Guide for Writing by and about Indigenous Peoples* (Brush Education, 2018).

Kathryn Yusoff, *A Billion Black Anthropocenes or None* (University of Minnesota Press, 2019).

Anam Zakaria, *The Footprints of Partition: Narratives of Four Generations of Pakistanis and Indians* (HarperCollins, 2015).

Alex Zamalin, *Black Utopia: The History of an Idea from Black Nationalism to Afrofuturism* (Columbia University Press, 2019).

Carl A. Zimring, *Clean and White: A History of Environmental Racism in the United States* (NYU Press, 2016).

Shoshana Zuboff, *The Age of Surveillance Capitalism: The Fight for a Human Future at the New Frontier of Power* (PublicAffairs, 2019).

Hafizah Augustus Geter is a Nigerian American writer, poet, and literary agent born in Zaria, Nigeria, and raised in Akron, Ohio, and Columbia, South Carolina. She is a PEN Open Book Award and Lambda Literary Award winner. Her poetry collection, *Un-American*, was an NAACP Image Award and PEN Open Book Award finalist. Her writing has appeared in *The New Yorker*, *Harper's Bazaar*, *Bomb*, *The Believer*, and *The Paris Review*, among many other publications. The poetry committee co-chair of the Brooklyn Literary Council, she is a Bread Loaf Katharine Bakeless nonfiction fellow, a Cave Canem poetry fellow, and a 92Y Women inPower Fellow and holds an MFA in nonfiction from New York University. Hafizah lives in Brooklyn, New York.

Twitter: @RhetoricAndThis

ABOUT THE TYPE

This book was set in Dapifer, a typeface designed by Joshua Darden. Fundamentally, Darden mixes elements from a number of different eras and usually-distinct classifications. Dapifer is a low-contrast old-style typeface, but without bracketing of the serifs. It expresses the canonical serif face within the rational framework of a slab serif.